Wrestling with Faith

Challenging problematic Bible stories to navigate crises of belief

Dan Harvey, PhD

Copyright © Daniel Joseph Harvey

Paperback ISBN: 978-1-64438-901-0
Hardcover ISBN: 978-1-64438-902-7

All rights reserved. No part of this publication may be reproduced, stored in a retrieval system, or transmitted in any form or by any means, electronic, mechanical, recording or otherwise, without the prior written permission of the author.

Published by BookLocker.com, Inc., St. Petersburg, Florida.

Library of Congress Cataloging in Publication Data
Harvey, PhD, Dan
Wrestling with Faith by Dan Harvey, PhD
RELIGION: Faith | Christianity | Christian Theology / Apologetics
Library of Congress Control Number: 2019908865

Printed on acid-free paper.

Booklocker.com, Inc.
2019

Unless otherwise indicated, Scripture quotations are from Common Bible: New Revised Standard Version Bible, copyright © 1989 National Council of the Churches of Christ in the United States of America. Used by permission. All rights reserved.

Unless otherwise indicated, chapter 14 scripture quotations are from Wright, N.T., translator. The Kingdom New Testament: A Contemporary Translation. 1st ed., Harper One, 2011.

Scripture quotations marked (CEV) are taken from the CONTEMPORARY ENGLISH VERSION copyright© 1995 by the American Bible Society. Used by permission. All rights reserved.

Scripture quotations marked (ESV) are taken from the (The Holy Bible, English Standard Version®), copyright © 2001 by Crossway, a publishing ministry of Good News Publishers. Used by permission. All rights reserved.

Scripture quotations marked (KJV) are taken from KING JAMES VERSION (KJV): KING JAMES VERSION, Public Domain.

Scripture quotations marked (LITV) are taken from Green, J.P. Literal Translation of the Bible (LITV). Copyright 1976 - 2000. Used by permission of the copyright holder, Jay P. Green, Sr. All rights reserved.

Scripture quotations marked (MKJV) are taken from the Holy Bible, MODERN KING JAMES VERSION copyright© 1962—1998 by Jay P. Green, Sr. Used by permission of the copyright holder. All rights reserved.

Scripture quotations marked (YLT) are taken from Robert Young's Literal Translation (YLT). Public Domain

Dedication

This book is dedicated to my granddaughters who no longer believe that Christianity is relevant.

Acknowledgments

I want to especially thank my daughter, Elisabeth McCumber, who is a freelance writer and founder of Invisible Ink Creative (invisibleinkcreative.com). She carefully read through the original manuscript and provided many important recommendations for improvement. I want to also thank Jekabs Bikis, Dean of the business school at George Fox University, who took time out of his busy schedule to critique my work and offer suggestions. I'm indebted also to Michael Gorman of St. Mary's Seminary and Ecumenical Institute (author of Reading Revelation Responsibly) for reviewing an early manuscript and pointing out where my research needed improvement. I am grateful to the folks at Booklocker (booklocker.com, namely Angela Hoy and Todd Engel) for their professionalism, encouragement, and helpfulness in guiding me though the production process. Additionally, the honest and professional critiques by Blue Ink Reviews and Kirkus were particularly helpful. Their insights helped bring about a better product.

Of course, I need to acknowledge Vivian, my wife of fifty years. She read aloud various versions dozens of times as we worked towards publication. I am grateful to family members who looked over an early manuscript and offered suggestions, which led to interesting family discussions.

Table of Contents

INTRODUCTION 1

PART 1 - THE REALITY OF FAITH 5

    CHAPTER 1 - PRELIMINARIES 7
    CHAPTER 2 - ADDRESSING THE SKEPTICS 20
    CHAPTER 3 - RATIONAL REASONS TO BELIEVE 43

PART 2 - SACRED SCRIPTURE 87

    CHAPTER 4 - AUTHORITY OF SCRIPTURE 89
    CHAPTER 5 - READING THE BIBLE 104
    CHAPTER 6 - MYTH OR HISTORY 121
    CHAPTER 7 - DENOMINATIONAL DIVISIONS 146

PART 3 - THE NATURE OF GOD 161

    CHAPTER 8 - MOSAIC LAWS AND RITUALS 163
    CHAPTER 9 - BIBLICAL VIOLENCE 194
    CHAPTER 10 - THE ANGRY GOD 214
    CHAPTER 11 - PEACE WITH GOD 236

PART 4 - END TIME FRENZY 251

    CHAPTER 12 - SIGNS OF THE TIMES 253
    CHAPTER 13 - THE BOOK OF REVELATION — INTRODUCTION 273
    CHAPTER 14 - JOHN'S REVELATION VISIONS 280
    CHAPTER 15 - CONCLUDING REMARKS 315

FINAL THOUGHTS 317

Introduction

At age fifteen, Eli Wiesel was deported from his childhood home in Hungary. The local authorities rounded-up Eli, his family, and all his friends. They packed them into box-cars, and three days later, the prisoners arrived at Auschwitz, the infamous Holocaust prison camp. Upon arrival, and on the very first day, Eli's mom and sister were burned to death. Meanwhile, he and his father were ordered to walk past crematoriums, seeing the bodies of thousands of dead Jews as they went. Eli and his dad were spared, at least for a time. He later recalled that day with the quote, "Never shall I forget those flames that murdered my God."

More than forty years later, in 1986, this same Eli Wiesel received the Nobel Peace Prize, and his young son accompanied him to the award ceremony. During his acceptance speech, he asked permission to recite a traditional Jewish blessing. He commented that it was not his right to be the end of a rich tradition that spanned some thirty-five hundred years. Somehow, through it all, though the pain remained, Eli Wiesel recovered his faith.

Few of us experience the grief, loss, and pain suffered by Eli Wiesel and other Holocaust victims. It is certain, however, that life will bring difficulties, even for those who skate through their years relatively unscathed.

I did not grow up in a Christian family, though for a time my parents were nominal Catholics. For most of my childhood, my father was an atheist, and my mother agnostic. It wasn't till my early twenties, shortly after I met my wife-to-be that I became a follower of Jesus.

For many years, this was enough. I listened to sermons from various preachers, and it all seemed good. In hindsight, I see how they carefully avoided the problematic areas. I don't remember any sermons about a young woman being cut up into pieces and sent to the twelve tribes of Israel. In fact, I recall little systematic teaching on the books of the Old Testament. There were bits and pieces.

Perhaps a pastor would dive into the books of Esther or Ruth, here a Psalm and there a Proverb. Occasionally, they might consider isolated verses from Deuteronomy or the prophets. Malachi is a popular way to convince the congregation to tithe.

Then in 1994, my seventeen-year old son died; a faith crisis ensued. My wife opened up about her traumatic missionary boarding school upbringing. In working with indigenous tribes and creating software to support their efforts to restore language and culture, I learned about the sorrows they suffered during the colonial period. This was more than I wanted to know. I also observed changes in the culture that the Church has been slow to reconcile. As a result, hearing the same sermons that I previously heard for twenty-five years no longer resonated. Nothing made sense any more.

I was at a crossroad. I could simply walk away as many have done in recent decades. Or, I could take a deeper look and determine whether the Christian faith still has relevance to me in this modern world. The question I faced was: "Are there answers to be had?" So, year by year, I decided to use research skills developed as a Computer Scientist to carefully analyze those areas that seem problematic, at least for me. For example, how can a loving God throw people into a literal, eternal furnace called hell? Is this just punishment for even the worst of people? Why does he seem slow to anger in some passages of scripture and quick to anger in others? Does the Bible teach that the Earth is 6,000 years old? What do we do with the theory of Evolution? Why are Christians so obsessed with end time prophecies? What do we do with past atrocities committed by the Church and by believers?

As I consider the testimony of Eli Wiesel; it causes me to reflect. In the West, growing numbers of people who were raised Christian report that they no longer consider religion important in their lives.[1] Many of these are convinced that religion does more harm to society than good. Scientific dogma tells us that belief in God is a superstition whose time is past. Historians recall the bloody wars and genocides of previous generations. Culture is leading us into an age of spiritual freedom, declaring that religion, especially Christianity, is small-minded, exclusive, and racially-based. Former believers often become the faith's most potent adversaries. At the same time, another religious

---

[1] Betsy Cooper, Daniel Cox PhD, Rachel Lienesch and Robert P. Jones PhD, "Exodus: Why Americans are Leaving Religion—and Why They're Unlikely to Come Back," *PRRI* (9/22/2016).

Introduction

tradition, Islam is growing rapidly, and it is contending to become the world's largest faith.[2]

My tradition is Christian and I do my best to follow the teachings of Jesus. What should I do? How should I respond to the challenges of our times? I could deny my faith, and quietly assimilate into the mainstream of twenty-first-century culture. I could embrace elements of other traditions, like Hinduism, Buddhism, and the like. Yet Eli Wiesel's testimony rings in my mind, and I realize that it also applies to me, and to every person of faith. We shouldn't be quick to cast off a Judeo-Christian tradition that spans thousands of years. The tradition lives on through the message and teachings of Jesus, and so it should.

It seems to me that the time has come for all of us who identify with the Christian faith to take a careful look at our sacred scriptures and our traditions. By saying this, I don't mean that we should discard certain texts as many are doing and have done. I also am not trying to transform the faith into something that it is not. We need rather to do what the Jews have always done in their Talmudic debates. That is, we need to challenge, probe, and express our doubts without guilt or fear. We should be able to evaluate ourselves, not by some special revelation received from God, by some miraculous event, or by some private new insight, but instead by whether we've thought of good questions to ask. Rather than judging our fellow believers by whether they agree with the denominational positions of our various congregations, we need to ask ourselves whether his or her way of looking at scripture could perhaps have some validity. We should be defined by the fruit of our faith, not by a rigid set of beliefs that determine whether we do or do not belong to this or that group or whether we worship in a designated way.

A goal for this book is to challenge some long-standing interpretations and to honestly face the Bible's troubling verses. The purpose is not to convert or even to persuade; it is to open a dialogue, a debate if you will. Is the Christian faith rational, or is it wishful fantasy? Is it a living faith, or will it inevitably die, like many other ancient religions? Is it possible to hold our sacred writings in high

---

[2] "The Future of World Religions: Population Growth Projections, 2010-2050," Pew Research Center, Washington, D.C. (April 2, 2015), http://www.pewforum.org/2015/04/02/religious-projections-2010-2050/, April 7, 2018.

regard, and yet still to ask questions, challenge accepted interpretations, express our doubts, and still be unified as fellow believers? Can we unearth possible explanations for well-known troubling verses? I believe we can.

I am fully aware that a book like this will not convince every reader. There simply is too much ground to cover. It also would be arrogant for me to think that I could definitively settle issues that have been debated for thousands of years. Nevertheless, I hope that this work can serve as a starting point for those who are on similar journeys. It is time to take a second look.

PART 1

The Reality of Faith

> Now Faith, in the sense in which I am here using the word, is the art of holding on to things your reason has once accepted, in spite of your changing moods. For moods will change, whatever view your reason takes. I know that by experience. Now that I am a Christian, I do have moods in which the whole thing looks very improbable: but when I was an atheist, I had moods in which Christianity looked terribly probable. This rebellion of your moods against your real self is going to come anyway. That is why Faith is such a necessary virtue: unless you teach your moods 'where they get off,' you can never be either a sound Christian or even a sound atheist, but just a creature dithering to and fro, with its beliefs really dependent on the weather and the state of its digestion.[3] — CS Lewis

Prior to the attack on the Twin Towers on September 11, 2001, there were those who did not believe in God, but they rarely attracted a worldwide audience. Yes, they did not want prayer in schools, and they fought to remove religious monuments from public spaces. Nevertheless, it did not normally appear that they were trying to destroy faith altogether. It was okay for people to worship in churches and within the privacy of their homes.

9/11 was a catalytic event, which immediately inspired Sam Harris to begin writing his bestseller *The End of Faith*. Shortly after this, a series of additional books appeared and they enjoyed widespread distribution. These authors sought to convince their readers that it is irrational to believe in an imaginary deity. According to these *New Atheists*, religious fundamentalism is largely responsible for wars, discrimination, and hatred. Religion is therefore dangerous to civilized society. Some of these authors, like Richard Dawkins, for example, were particularly aggressive. When asked how one should

---

[3] CS Lewis, *Mere Christianity*, 125.

react to a person of faith, he replied with his famous answer: "Mock them." Are they right? Are there answers to their charges? If so, what are they? We'll explore these questions in the first part of this book.

Chapter 1

Preliminaries

What would the atheist Nobel Laureate Bertrand Russell say when confronted by God? His answer: "Sir, why did you not give me better evidence?"[4] This is very similar to the mockery Jesus received while hanging from the cross. "If he is the King of Israel, let him now come down from the cross, and we shall believe him (Matt. 27:42)."

The question we could ask is, "What kind of evidence is sufficient for one to believe that a God exists who is personal and involved in his creation?" Is any amount of evidence sufficient? Who decides?

Extraordinary Claims

A popular charge made by skeptics is that belief in God is an extraordinary claim. It must, therefore, be backed up with extraordinary evidence. The argument goes:

> I believe in God.
>> What is the evidence?
>
> What kind of evidence would you find acceptable?
>> Something that cannot be explained by naturalistic processes.
>
> How about the existence of the first living replicating machine, the cell?[5]
>> No, not good enough.
>
> Why not? Do you have a naturalistic explanation?
>> No, but one is forthcoming.,
>
> When?
>> When science progresses enough.

Carl Sagan in a 1980 PBS program called *Cosmos, a Personal Voyage* popularized the expression: an extraordinary claim requires

---

[4] Leo Rosten, "Bertrand Russell and God: A Memoir," *The Saturday Review* (February 23, 1974).: 26

[5] "Inner Life of a Cell," https://www.youtube.com/watch?v=B_zD3NxSsD8, visited 7/27/18

extraordinary proof. He was referring to the existence of alien life, not God. He loosely quoted Marcello Truzzi, who in 1987 stated that the skeptic has nothing to prove since they assert nothing. It is the job of one making a claim, or another refuting that claim, that has the responsibility.[6]

Is this a valid argument when it refers to belief in God? Anthony Flew, a famous twentieth century English Philosopher could shed some light on this question. When he was an atheist, he wrote two well-known articles that are widely circulated in skeptic circles. In the first, titled *Theology and Falsification*,[7] he starts with a parable of two explorers who come to a jungle clearing containing a combination of flowers and weeds. One explorer believes that there must be a gardener; the other is a skeptic who disagrees. They test the hypothesis over and over in various ways causing the believer to back off after each test and refine his hypothesis. It gets to the point where he claims the gardener to be "invisible, intangible, insensible to electric shocks, has no scent, makes no sound, and who comes secretly to look after the garden." The skeptic explorer then asks how this is different from believing that there is no gardener at all. Flew then applies this argument to a God who loves us, has a plan, and is intricately involved with our lives. In other words, there is no way to falsify the claim because the believer would continue to come up with even more unlikely scenarios. Eventually, the whole thing becomes an exercise in futility.

The argument is a strong one, but it goes both ways. At the time of Darwin, the cell was thought to be a simple structure. This hypothesis was proven to be incorrect. During the twentieth century, biologists conducted many lab experiments trying to emulate conditions on the early Earth. They struck simulated environments with electric pulses, which hit molecules thought to exist at that time. All of these experiments failed. In time, scientists discovered DNA, which is at the heart of all living things, and probably has been from the very beginning. We learned that the simplest cell is not pond scum, but a very complex factory of molecular nanomachines. The explosion of

---

[6] Marcello Truzzi, "Pseudo-Skepticism," *Zetetic Scholar*, 12-13 (1987): 3-4.
[7] Antony Flew, "Theology and Falsification," *University*, (1950-51), from Joel Feinberg, ed., *Reason and Responsibility, Readings in Some Basic Problems in Philosophy*, (Dickenson Publishing Company, Inc. 1968), 48-49.

Preliminaries

life in the Cambrian period occurred within a few million years, not over the long periods of time previously thought. The Universe is not eternal as steady-state theories maintained, but had a beginning. Time itself is not constant but flows at different rates in the presence of gravity and slows down as we approach the speed of light.

We are discovering each year more fine-tuned aspects of the Universe that imply a transcendent cause. For example, the strength of gravity must be within an extremely narrow range (1 part in 10 followed by 60 zeroes). A stronger gravitational constant would have caused the Universe to collapse; a weaker constant would have caused it to fly apart. In either case, life would not be possible. There are many dozens of examples like this which led to the following quote by the Physicist Freeman Dyson:

> The universe is an unexpectedly hospitable place for living creatures to make their home in. Being a scientist, trained in the habits of thought and language of the twentieth century rather than the eighteenth, I do not claim that the architecture of the universe proves the existence of God. I claim only that the architecture of the universe is consistent with the hypothesis that mind plays an essential role in its functioning…The more I examine the universe and study the details of its architecture, the more evidence I find that the universe in some sense must have known that we were coming.[8]

There are ever more intricate mathematical models to explain these things naturalistically. Some hypothesize the existence of an infinite number of universes or a single universe that oscillates in and out. Regarding the origin of life, some scientists propose things like the aliens did it, or crystals seeded life. I recently heard a physicist during a debate attempt to compare the complexity of life to that of snowflakes. We like to say that we are rational beings, but this does not prove to be true.[9] Most of us, whether we be scientists, atheists, or

---

[8] Dyson, *Disturbing the Universe* (1979): 250-251.
[9] Refer to Daniel Kahneman's work on the psychology of judgment and decision-making and behavioral economics, leading to the 2002 Nobel Memorial Prize in Economic Sciences

religious, cling with bare knuckles to our beliefs and prejudices, especially those that are strongly held.

Anthony Flew wrote another popular article called *the Presumption of Atheism*.[10] He first redefines the meaning of the word, atheist, to mean one who is not a theist. Next, he makes the argument that the burden of proof is on the theist. They first must describe their concept of God and next, they must prove that such a God is applicable in our world. Throughout the article, Flew equates the argument for existence of God to a court case where the accused has the presumption of innocence. The one proclaiming that God exists is the prosecutor, and the skeptic is the one holding that presumption of innocence. Atheism is the default position.

My first question is to ask, burden of proof to whom? Who is the jury and judge? Second, is it only the believer that has this burden? Is atheism really the default position?

Within an academic debate, there could be strict rules to follow. One of these might force the believer to deliver a compelling proof and demand nothing from the skeptic. If this is true, it is where things will stand. Nothing else is allowed.

In 2009, a debate was held between William Lane Craig, a well-known Christian apologist, and Christopher Hitchens, a famous atheist. The following is a quote taken from Hitchens's closing remarks:

> It seems to me, to put it in a condensed form: extraordinary claims—such as the existence of a Divine Power with a Son who cares enough to come and redeem us—extraordinary claims require truly extraordinary evidence. I don't think any of the evidence we heard from Dr. Craig, brilliantly marshalled as it was, was extraordinary enough to justify the *extreme* claims that are being made and backed by it.[11]

---

[10] Anthony Flew, "The Presumption of Atheism," *Canadian Journal of Philosophy* 2, no. 1 (1972):29-46.

[11] William Lane Craig and Christopher Hitchens, "Does God Exist?" debate (Biola University, California, 2009).

Hitchens leaned on the extraordinary claim premise. I suspect that he also had Flew's burden of proof hypothesis in mind. He failed to consider that this kind of public debate places the burden on both presenters. The listening audience is judge and jury. Each individual listener judges and decides who won and who lost. It is a dangerous tactic in such a forum to simply say, "I don't need to prove anything, that's your job." It is like a lawyer forgoing the closing argument. In any case, a debate situation proves very little; it only reveals who is better prepared on a given day.

Debates and academic rules don't apply in our everyday experience. We each form a worldview, and it begins to take shape very early in life. In my case, my parents were nominal Catholics; I don't remember them ever going to church, not even on Christmas or Easter. God was not a topic that we talked about. I went to Catholic School till I was eight. After that, my father became an atheist and transferred me to a public school. From that time on, he considered religion to be a money-making racket. His new-found position didn't shake my faith though, even at that young age. I can say that I never remember a time when I didn't believe in God. I didn't know why or what kind of God he was. I had little idea of what I believed, but I did believe that there was a God of some kind. In my case, this is my default position. It is my default worldview.

Without extraordinary convincing, we are unlikely to budge. Sometimes, maybe even most of the time, life experience provides the basis for major shifts in thinking. Shifts of thinking could stem from a major tragedy, abuse by a respected religious leader, being swindled by a faith organization, some important or unimportant unanswered prayer, or simply hating all the rules and expectations. It could be intimidation, being shamed by colleagues, loss of funding, peer pressure, the lures of culture, and many other things.

On the other hand, we could be moved by a vivid dream, a miracle, or a perceived supernatural presence that is as real as it can be. Or, as in my case, we might always have believed, and still do.

For some of us who have a rationalistic nature, we research. This impulse usually comes much later, certainly not to an eight-year old. But where is the burden of proof? In life, each one of us is judge and jury. If I am trying to convince Richard Dawkins that the Christian God is real, it is my responsibility, my burden of proof. If he is to convince me, then the burden falls to him. He tried in his book, *The*

God Delusion. He failed; I found his arguments weak. The burden is always on the one who is trying to change another's worldview.

In any case, it is an uphill project to change a person's mind, and many books set out to convince. This book is not like that. I hope to present a different way to see things, to provoke thought and spark debate, to encourage you to wrestle with your beliefs, not necessarily to change your mind. You could say that God has the burden to make himself known, should he choose to do so. In some cases, as I describe my positions, evangelicals might cheer; in others, they may strongly disagree. Nevertheless, doctrinal differences need not lead to serious divisions.

I want to point out that I don't simply ignore those things that trouble me about faith in general, and the Christian faith in particular. Over the years, I've seen many who left the faith, and others who walked away and later found their way back. For some, their faith is hanging by a thread. I've also witnessed evangelistic fundamentalists who later became either extreme atheists or political radicals. They simply changed teams, sometimes very aggressively. I try to listen to valid arguments and I do my best to resolve them in my mind. In some cases, this leads to a crisis that I work to reconcile.

God of the Gaps

> The madman jumped into their midst and pierced them with his eyes. "Whither is God?" he cried; "I will tell you. *We have killed him* you and I. All of us are his murderers....God is dead. God remains dead. And we have killed him. ... How shall we comfort ourselves, the murderers of all murderers? ... What festivals of atonement, what sacred games shall we have to invent? Is not the greatness of this deed too great for us? Must we ourselves not become gods simply to appear worthy of it?"[12]—Friedrich Nietzsche

Did the birth of modern science and philosophical thought lead to the inevitable death of God? I recently listened to a PBS debate arguing

---

[12] Friedrich Nietzsche, "The Parable of the Madman," (1882).

the premise, "Does Science Refute God?" Four debaters presented their cases, two in favor of the premise and two against. The audience voted both at the beginning and end of the debate; the side that changed the most minds was declared the winner. It turns out that the audience voted in favor of the premise; "Science refutes God."[13] Does this settle the issue? Did the audience, in this case, perform the burial? Has God, in light of 21st century enlightened thought, ceased to be relevant? Let's take a closer look.

In ancient times, people did not understand the workings of the natural world. They made sense of the cosmos by their observations, as limited as they were. They hypothesized the existence of gods and used various sacrificial and magic rituals in an attempt to control the future. Sacrifice today and hope for a better tomorrow. Scientists call these things superstitions.

The scientific revolution changed much of this. We know that Earth is just one small planet in an unbelievably large universe. It is not at the center but positioned at an unlikely place among the billions of medium sized galaxies. Stars and comets are not living heavenly beings, but astronomical bodies, which we can investigate and eventually understand. We know that sickness comes from germs, not from angry gods. The Universe operates in predictable ways which we accurately describe using mathematical formulas. Volcanoes, earthquakes, floods, and famines are natural events. Paul Henry Thiry d'Holbach, a prominent French Enlightenment philosopher states: "If the ignorance of nature gave birth to such a variety of gods, the knowledge of this nature is calculated to destroy them."

Nietzsche's *Parable of the Madman* (cited above) contains the famous expression, *God is Dead.* Yet his statement is often misunderstood. It is not meant to be a statement of triumph. Nietzsche posits various questions in his writings: What comes next? How do we derive meaning without God? Is there anything transcendent that we must answer to? Can we even survive as a species? Can we avoid oscillating between nihilism and totalitarianism?

Many scientists believe that God is dead. They often go a bit further. Our ability to explore and think objectively and rationally, eliminates any need for God. This worldview explains how the God of

---

[13] "Does Science Refute God," *NPR Intelligence Squared Debate* (December 11, 2012).

the Gaps charge originated. What we know is science, what we don't know is ignorance, and God lives on the ignorance side of the equation. I could quote dozens of leading scientists who adhere to this belief. The popular astrophysicist and TV personality, Neil deGrass Tyson is one example. He claims, "God is an ever-receding pocket of scientific ignorance." Some scientists go even further than this. They posit that belief in God prevents a person from doing good science. Consider the following quote from James D. Watson, a co-discoverer of DNA: "The biggest advantage to believing in God is you don't have to understand anything, no physics, no biology. I wanted to understand."

Is God dead? Does God live in what we don't know? Robert Jastrow was an agnostic and a NASA-based American astronomer and planetary physicist. Starting in the late 1960s, he observed anger and frustration expressed by his colleagues. It was becoming evident that the Universe had a beginning. Long held steady state theories of the eternal cosmos were wrong. If the Universe began, God's foot was back in the door. Jastrow wondered why his colleagues should care. Science is supposed to be an objective pursuit of the truth. Data is to be followed wherever it leads, even if this points towards a supernatural beginning. So Jastrow was inspired to write his book, *God and the Astronomers*. Its purpose was to document the scientific history of Big Bang discoveries and the reactions to it by scientists. The following are a number of powerful quotes from his work.

1. There is a kind of religion in science; it is the religion of a person who believes there is order and harmony in the Universe. Every event can be explained in a rational way as the product of some previous event; every effect must have its cause; there is no First Cause. ... This religious faith of the scientist is violated by the discovery that the world had a beginning under conditions in which the known laws of physics are not valid, and as a product of forces or circumstances we cannot discover. When that happens, the scientist has lost control. If he really examined the implications, he would be traumatized. (113-114)
2. Consider the enormity of the problem. Science has proved that the Universe exploded into being at a certain moment. It asks: What cause produced this effect? Who or what put the matter

or energy into the Universe? ... And science cannot answer these questions, because, according to the astronomers, in the first moments of its existence the Universe was compressed to an extraordinary degree and consumed by the heat of a fire beyond human imagination. The shock of that instant must have destroyed every particle of evidence that could have yielded a clue to the cause of the great explosion. (114)
3. Now we see how the astronomical evidence supports the biblical view of the origin of the world. The details differ, but the essential elements in the astronomical and biblical accounts of Genesis are the same: the chain of events leading to man commenced suddenly and sharply at a definite moment in time, in a flash of light and energy. (14)
4. For the scientist who has lived by his faith in the power of reason, the story ends like a bad dream. He has scaled the mountains of ignorance; he is about to conquer the highest peak; as he pulls himself over the final rock, he is greeted by a band of theologians who have been sitting there for centuries. (116)
5. It turns out that the scientist behaves the way the rest of us do when our beliefs are in conflict with the evidence. We become irritated, we pretend the conflict does not exist, or we paper it over with meaningless phrases. (16)

Apparently, God is making a comeback. Perhaps he is not dead after all. Yet there are many with dug-in positions. When someone who is normally on the skeptic-side appears to agree with the theists, they temporarily become friends. When Einstein says, "God doesn't play dice," he becomes a theist. Another time he denies the possibility of a personal God, and he becomes a skeptic. Too bad that we cannot ask him. Instead we argue back and forth about what a dead guy thought.

Of course, the scientific or faith community expects those who share their views to remain faithful in their allegiance. But what if a leading figure changes sides? Suppose, hypothetically, that Franklin Graham schedules a news conference for a major announcement. He declares that he can no longer believe in the Christian God; the scientific evidence is just too strong. Evangelicals would be horrified, and they likely would feel betrayed. Negative comments would come from every direction. This is what happened when Anthony Flew changed teams. He was a leading atheist whose papers (discussed above) were copied and cited over and over for a half century, a hero if you will. Then he did the unthinkable; he co-authored the book, *There is a God.* One day he was enlightened, the next day he was a senile old man. It was the ultimate betrayal.

Ignorance is a condition from which we all suffer, both scientists and theists. Even if the body of scientific knowledge has all the answers, nobody knows, or even comes close to knowing those answers. We live by experience and intuition. It is not possible for anyone to understand everything there is to know about every subject. We cannot be experts in all fields, so we know what we know and come to some conclusions about those areas that we don't. Our *a priori* biases play a huge part in informing our positions.

Every year there are tens of thousands of journal articles published. No one can read but a small fraction of these. And most would glaze over at the details of the overwhelming majority of them, especially those outside of one's field of study. Yet they all contribute to the scientific body of knowledge.

I sometimes joke that the definition of a Ph.D. is a pursuit where a person learns everything there is to know about something which almost no one in the world cares about. Many times, the effort requires spending decades trying to make a breakthrough in a very specialized area. Outside of that area, the person with a Ph.D. frequently knows very little. If that person is working twelve to sixteen hours per day in their area, there simply is no time left. In most cases, it is disingenuous for one schooled in Physics to speak with assumed authority about Evolutionary Biology, Astronomy, or Synthetic Chemistry. Their Ph.D. does not provide them the credentials to be recognized as an expert in every area.

If I were to ask a typical member of the Freedom from Religion group what's the reason for them being against religion, I seriously doubt that they would cite some article in *Nature*. Most skeptics have not considered all the arguments for and against to come to a sound decision. Neither has the average church-goer. I don't say this to be critical. It is how we humans navigate the few years of our lives. We learn as much as we can and go with that. We tend to avoid those data that conflict with what we hope to be true. I know this is true in my case; I try to force myself to fight the tendency.

So, is belief in God synonymous with ignorance? Well, I hope I've shown, we are all ignorant, some more than others. Some of us, religious and irreligious, are trying to learn with an open mind whatever we can in the time available to dedicate to the effort.

Regarding the *God of the gaps* charge, I am convinced that there will always be gaps. The complexity of reality is far beyond humanity's ability to comprehend and measure. Every new discovery inevitably leads to even more gaps. Often, things that were thought to be settled suddenly, and unexpectedly, become open for debate.

I believe in God. I have read books by both theists and skeptics and enjoy doing so. I've considered arguments from both sides, and at times wrestled with opposing points that seem valid. I can say that I've not found compelling arguments to change my view. The God in whom I believe transcends the gaps. His creative power explains both what we know and that which we don't know. He is not defined by primitive speculations, and he certainly is not like the Greek gods who were confined to the cosmos.

Nevertheless, to those who want to persuade me otherwise, I say, "Do your research. Close the gaps without opening even larger ones. Prove by observation that the space, time, energy, and matter did not have a beginning. Show empirically how life spontaneously came to be." These and many other gaps exist. They are real, significant, and important. I predict that ongoing scientific inquiry will reveal increasing evidence for design. This will demonstrate that the creation model has predictive power.

As I've shown, the gaps argument does not refer solely to the receding place occupied by God in our explanations. It more commonly refers to unanswered questions in general. People of faith always strive to answer legitimate challenges proposed by skeptics and by issues of everyday life. Similarly, scientists work to better understand the workings of our reality. Each new answer eliminates a gap. Perhaps with this in mind, it is possible for science and faith to work together to minimize the gaps in the traditional patterns of thought that we all have. Faith can lead to better science, just as science can strengthen faith.

Religion

Religion has dozens of definitions. Many of these relate to belief in an all-powerful, transcendent being. I prefer a wider definition. The following quote is one example: "Any activity pursued on behalf of an ideal end against obstacles and in spite of threats of personal loss because of its general and enduring value."[14]

This wider definition of religion will normally embody the following characteristics.

1. Adherence to a well-defined set of principles
2. A desire to spread the doctrine to the ignorant, unenlightened, or lost
3. Great exuberation upon experiencing victory
4. Faith that important benefits will spring from the ideology

Religion, as I'm defining it, might relate to any strongly held set of beliefs that contains precepts that are non-negotiable. In this case, the dogma can easily become a replacement for God. The question I pose is: Are humans wired to be religious? Can we avoid it?

I think that it is safe to say that religion is everywhere. As an example, let's consider the political sphere. As our institutions fracture and become more partisan, activists fight for things that they consider to be self-evidently righteous. Therefore, those who resist are either ignorant or evil, not people of goodwill who also want what is best. Negative advertisements portray the opposition to be dangerous, holding positions designed to harm people and bring widescale destruction. In extreme cases, average citizens experience harsh personal attacks, simply because they support the wrong candidate or policy.

This being said, religious beliefs are not necessarily bad. Christians are generally quite happy when they are able to lead someone to the faith. Similarly, political pundits celebrate when their favored candidate wins an election. But what happens when a person turns away from the faith or the other party wins? Do relationships persist, or is there hostility? One's faith becomes a problem when it negatively affects how we treat those that don't agree with us.

---

[14] John Dewey, *A common Faith* (1934): 27.

Ideology can be dangerous, whether it pertains to a political persuasion, a particular manner of living, or a concept of God. It is easy to feel superior to those who differ, labeling them with derogatory phrases. Over time adherents become less able to consider alternative points of view and begin to defensibly react with anger to criticism. Sometimes, this can even lead to violence.

A popular quote attributed to the Swiss Psychologist Carl Jung states: "People don't have ideas, ideas have people." This is a dangerous thing. If one is not careful, an ideology can take on a life of its own and replace one's persona. I often observe political interviews where respondents seemingly are no longer present; instead, a living doctrinal spirit emerges that robotically spews out prepared talking points. If unrestrained, this phenomenon can lead to intolerance and fanaticism. It separates people and leads to wars. It can cause great civilizations to fall. It is well to consider a couple other quotes by Carl Jung: "Everything that irritates us about others can lead us to an understanding of ourselves." And: "Knowing your own darkness is the best method for dealing with the darknesses of other people."

The point is this. Belief in the God of the Bible may be losing its appeal in the twenty-first century, but this does not eliminate religion. Humanity requires gods. The question at hand is, "Which gods will they be?" The pull of the crowds and the need to conform always dominate reason. We rarely use logic to decide which positions to hold. Instead, we use our intellect to justify positions already held.[15] Although we cannot change our nature, it is important that we are aware of the dangers, and resist the evil parts of these tendencies.

---

[15] Haight, *The Righteous Mind*, 52-71.

Chapter 2

Addressing the Skeptics

> The common man cannot imagine this Providence otherwise than in the figure of an enormously exalted father. Only such a being can understand the needs of the children of men and be softened by their prayers and placated by the signs of their remorse. The whole thing is so patently infantile, so foreign to reality, that to anyone with a friendly attitude to humanity it is painful to think that the great majority of mortals will never be able to rise above this view of life.[16] — Sigmund Freud

The above quote is typical among skeptics who consider themselves champions of science and reason. Without presenting counter evidence, they trivialize the average person, who they believe is imprisoned by ignorant superstitions. Of course, attack by insult rarely works. They may energize those holding similar positions, but they are guaranteed to alienate those who disagree. As a result, people retreat to their social circles, and meaningful dialogue becomes impossible.

This being said, there are challenges that people of faith should consider. Let's check out a few of these.

God's Attributes; are they self-contradictory?

I'm going to tell you what a rose is.

> A rose is of the domain, Eukaryote, in the Plantae kingdom, of phylum Magnoliophyta, class Magnoliopsida, of order Rosales, family Rosaceae, genus Rosoidaea, of species Rosa L, having the scientific name Rosa and common name, Rose. It is an angiosperm of the monophyletic, Rosid clade, having been called tricolpates or non-magnoliid dicots by

---

[16] Sigmund Freud, *Civilization and its Discontents* (1930).

> previous authors. It is an Eudicotidae. It has prominent colored anthers.

I don't understand. What is a rose?

I know nothing about botany, so please excuse any mistakes that I've made in the above technical description of a rose. Suffice it to say that I know one when I see it, and somehow it conveys much more to me than scientific jargon. Yet this is what we do in Western culture. We dissect, categorize, and describe every detail. I think this is one reason English has many more words than biblical Hebrew, which only has a few thousand. We kill things by describing them in this way.

I don't mean to impugn our Western way of doing things. In some ways, this approach can be quite beneficial. When I as a computer scientist build a complex system, I break the whole into parts, those parts into sub-parts, and so on, eventually getting to something simple enough to implement. In other disciplines, I'm sure it's important to understand the smallest components and how they interrelate. By working upward, we can eventually come to understand entire systems.

This divide and conquer strategy doesn't always work, though, and if taken to the extreme, it can be ridiculous. In the case of a rose, after splitting it into an absurd number of pieces and categories, we kill the life of the thing. We lose the ability to appreciate the whole: that is, seeing, smelling, and admiring it on its own terms. Words do not always convey the wonder we feel with our senses. When we try to describe God, one who is beyond our scientific instruments, in terms of a list of attributes, we undoubtedly will miss the mark.

Skeptics say, "There is no such being." Okay, but let's suppose, for the sake of this discussion, that God does exist. Let's also suppose that this God is the one described in the Bible.

How do we describe such a God? As I said already, we pile on a list of attributes. God is omniscient, omnipresent, omnipotent, omni, omni, omni, and more omnis. There is an obvious problem. None of these things accurately describes God. It also leaves us open to logical circular contradictions.

For example, we say that God is eternal. But what does this mean? I define eternity as beyond time and space. This concept agrees with science, which now understands that before the *Big Bang*, there was no such thing as time. Scientific experiments also show that time does not flow at a constant rate. If we could travel at the speed of light, time would stop, yet we might still exist. If we could travel very close to the speed of light, our relative time would slow to a crawl, yet time would still progress normally on planet Earth. The Creator, the Eternal God, is one who lives outside the bounds of time and space. Eternity wraps around our past and our future.

Most of us live seventy to eighty years. We speculate that God, who created everything, lives longer. The longest we can imagine is infinite, so we think that infinite is equivalent to eternal. Unfortunately, as just explained, we don't even know what it means to be eternal. God's existence is another item altogether. It cannot be defined using time as a metric.

When Moses asked God for his name, he replied, "I am that I am." When Jesus was asked how he, being less than fifty years old, could have seen Abraham, he replied, "Before Abraham was, I am." "I am" is sufficient. Nothing more needs to be said. That is probably the best one can do to describe the duration of God's existence.

Let's consider the God attribute, omnipresent. How can he be everywhere at once? I wondered about this when I was younger. How can God hear every prayer of billions of people at the same time? In the era before Google, it was a valid question. Now, with a clumsy network of servers, wires, and signals, Google has no problem. Billions ask, and Google answers.

What does it mean to be omnipresent? Is God physically present at each place? I think not. We cannot use God's physicality as a metric, because God is spirit.

Consider the following logical argument.

1. If God exists, he is transcendent, outside space and time
2. If God exists, he is omnipresent
3. A transcendent being cannot exist anywhere in space
4. Hence, a transcendent being is not omnipresent
5. Therefore, there is no God

The argument fails. It is simply a game of words. Do we even know how to describe one who is transcendent? I think not. Furthermore, who says that transcendence precludes existence? The description, "I

Addressing the Skeptics

am that I am" covers it, doesn't it? God certainly is aware of what each of us is doing, and a physical presence is not needed.

Let's try another one of these logical arguments.

1. If God exists, then he is non-physical
2. If God exists, then he is a person
3. A person needs to be physical
4. Hence, God doesn't exist

This argument has the same fallacy. Why does a person need to be physical? What does it even mean to be physical? Does physical mean having a body that we can touch and see? God's substance is entirely another matter.

What about, God is Omnipotent?

1. If God can create a stone that he cannot lift, he is not omnipotent
2. If God cannot create a stone that he cannot lift, he is not omnipotent

Again, the argument reduces God to a word game. We have some strength, so we measure God as having infinitely more strength. But God's strength is different from ours. Our strength is not a valid metric. Perhaps almighty is a better word than omnipotent. Even that misses the point. "I am that I am" also works in this case.

Now, let's attack God based on virtue.

1. God, by definition, is one where none greater can be conceived
2. God, then, is the most virtuous
3. Virtue includes the ability to overcome pain and danger
4. To overcome pain and danger requires the risk of being destroyed
5. A God who can be destroyed is not the greatest that we can conceive
6. Therefore, God doesn't exist

In this case, the metric is our ability to conceive. God's existence does not depend on our conceptions. His existence certainly does not depend on arbitrary logical assumptions that we make. The argument, therefore, is logically incoherent.

I'll consider one more of these.

1. God is righteous and all powerful
2. Because God is righteous, God hates evil
3. Evil exists
4. Because evil exists,
    a. God either doesn't care, in which case he is not righteous, or
    b. God cannot to do anything about evil, in which case he is not all powerful
5. Therefore, God doesn't exist

There are several fallacies here. What does it mean for God to hate? The assumption is: We hate, so God's hate must be of the same nature as ours. But how do we know this? The Bible describes God in terms of human emotions. These are the authors' best attempt to describe the indescribable.

A second fallacy involves the premise concerning evil. It assumes a binary choice: either God doesn't care or God is impotent. But what if reality is not reducible to either this or either that. The argument assumes that evil exists, so it will always exist. I believe all things will be made right. It won't be in this life, but it will happen. I see evil as a temporary part of our current existence and God's kingdom will bring it to an end. I don't know why God allows it presently, but I recognize that I don't have enough information to judge.

I can say this. Maybe God's priorities are not the same as ours. Perhaps an imagined utopia is not the same thing as goodness. The cosmos is a dangerous, dynamic, place packed with powerful natural forces. This entails risk, and with risk comes the potential for pain and loss. But without risk would there be reason to strive, to improve? Would we become lazy and bored? Nature has great power, and so do we. We have a choice. Should we use our power to help each other? Should we strive to live in harmony with the natural forces? Or, should we stubbornly choose to ignore or destroy the environment and hurt each other? God respects our choices.

I didn't make up the logical arguments that I described above. I extracted them from popular books written by skeptics. In my opinion,

Addressing the Skeptics

the reasoning is quite fallacious. The cases presented are funny in a way; I enjoy seeing them. I'm surprised people take them seriously. It takes a Western *enlightened* mind set to come up with these pseudo-proofs. God is not one who can be dissected, like we dissect a rose. If the God of the Bible doesn't exist, surely there must be a better way to make the case than playing with the man-made list of omni-characteristics.

Things are not right; it's not fair

> Three blind mice, three blind mice, see how they …
>
> Twinkle, twinkle little star, how I wonder what you are. Up above the world so high, like a diamond in the …
>
> There was an old lady who swallowed a fly
> I don't know why she swallowed a fly; perhaps she'll …

I'll bet that you had to fill in the missing words. Why? I think it has something to do with the way our brains are wired. And it extends beyond nursery rhymes. Try listening to a chorus of music and leave out the last note; I bet, even for those of us who are musically challenged, we simply cannot let it stay that way. For example,

> Amazing Grace, how sweet the sound,
> that saved a wretch like me.
> I once was lost but now I'm found,
> was blind, but now I …

Could you hear the melody? I bet you could. Did you fill in the last note? I bet you did. Now, let's try changing some words. Can we stand the difference?

> Amazing cat, how sweet the meow,
> that saved a mouse like me.

No! No good! That just won't do. It is not right.

What about movies? A few years back, my wife Viv and I saw a movie called *Premonition*. When the plot begins, the police come to the door and tell Linda Hanson that her husband was killed in a car crash. But then she finds him alive and well. The scenario repeats over and over, and she tries everything she knows to do to prevent the crash from happening for real. In the end, the movie winds up with her husband dying anyway. When I was leaving the theatre, I wondered why I ever watched such a thing. It wasn't fair; it just was not right.

Action adventure movies typically feature the bad guy, often with super powers, that appears to be invincible and is very evil. The plot progresses from one special effect scene to another until finally, in some unlikely sequence, the good guy vanquishes the bad guy. Of course, there is usually some stone left unturned so we will want to return for a sequel. Movies like Star Trek often portray humanity at risk, but there always is the hero who saves the day and brings salvation from the edge of destruction.

Movies are supposed to reconcile. Most of us are not willing to spend money for those that don't. Our psyche won't allow it. According to the psychologist Jordan Peterson: "Chaos and order are fundamental elements. ... The fundamental reality of chaos and order is true for everything alive, not only for us. Living things are always to be found in places they can master, surrounded by things and situations that make them vulnerable."[17]

Generally, actors read the script before they agree to play a role. But what if they don't? They then would have to put complete trust in the producer, director, and script writer. I suppose that if they didn't like where things were going, they could quit in the middle. That is, if they didn't have an iron-clad contract.

In life, we participate in the drama of the Universe, which we experience firsthand, not as observers. For many of us born in Western cultures, things are good, at least for a while. For me, that is the way it was early August 1994 when I was living in Duncanville, TX. Then one night just after midnight, the police called. "Your son is in the hospital; there's been an accident." Within a few hours, after rushing to the hospital, my seventeen-year-old son was dead. He had climbed up to the top of a parking garage with a friend and was running around on the roof when a skylight gave way. His spine broke in three places

---

[17] Jordan Peterson, *Twelve Rules for Life*, 40.

and his brain was hemorrhaging. Nothing could be done. I've heard of miracles after accidents like this. In my case, though, none were coming. God didn't intervene this time.

In the weeks that followed, my wife thought, "Why does the Sun shine and the grass grow? My son is dead." She blamed herself for not praying enough. For me, I was numb; I was there but not there. I went through the motions of life, but inside, I felt dead. This is one of the few times in my life where I heard a voice, which I believe was God. He asked, "Will you still follow me now?" I responded, "To whom else could I turn?" At that point, I knew that my faith would persist. Still, my son's death was the most painful thing that I experienced in my life.

Others experience loss that is much worse than mine. I can't imagine the pain experienced by Christians and Yazidis forced from their homes, having to watch family members killed in front of them, and then see their young daughters taken away to be sex slaves. Parts of the world regularly experience famine, disease, and starvation. Add to this volcanoes, earthquakes, and tsunamis; we quickly realize that nothing is guaranteed. Live long enough and loss is certain.

So, especially in the West, we ask: "why?" If God exists, why doesn't he intervene? Doesn't he care? Is he too weak? We want answers, but they don't come. Some propose answers, but often they don't help. In Muslim communities, the answer simply is "Allah willed it," and that is it. For some in the East, "It's karma." An atheist would say, "There is no God and all is subject to chance. Get used to it." Some Christians say, "It's God's judgment because of sin." When my son died, well-meaning people would say, "God loved your son so much that he took him to heaven right away," or "He's in a better place."

I refuse to accept or be comforted by any of the above explanations. Each of us has life, we live through our experience, and then we die. If this life is all there is, the atheists would have a point. But I don't believe this; I find that possibility repugnant. There must be something that follows death. Without this, things can never reconcile. The powerful always will oppress the weak; the poor will always be at the bottom. The evil ones simply die without justice. Culture decides good and evil for itself without consequence. In the end, humanity will go extinct, and all life on this planet will end. I will not live my life with this pessimistic worldview. I instead will accept the promises of Jesus recorded in Matthew chapter five:

> Then he began to speak, and taught them, saying: Blessed are the poor in spirit, for theirs is the kingdom of heaven. Blessed are those who mourn, for they will be comforted. Blessed are the meek, for they will inherit the earth. Blessed are those who hunger and thirst for righteousness, for they will be filled. Blessed are the merciful, for they will receive mercy. Blessed are the pure in heart, for they will see God. Blessed are the peacemakers, for they will be called children of God. Blessed are those who are persecuted for righteousness' sake, for theirs is the kingdom of heaven. (Matt. 5:2-10)

If we consider the events of the Universe as a cosmic drama, we as participants simply don't know how the whole story plays out. I choose to believe that there will be a time when all is made whole. I choose to put my trust in the creator of all things, even when I don't like or understand the way things are going. I'll go with Colossians 1:20: "It pleased the Father to reconcile all things to Himself through Him, whether the things on earth or the things in heaven."

What is my evidence? It is true that the second law of thermodynamics implies that chaos will prevail over order and ultimately, the Universe will go dark. But is this the final word? Perhaps, in the end, order will triumph and everything will be set right. We see signs of this as we wonder over the goodness of nature. We see it in how we are wired. This is enough evidence for me. Things must reconcile.

What is the nature of this God who will eventually bring everything into balance? I don't try to reduce God to a list of attributes. He is alive; he is a person; he feels; he loves. He is not a cold-hearted, distant, angry, judgmental mastermind that forces, or concocts, some divine plan prescribed by a rigid, predefined blueprint. We, his creations, each have a say in shaping a new creation. God respects our desires, and willingly yields to them. God is sovereign but not necessarily in control. He places limits on his power. He is a master artist who works with our imperfections and in the end, he will complete a great, amazing masterpiece. Despite the darkness of all of the evil of this world, he is well-able to bring forth goodness and redeem whatever is broken.

You might say, "You can decide to believe these things, but that doesn't mean you are right." Maybe so, but I still have a right to choose. My faith empowers me to be an active participant to bring about the kingdom and strive in a small way, to make this world a better place.

God vs. Science

> While media attention goes to the strident atheists who claim religion is foolish superstition…a majority of the people I know have no difficulty accepting scientific knowledge and holding to religious faith.
> —Physics Nobel Laureate William D. Phillips

According to the popular narrative, scientists are anti-God and people of faith are anti-science. The above quote illustrates that this is not true. Many scientists maintain a strong religious faith, and many Christians are strong supporters of scientific inquiry. This being said, there are a growing number of skeptics who believe that religion's impact on society is destructive, and they fight to reduce or eliminate its presence. Naturally, Christian apologists work to counter these efforts.

Many times, over the past hundreds of years, Christian apologists and skeptics intellectually went toe-to-toe in hot debate. Both sides landed their share of body blows that the opposing side now tries to forget. And of course, the opposition makes certain that this will not be the case.

For example, the skeptics don't like to be reminded that Stalin, Pol Pot, and Mao Tse-tung were atheists who murdered close to a hundred million of their own citizens. This dispels the myth that belief in God is the source of the worst evils. Skeptics don't like being reminded that it was the intellectuals, including Darwin himself, that promoted forced sterilization and even murder of those considered inferior. Eugenics was thought to be good thing that would speed up evolution by breeding away the races that were "less evolved." Skeptics don't like hearing that the God of the gaps is making a strong comeback; those seemingly small cracks in scientific understanding have widened to large caverns in the past 75 years.

On the other side, the apologists hate hearing about the Crusades, of course, but also other forms of intolerance. Galileo pushed his friendship with Pope Urban VII to the limits by poking fun at him in his book, *Dialogue Concerning Two World Systems*. As a result, he wound-up in-house arrest for the rest of his life. One didn't challenge the Vatican in those days and when others tried it, they didn't fare as well as Galileo. John Wycliffe who fought to relieve wealthy monks of their large land holdings, was declared to be a heretic several decades after his death. The Church ruled that his bones could not remain in holy cemetery grounds, so workers promptly dug up those bones, burned them, and threw their remnants into the river Swift. Others had even worse fates awaiting. The Church (Catholics and Protestants) were not hesitant to burn people at the stake to cleanse the land of their perceived evils (ex. Jan Hus July 4, 1415). Torture was commonplace. So much for the command to love your enemies.

The Scopes trial is a more recent body blow to the faith community. In the early twentieth century, evolution theory was gaining ground. It presented such a threat that it had to be opposed and destroyed at all costs. It certainly had to be kept away from the developing minds of our children. A new Christian doctrine took hold. "He who accepts evolution will become an atheist and will be forever damned to the eternal fire." The tension reached a climax when the substitute science teacher John T. Scopes, dared to commit the high crime of teaching evolution illegally to a high school class in Dayton, Tennessee. A court trial followed that was humorous to some and deadly serious to others. The event captured the attention of the entire country. Reporters dubbed the proceedings as the "monkey trial." The honor of God was at stake. The question was: did we evolve from monkeys? Are we no more than an advanced race of apes? The following quote summarizes the goings on.

> More than two hundred reporters, from as far away as London, descended on Dayton during that hot summer of 1925. For the first time in history, a radio station broadcast the court proceedings live. Pictures of grinning monkeys sipping soda and holding medicine

jars adorned billboards and shop windows across town, and Robinson's Drugstore proudly displayed a banner proclaiming "Where it All Started." Protestors, activists, and preachers made pilgrimages to Dayton, so residents erected a giant platform on the courthouse lawn to accommodate any impromptu lectures or debates. (It was rumored that Gorge Rappleyea actually staged a fistfight there.) People could pay to get their picture made with a live chimpanzee, and the town constable even put a sign on his motorcycle that read "Monkeyville Police." A *New York Times* reporter wrote that "whatever the deep significance of the trial, if it has any, there is no doubt that it has attracted some of the world's champion freaks."[18]

The monkey trial ensued and after a week or so of excitement, the result was anticlimactic. Scopes was found guilty and had to pay a $50 fine. The fundamentalists, who engaged the battle with fervor, looked ridiculous to the country and to the world. Their biggest victory became their biggest defeat. To this day the faith community has not fully recovered, at least not in scientific circles.

Recently, skeptics are in danger of repeating the same "monkey" mistake. Try going into most any evolutionary biology lab and saying the words, *Intelligent Design*. At best, you'll get sneers of mockery. More likely, you'll get shouted out. If you are a professor, you will immediately lose status. I suspect that many more scientists believe in God than the polls reveal. In the current scientific environment, they must be careful and keep their views private to avoid censure and even dismissal.

There are numerous examples of scientific discrimination that I could cite, but I'll summarize one egregious example. It concerns Dr. Richard Sternberg, who was a Research Associate from the Smithsonian Institute of Natural History. In 2004, after a standard peer review process, Sternberg chose to publish a paper authored by Steven Meyer. It was titled *The Origin of Biological Information and the Higher Taxonomic Categories*. Steven Meyer is an Intelligent Design

---

[18] Rachel Held Evans, *Faith Unraveled*, 53.

proponent, Sternberg is not. Nevertheless, he thought the topic was worthy of discussion.

There were repercussions. It started with a concerted effort by colleagues to have him dismissed. After not taking the hint that he should resign, an investigation ensued. Sternberg was cleared of wrong doing and temporarily retained his position. Things were not settled. Retaliation followed. Sternberg was transferred to a hostile supervisor, he lost his office space, he was required to submit additional and unnecessary work reports, he lost access to museum specimens needed for his research, and his access to the museum itself was restricted. In addition to all this, Sternberg was pressured to release the names of others who approved the publication. He was smeared with false allegations, and his political and religious beliefs were investigated. Finally, when it came time for his position to be renewed, he was demoted without explanation.

Sternberg committed the unforgivable sin; he allowed an article critical of Neo-Darwinism to be published in a scientific journal. He failed to reject unpopular positions concerning unexplained natural phenomena.

There are other very public examples of scientific discrimination. I've heard report that Richard Dawkins believes that a person should be denied admission to Oxford if they profess a belief in God. He is not alone. Some believe that you cannot do good science if you believe in God. I have a friend that bounced around between three advisors for this reason. He eventually earned his Ph.D. but had to endure several years of extra grief in the process.

It is true that our worldview can get in the way of our scientific research. But this can go both ways. When junk DNA was discovered, many on the evolutionary side of the fence declared victory and went home. Now we learn that the junk may not be so much junk after all. In fact, the name for it has changed. No longer junk, it is now called intergenic DNA. Its functions are extremely complex, not well-understood, and its mechanism for controlling the timing of gene activation seems to be in its own language. The protein coding portions of DNA between humans and Bonobo monkeys have 98.8% commonality. When we consider this intergenic area, the common percentage decreases significantly.

Another example is described in the book, *Irreducible Mind: Toward a Psychology for the 21st Century,* produced by a reputable group of professors from the University of Virginia. This book describes the research of Fredrick Myers and William James near the end of the 19th century. Because the psychology community at the time wanted to be considered a *true* science, it went along with the prevailing pressure of the times and accepted that everything that happens in the human body is controlled by the neurology of the brain. Well-documented paranormal phenomena like near death, out of body experiences, telepathy, etc. were largely ignored for about fifty years. Only recently are studies being devised to analyze these things and determine whether they are real. This is a case where a materialistic bias inhibited progress.

There was great resistance to the big-bang theory, when it first came to light. Early discoveries were largely ignored for more than a decade. Resistance is common in science for a number of reasons. Any new theory that goes against the prevailing winds must face the rigor of all challenges before the mainstream accepts it; this is a good thing. Then, there are those scientists that dedicate decades to their research. To find out that one's life work is wrong is a hard thing to face. This is only natural, because scientists, human like all of us, will fight tooth-and-nail to hold their positions. There is so much at stake for them. But when we add God to the equation, the issue rises to a whole new level. Richard C. Lewontin of Harvard University illustrates this in a famous quote. It has nothing to do with science and everything to do with his worldview bias:

> It is not that the methods and institutions of science somehow compel us to accept a material explanation of the phenomenal world, but, on the contrary, that we are forced by our a priori adherence to material causes to create an apparatus of investigation and a set of concepts that produce material explanations, no matter how counter-intuitive, no matter how mystifying to the uninitiated. Moreover, that materialism is absolute, so we cannot allow a Divine foot in the door.

Not all God believing scientists face discrimination. There are many that do not. Jim Tour, arguably the top synthetic chemist in the world, is one of these. He has over a hundred patents, more than 650 peer-reviewed articles to his credit, and he is cited many thousands of times.

He has an open challenge to anyone who can explain to him the chemical mechanism that could lead to the first self-replicating cell or that could explain the mutations leading to varied body types. He is not asking for high-level arm-waving. He wants the actual chemistry behind the theory. No takers have come forward. Not only do all current explanations fall short, there are not even proposals showing how things might work chemically.

Tour describes evolutionary biologists as flying high over the city of molecular life. He works in the streets creating molecules at the bottom level. Getting anything to work at that level is a monumental challenge. Evolutionary time is the enemy, not the friend. As soon as an appropriate compound is formed, it is immediately subject to degradation. It will not stay around for years or centuries waiting for the next compound to appear to join with. Synthetic chemists take extraordinary care to preserve molecules needed in their creation of nanomachines. Nature does not have this luxury. Synthetic chemists carefully remove artifacts that will conflict with their procedures. Nature does not have this ability. Most importantly, synthetic chemists know what they are trying to build. According to evolutionary theory, nature has no clue; it is all by chance.[19]

There doesn't have to be an ongoing philosophical fight between God and science. This is not because, as many say, science and religion are separate domains, science the how, and religion the why. This is an over simplification. In 1978, the scientific community had a valid reason to want to analyze the Shroud of Turin. Was it really the burial cloth of Jesus? Carbon 14 dating implies no, but new evidence since arose, and the debate about this continues to this day. Similarly, the Bible seems to make statements about the how of creation, and so it crosses into the realm supposedly reserved for science. Both sides propose and re-propose, investigate and reinvestigate, interpret and reinterpret. In the end, we are simply trying to figure things out.

I am a computer scientist and have worked with many scientists over the years. Some are Christians, some are not. We work together and get along quite well. Most of us do our research in a professional manner and, believe it or not, very little of science has any direct

---

[19] Jim Tour, "Animadversions of a Synthetic Chemist," *Inference – International Review of Science* 2, no. 2 (2016) and "An Open Letter to my Colleagues 3," no. 2 (2017) in the same journal.

implication for evolutionary theory or for faith. I've worked quite a bit on trying to devise algorithms that will allow for language-independent speech recognition without requiring dictionaries, grammar, or training data. This is a very difficult problem, and after spending way too much time on this, I've had some very limited success. Belief in God has nothing to do with this research.

Recently, at a church service, a lady collapsed. Immediately, two doctors were by her side. Within minutes she was stabilized; professionals arrived and took her off to the hospital for further treatment. The competency of those doctors had nothing to do with their faith.

Times change, culture changes, the horizons of knowledge change. I think we all need to keep an open mind and not dismiss each other out of hand. Digging in to entrenched positions does no good for anyone. I believe that we need to be willing to listen and even to adapt our own views where necessary.

Darwinism

> **Evolution:** Changes in the populations of living things over time.
>
> **Darwinism:** The theory that all life on earth descended from the last universal common ancestor through the processes of natural selection and random mutations.
>
> **Intelligent Design (ID):** The hypothesis that certain features of the Universe and living things are best explained by an intelligent cause.
>
> **Third Way:** The imperative to seek approaches to explain the process of evolution that are not adequately explained by either Darwinism or ID.
>
> **Naturalism:** The belief that the natural world is a closed system that is completely knowable apart from any supernatural causes.

Panspermia: The belief that life exists throughout the Universe, distributed by meteoroids, asteroids, comets, planetoids, and, also, by spacecraft in the form of unintended contamination by microorganisms.

Epigenetics: The study of external or environmental factors that affect how cells read genes to cause cellular and body structural variations without requiring changes to DNA.

Based on the above definitions, all scientists accept evolution (changes over time). This is not controversial. A scientist can hold any of the above positions, but you cannot be both a Darwinist and an ID proponent. Darwinists hold to Naturalism which denies the possibility of supernatural causes. They assume that ID is a backhanded way of bringing religion into the classroom. Note though, that according to ID, the Universe might not have originated from an all-powerful God in the traditional sense. We could, for example, be part of some huge matrix, a computer game developed by creatures in a higher-level Universe. That would be weird, wouldn't it?

Darwinists can promote Panspermia (ex: Francis Crick, who with James Watson discovered the DNA structure). This position is possible because, even though it is not falsifiable and begs the question of life's origins, it is naturalistic.

It is possible for a Third Way proponent to accept some of Darwin's proposals, but the Third Way recognizes serious deficiencies in his approach. Epigenetics is a recent Third Way area of research that explores how living organisms can restructure themselves quickly according to stimuli in the environment.

Fundamental Darwinists tend to be hostile to ID proponents and also skeptical of the Third Way. They fear that both threaten their naturalistic view of science. They are particularly hostile to ID proponents because most, but not all of them are Christian.

Darwinists actively seek to mock, censure, and punish any scientist that publicly criticizes their beliefs. As a result, many scientists keep their views private. Only a few speak out, particularly those who already have earned tenure or who have impeccable careers that cannot be impugned. In some sense, I understand the hostility. The Enlightenment followed the age of Catholic/Protestant religious wars.

Addressing the Skeptics

That age produced inquisitions, burnings at the stake, horrible torture devices, and many other things too awful to describe; all of this was done in the name of God. Darwin gave intellectuals an excuse to remove God from the equation and this freed them from religious dogma.

One common charge against ID proponents is to say that they hold to a God of the gaps paradigm. However, one could say that Darwinists hold to a Natural Selection of the gaps position. Those that explain the origin of life by panspermia could be charged with panspermia of the gaps, and those who believe in an infinite number of universes as universes of the gaps. In my opinion, any of these positions are fine for a scientist to hold. It is not okay, though, to let beliefs interfere with research. It is not okay to nastily tear down those who disagree. Science should be systematic and objective, not political. Scientists are supposed to be trained to put aside their pre-conceived biases and follow the evidence wherever it leads. Challenge the ideas with data and facts, not with sarcasm and mockery.

I am a computer scientist and in my career, I've coded and debugged millions of lines of computer instructions. I don't say this to brag; sometimes after a long sixteen-hour day, I come back to reality not quite knowing whether I am still fully human. It's a weird feeling. I'm sure lab scientists, after long days performing experiments with the latest technological equipment, feel the same phenomenon.

In this section, I will present why from a Computer Science point of view, I am skeptical of Darwin's hypotheses, namely common descent and natural selection through random mutations. I will not address or present challenges to Darwinism that are outside my field of expertise. There are long difficult-to-read books and many articles written on these matters. Have at it if you wish.

Before I start, I want to emphasize that my challenges to Darwinism are not why I'm a Christian. My faith would not be destroyed if Darwin proves to be correct. I also am not going to try to prove God exists using Science. The Darwinist theory simply makes no sense to me as a computer scientist.

Computer Science is the discipline that solves real-world problems using digital technology. Essential to this discipline is the study of algorithms and information. Natural selection through random mutations is an algorithm subject to evaluation.

In my field, there are many problems that are intractable. This means that no matter how fast computers ever will get, there will never be an algorithm that can arrive at an optimal solution to one of these problems in a reasonable amount of time. By a solution in a reasonable amount of time, I mean before all life ends on the planet. I'll spare you the mathematical proof of this assertion.

An algorithm is a step-by-step process that arrives at a desired result. There are systematic techniques that we can use to evaluate them and there are classes of algorithms used to solve whole groups of similar problems. Natural selection through random mutations falls into a particular computer science classification known as *greedy algorithms*.

Let me illustrate. Suppose you were blindfolded in an open area of one-mile square. Your task is to get to the highest point. How would you proceed? No, you can't cheat and remove the blindfold. One approach is to pick the direction of steepest ascent and take a step (*the greedy step*). After some fixed number of similar steps, you will converge at a point that is the highest. Unfortunately, that point is unlikely to be the maximum. Taking a counter-intuitive step that goes downward might get you to a point where another series of ascents will turn out to be better.

Nature's natural selection algorithm is somewhat more powerful than what I just described, but not much. Computer Science often employs a technique called parallel programming. This means, instead of the blindfolded person taking a single step at a time, they can simultaneously take many steps in different directions. The algorithm then proceeds from each of those new positions in parallel. Sometimes this kind of algorithm can be useful in finding heuristic (approximate) solutions to intractable problems.

Natural selection, in a manner, resembles parallel programming. Because the population size of a particular species is greater than one, by natural selection, more than one mutation can occur in a single generation.

Many questions come to mind. How many simultaneous steps (mutations) can natural selection take? This depends on the population size and the likelihood of a mutation occurring. We expect more mutations to occur within a single generation of large populations than smaller ones. There will be fewer impactful rhinoceros mutations than in strains of bacteria.

Addressing the Skeptics

The next question: What percentage of mutations result in an advantageous change (going up-hill)? From what I've read, most mutations, being copying errors, are destructive. Those that are positive, are mostly in response to a particular situation, like enabling malaria parasites to become resistant to antimalarial drugs. This kind of mutation deactivates a gene from being expressed, which in the long run makes the organism less resilient. It is extremely rare for a mutation to create a new protein that is useable in an organism.

A third question is: How likely is it that a mutation will travel through the entire population? This depends on how advantageous the mutation is with respect to the whole and also whether the whole is within geographic reach.

Genetic algorithms are an approach often used in Computer Science. The effectiveness of them is dependent upon how *smart* they are. Algorithms programmed with complex logic to decide whether a mutation is beneficial will be more effective than one without this sophistication. Natural selection is not very intelligent. It only knows about procreation. It knows nothing about the type of creature that it wants to develop. If most of the offspring procreate successfully, we have a success.

Mutations occur by chance, and most are damaging. This raises a question. What kind of complexity can we expect to arise from this mechanism?

Many of us have heard of the Monkey Theorem. Get a bunch of monkeys together with a set of typewriters, wait long enough, and they will produce Shakespeare's plays. At first glance, this seems very plausible, does is not? It is not. Suppose that every atom in the Universe was a typewriter, and a random key was simultaneously struck on each of them every second from the beginning of time. The monkeys would not even be able to successfully type out a single Shakespeare sonnet. The probability of 288 consecutive correct keyboard strikes is so small that in a practical sense we could say that it is impossible. The Monkey Theorem has been falsified by mathematicians; this is a well-known scientific fact.

Considering life on the planet, no one even knows how many mutations are necessary to build a single mammal, let alone all the other forms of life. The number has to be enormous. Even if nature conserves each successful step as a precursor for the next advancement, there has simply been not enough time to explain all of the billions or trillions of positive mutations that must have occurred. Making matters even worse, it is likely that simultaneous beneficial mutations are needed to explain some of the genetic improvements. The probability is extremely small for this to occur, to impact the reproductive system, and then to rapidly spread through a population. Generating the number of mutations needed to explain the diversity of life is a far more difficult task than monkeys randomly typing out a Shakespeare sonnet.

This brings me to my evaluation. I am quite skeptical that Natural Selection through random mutations is a powerful enough algorithm to explain all life on earth. Greedy algorithms simply are not this good. Better explanations are needed.

Now let's consider the complexity of the cell. In the simplest of living cells, we have proteins that decode, copy, splice, and transport DNA/RNA sequences appropriately to create needed cellular proteins. We have other proteins that carefully shape proteins into unique three-dimensional structures and usher them to places in the cell where they are needed. More proteins clean out waste material so the internal workings are not gummed-up. Proteins build temporary scaffolding, which serve as roadways to assist in moving proteins around. This sounds to me like self-healing computer architecture. There is significant research in Computer Science to build this kind of hardware, but it has a long way to go. I seriously doubt that nature, not knowing what it is building, simply by chance, would come up with such an exquisite system.

Next, we have the information in the cell. Information theory has specific well-defined definitions to explain what comprises information; allow me to give you a few highlights.

The genetic code is incredible and as far as we know, it goes back to the very earliest forms of life on earth. DNA is a string of the letters A, C, T, and G, where each letter maps to a specific chemical base molecule. Every three of these has 64 possible arrangements, and the genetic code translates these to the 20 amino acids used in all known living cells. The translation from 64 down to 20 is near optimal with sophisticated error correcting features. This means that if there is an error, the translation automatically corrects for it. Error correcting algorithms, especially those that are near optimal, are difficult to devise, and they require a skilled computer scientist to create them. I don't believe nature could come up with this code on its own randomly without knowing what it is doing.

Syntax is an essential feature of information. English grammar follows a particular structure; we cannot plop words anywhere we want. DNA follows an exact syntax. Why do all DNA sequences map exactly three ACTG letters to a single amino acid? Why not, sometimes two, sometimes four, and sometimes other values? How did nature figure out how to use a start code and an end code so the cell mechanisms can properly decode the in-between ACTG letters to make a protein? Why does DNA only specify the amino acids needed for life, not others? I'll stop here, but there are lots of other questions like this that we could ask.

The specified order of DNA is another mystery. When I write a computer program, the instructions must follow an exact order. I can vaguely recall maybe a half-dozen times over my forty-five-year career where I wrote some series of instructions that did something I didn't expect, and it turned out to be minimally helpful by accident. In all other cases, when I wrote instructions that were not properly expressed, they either degraded or broke the logic. That caused me to spend lots of time debugging and correcting the errors. A single cellular protein requires an exact DNA sequence of A, C, T, G letters that is hundreds long. The idea that nature can randomly produce such sequences specifying, not one, but many proteins needed by even the simplest cell seems impossible. Each of these not only must have proper function and correct three-dimensional shapes, but must work cohesively within the cell's architecture.

Finally, there is the issue of life's origin. Scientists universally concede that no one knows how the first cell came to be. The pre-biotic soup explanations where lightning hits some group of chemicals to produce the first cell have long been refuted. The cell is far too complex to support any hypothesis for spontaneous generation. There are additional problems. Cell types significantly differ in their architecture. It is unlikely that one type can evolve into another. This would be like the operating system inside a microwave oven evolving into Microsoft Windows.

I could go on, but I won't. My purpose here is not to bore everyone with technical information. For that reason, I tried to keep the above discussion as high-level as possible. My comments are not intended to be something that one would present in a scientific article. Also, this was not some kind of proof for God, or even a proof for the existence of an intelligent agent. I simply want to present the reasons why I don't believe Darwinism (in the long run) will be able to withstand scientific challenges. Other explanations are needed. You could say that I am a skeptic

Chapter 3

Rational Reasons to Believe

> Faith isn't the ability to believe long and far into the misty future. It's simply taking God at His Word and taking the next step. —Joni Erickson Tada

> Faith is taking the first step even when you don't see the whole staircase.[20] —Martin Luther King

Joni Erickson Tada believes in God, even after experiencing a swimming accident that left her paralyzed for life. Martin Luther King, also a believer, needs no introduction. Their above quotes provide similar definitions of faith. They acknowledge that the world is a complex place, and the future can be unknown and scary. Whether we are religious or not, we all attempt to make sense of the chaos of life and through faith, we set our course. The questions are: "Are we alone?" And: "Is there is a God who, through the Holy Spirit, is willing to walk with us, even when things don't go well?" If we say yes, we might ask: "Is this kind of faith blind? Is there evidence?" Let's consider this issue.

The Moral Law

> The first time it was reported that our friends were being butchered there was a cry of horror. Then a hundred were butchered. But when a thousand were butchered and there was no end to the butchery, a blanket of silence spread. When evil-doing comes like falling rain, nobody calls out "stop!" When crimes begin to pile up, they become invisible. When sufferings become unendurable the cries are no longer

---

[20] Martin Luther King Jr, *Let Nobody Turn Us Around: Voices on Resistance, Reform, and Renewal an African American Anthology*.

heard. The cries, too, fall like rain in summer.[21]
—Bertolt Brecht

My people are few. They resemble the scattering trees of a storm-swept plain…There was a time when our people covered the land as the waves of a wind-ruffled sea cover its shell-paved floor, but that time long since passed away with the greatness of tribes that are now but a mournful memory.[22] —Chief Seattle

The history of interactions among disparate peoples is what shaped the modern world through conquest, epidemics, and genocide. Those collisions created reverberations that have still not died down after many centuries, and that are actively continuing in some of the world's most troubled areas.[23] —Jared Diamond

There aren't just bad people that commit genocide; we are all capable of it. It's our evolutionary history. — James Lovelock

The above quotes provide examples where humanity violated standards of morality that most of us would consider absolute. In light of these lessons from history, does our species have the ability to ultimately judge for itself between good and evil? The answer is not at all obvious. If there is no God, and if we are bound by evolution, what can we expect? This is a question that I'll explore in this section.

On Sunday, March 15, 2015, Leslie Stahl hosted a sixty-minute special, *Back to the Wild*. It documented an attempt by the Aspinall Foundation to reintroduce a family of gorillas into their natural habitat. Silverbacks are highly endangered and Damian Aspinall's passion is to do what he can to preserve the species.

The alpha male of the family to be reintroduced is Djala. As a youngster, he saw his family massacred and probably eaten. He was

---

[21] Bertolt Brecht, *Selected Poems*.

[22] Chief Seattle's, "1854 Treaty Oration," (Seattle Sunday Star Oct. 29, 1887), column by Dr. Henry A. Smith.

[23] Jared Diamond, *Guns, Germs, and Steel: The Fates of Human Societies*, 16.

chained and tortured, but fortunately, he was rescued and taken to England. When he became too much to handle, the Aspinall Foundation agreed to look after him in their protected facility.

Djala was nervous in captivity and had a habit of repeatedly pulling at his arm hair. Nevertheless, he grew to be a fine full-grown silverback, with seven wives and thirteen children. Damian decided that it was time to give Djala and his family the chance to live in their indigenous habitat. Single silverbacks were previously reestablished; this was the first attempt to reintroduce an entire family. They initially were transported to a sixteen-acre river islet, Gorilla Island, in the protected reserve in Gabon, Africa.

The family appeared to be doing well. On the island, Djala was no longer nervous, and even fought off a wild silverback who crossed on a log to the island. A year passed and Damian was confident enough to construct a bridge to the main reserve. Once built, the gorillas were encouraged to cross. The female gorillas crossed first, followed by their enthusiastic children. Djala hesitantly crossed last. After an hour all were on the mainland. Unfortunately, a month later, five of Djala's wives were found dead along with one of his children. The head and body wounds suggested attacks from one of the wild male silverbacks. Djala and those that remained retreated back to the island. It was a heartbreaking loss

From a human point of view, it was hard to learn of the deaths. Some might blame Damian for embarking on a project doomed to fail. Nobody, though, would think to blame the gorillas. We would not think to say that gorillas are immoral. It is unthinkable to ascribe human morality onto these fine animals. Gorillas do what gorillas do. Instead, we continue our efforts to restore their numbers.

How do we view those native people that killed Djala's family when he was a youngster? I know my reaction. I'm quite a lot less sympathetic. Should I be? Don't most meat-eaters, myself included, do the same thing? We don't do it directly; others do the killing. We are really not in a position to blame the local African tribal people, are we?

One of the arguments for the existence of God is that we humans have a moral framework. We distinguish right from wrong, good from evil. We have a conscience. We supposedly hold ourselves to a higher standard than we hold other creatures. We feel superior in this way; we are human. One does not need to be a Christian to wonder about the moral law that is embedded within us. The philosopher Immanuel Kant, for example, stated: "Two things awe me most, the starry sky above me and the moral law within me."

From where does this moral framework come? A theist would argue that it originates from a higher intelligence, from God, who instills a moral consciousness into our being, our intellectual wiring. We are God's image bearers, which means that we are entrusted with bringing his will to earth. Skeptics counter that our moral framework has nothing to do with God. It is simply a product of evolution.

For argument's sake, let's assume in this section that evolution explains the origin of our morality. How much of a moral framework can we expect could emerge from this view?

The scientific consensus is that Chimpanzees are our closest relatives in the animal kingdom. Jane Goodell spent fifty-five years observing Chimpanzees in the Gombe Stream National Park, Tanzania, starting in 1960. Her 1986 book, *the Chimpanzees of Gombe* describes twenty-five years of observed behaviors.[24] These animals, like silverbacks, live in communities. They form social traditions and intra-tribal norms. Within the group there is affection and relationships, often lifelong.

There is also a darker, violent side. Chimps, like humans, establish territorial boundaries which are patrolled regularly. They aggressively raid neighboring groups. Their younger members appear excited by conflict, often adventuring close to danger to provoke encounters.

One group of chimps, the Kasakela, split into two, forming a new group, the Kalama, that moved to the south. The former retained more warrior chimps and over a five-year period annihilated the latter and assumed their territory. The winners displayed great excitement when they killed the males of the losing group, even those that were formally treated as insiders. Eventually, another group further south pushed the victorious group back to the north. Apparently, as soon as the Kalama lost membership in the original group, they were no longer kin. They became prey.

Cannibalism was observed among invading chimps. Older females did not fare well; they were specifically targeted. Goodall speculated that this could have served to break mother-daughter bonds. That way,

---

[24] Much of the information here comes from Docket, *Origin of Violence*.

the younger female chimps are more likely to assimilate with the attackers.

This behavior reminds me of ancient human warfare as described in the Bible and in Middle Eastern archaeological records. Chimps do not have human intellectual ability, yet the roots of violence among our supposed closest cousins are well-observed. Ancient tribal warfare in the Middle East was frequent and violent. The intent was commonly extermination, killing all men, women, and children. In biblical terms, enemies were placed *under the ban*. Ancient human tribal warfare is similar to that of their chimp counterparts. Older married women were eliminated. Virgins were spared.

Humans are more sophisticated than chimps, so other outcomes in these situations are available. The facility of speech enables the victims to plead for mercy and unconditionally surrender. This can lead to men becoming slaves, the conquered towns being forced to pay tribute, or to serve the victors in other ways.

There are also similarities between chimp and human culture in sexuality. The more aggressive chimps yield more offspring. Apparently, this leads to an evolutionary advantage. The relationships are not monogamous and males are known to kill the offspring that are not their own. Human polygamy and patriarchal societies have similar tendencies. Chimps kill the offspring of disloyal females; humans, in the past, stoned the women who were considered unfaithful. The aggressive and powerful human males traditionally gathered more wives. Men could divorce, women could not. Women were at the mercy of their husbands; they had few opportunities of their own.

Ancient cultures, like troupes of chimps, distinguish those inside the group from those on the outside. There are different rules, even at times of peace. The Israelites were not allowed to charge interest to a fellow tribesman, but they could charge any amount to those outside. They could not eat a dead animal found on the road, but they could sell the meat to an outsider. A fellow Israelite could be financially bankrupt and made into a slave, but they must be released with gifts after seven years. A foreigner was considered inheritable property; no such limit was required. Marriage to a foreigner was forbidden. To the ancient Israelites, to *love your neighbor* meant to love a fellow Israelite.

Severe punishments were common in the ancient Mesopotamian law codes. Stoning, burning, amputation, and castration were the most popular techniques. Later, the Romans and Greeks added beheading and crucifixion.

To summarize, these ancient societies were patriarchal. Women were most certainly not equal. Men could divorce for almost any reason, women could not. The laws were harsher to women than to men. The powerful could accumulate hundreds of wives, and more hundreds of concubines. Warfare was brutal. Throughout the West, ancient cultures besides the Israelites exhibited similar patterns of behavior. It was the way things were.

Returning to the topic of morality, what can we expect from evolution? I suppose an evolutionary biologist would assert that human adaptations over time could easily lead to societies that resemble those of the ancient world, including their extreme patterns of violence and genocide. If this were true, I can envision close family structures and relationships and some level of morality within a group setting. I could see the importance of treaties and vows where tribes, groups, or countries might temporarily join together to repel a larger threat. Where the Ten Commandments are concerned, it's believable that evolution could lead to some intra-group standards against lying, stealing, murder, adultery, and disrespecting parents. The prohibition against coveting could stem from the understanding that it leads to violations of one or more of the other principles. These prohibitions would be in place not because they are morally wrong, or because of any deep-seated concern for another person, but to maintain order and to avoid unpleasant consequences within the group.

I suppose the worship of one god by a particular group could arise, being that the tribal god would become angry if the people worshipped others. For similar reasons, the prohibition against taking the Lord's name in vain might be established. One would never want the big tribal god to withdraw, causing battles to be lost.

Other moral principles in the Ten Commandments are more difficult to explain. Why the prohibition against graven images? I would think the tribe would like to imagine some physical portrayal of what their god looks like. What about the sabbath? This one makes the tribe vulnerable to attack, so it is counter-intuitive.

Among the ancient Hebrews, the most difficult moral law for evolution to explain is concern for the weak, the sick, and the disabled, especially those outside the group. This flies in the face of evolution, as demonstrated by the eugenics movement in the late 1800s and early

1900s. There were real concerns that lasted for nearly a century after Darwin, which intellectuals labeled the Descent of Man. Scholars posited that humanity's moral concern for the weak was causing the human species to be in a process of degrading. Consider a couple quotes by Charles Darwin on these matters:

> One general law, leading to the advancement of all organic beings, namely, multiply, vary, let the strongest live and the weakest die.[25] —Charles Darwin

> With savages, the weak in body or mind are soon eliminated; and those that survive commonly exhibit a vigorous state of health. We civilized men, on the other hand, do our utmost to check the process of elimination; we build asylums for the imbecile, the maimed, and the sick; we institute poor-laws; and our medical men exert their utmost skill to save the life of each one to the last moment. There is reason to believe that vaccination has preserved thousands, who from a weak constitution would formerly have succumbed to small-pox. Thus, the weak members of civilized societies propagate their kind. No one who has attended to the breeding of domestic animals will doubt that this must be highly injurious to the race of man. It is surprising how soon a want of care, or care wrongly directed, leads to the degeneration of a domestic race; but excepting in the case of man himself, hardly any one is so ignorant as to allow his worst animals to breed.[26] — Charles Darwin

The educated classes, freed from religion after Darwin, saw no problem with forced sterilization or elimination of those deemed less worthy to live. They viewed some people groups less evolved than others. Those groups deserved forced slavery to serve to the benefit of the more evolved. They deserved slaughter if they refused to submit or they were not able to be useful. As such, the nineteenth century saw

---

[25] Charles Darwin, *The Origin of Species*.
[26] Charles Darwin, *The Descent of Man*.

colonialism to be a good thing. The more evolved, would take, by force if necessary, the resources from the less evolved. The book, *From Darwin to Hitler,* by R. Weikart is a good reference.

As much as we'd like to deny it, there was widespread support for Hitler as he rose to power. He favored helping evolution along to produce a better, superior human. Under the Soviet Union, dissent was considered to be a psychological problem. Those who were no longer useful to the state were considered to be "former persons."[27]

Skeptics often criticize ancient cultures, especially the Israelites, on moral grounds. In one sense, this is amusing. The people that do the attacking are often the same ones that deny the existence of absolute truth. If there is no absolute standard, why would ancient cultures be any more subject to attack than the morality of chimps?

But let's put this objection aside for a bit. From a modern perspective, the ancient peoples were immoral. Their wartime behavior, by today's standards, were criminal. The ancients, of course, did not see it that way. Victory meant God's favor; loss meant God's rejection. A more complete victory implied a greater blessing. When I read the Old Testament, I do not see a tinge of remorse over accounts that we find objectionable. Jephthah sacrificed his daughter as a burnt offering to satisfy a vow. When his daughter agrees, the author narrates her decision as if it was the way things should be, even virtuous.

Where morality is concerned, the greatest challenges to evolution come from the teachings of Jesus. The idea of loving your enemies and doing good to those who seek ill goes in the opposite direction. The idea that the meek will inherit the earth is preposterous. The world now, and in the past, is run on power and violence, sometimes physical, other times verbal, and often legal.

Jesus teaches that love is an alternative, but not in some feel-good emotional sense. The love he promotes is demonstrated in action. It is instantiated when we listen to the internal voice that we all hear, avoid the temptation to immediately dismiss it, and then embody the good within our personal domain. It promotes doing that which is counter-intuitive because it is right, even in the face of personal risk. How could it be that this kind of love can prevail over current world systems? Jesus demonstrated his solution on the cross. He submitted

---

[27] Doug Smith, *Former People: The Last Days of the Russian Aristocracy,* documents the Red-Terror from 1918-1922.

willingly without complaint, though he travailed and wished that another way be possible. On the cross, he didn't call for revenge, but for forgiveness. Could his approach really succeed, or is it foolhardy? Everything naturalistically points to the latter.

Even in our time, the teachings of Jesus seem idealistic, and impractical. Immediate objections arise. What if *this*? Or what if *that*? In almost every case, the *this* or *that* is hypothetical; they didn't happen. If the sermon on the mount and the call to love one's neighbor become life patterns, we can deal with the *this* or *that* when they come up. In the meantime, why not try to live by their principles? All this makes no sense from a Darwinist perspective. It is contingent upon a reality beyond strict materialism, a bigger picture if you will.

The distant past fades from our collective memory. We discount early Christianity's impact in Roman culture. It was so long ago. The world changed because of the explosive effects that Jesus' teachings had on humanity. When the rich and powerful ran from calamity, Christians ran towards it to assist. Examples of this include two major epidemics that swept through the Roman Empire (AD 156 and AD 251). Historians estimate that each of these plagues killed about 30% of the total population. The wealthy, including the famous physician Galen fled. Christians stayed and cared for both believers and those outside the faith.

When people became destitute, Christians provided help. The emperor Julian, no friend of Christianity, implored the pagan priests to match the benevolence of this rising faith, but to no avail.[28] People, in those days, were attracted to Christianity, not primarily because of its doctrines, but because its followers were transformed humans who followed Jesus. Those who previously were heartless became compassionate. They became *more human* than they were in the past. The following quote provides a glimpse of the early Christian community.

> Christianity served as a revitalization movement that arose in response to the misery, chaos, fear, and brutality of life in the urban Greco-Roman world...Christianity revitalized life in Greco-Roman

---

[28] Rodney Stark, *The Rise of Christianity*, (Princeton University Press 1996): Chapter 4.

> cities by providing new norms and new kinds of social relationships able to cope with many urgent problems. To cities filled with the homeless and impoverished, Christianity offered charity as well as hope. To cities filled with newcomers and strangers, Christianity offered an immediate basis for attachment. To cities filled with orphans and widows, Christianity provided a new and expanded sense of family. To cities torn by violent ethnic strife, Christianity offered a new basis for social solidarity. And to cities faced with epidemics, fire, and earthquakes, Christianity offered effective nursing services ... For what they brought was not simply an urban movement, but a new culture capable of making life in Greco-Roman cities more tolerable.[29] — Rodney Stark

There are more recent examples; I'll mention just one. Lepers traditionally are separated from their communities, and for good reason. Father Damian, a Belgian priest, served a leper colony in Hawaii from 1873 to his death in 1889. As he searched for a cure, he personally cared for leprous patients. He built schools, hospitals, and churches. He supported the quarantined people, both medically and emotionally. One day, when he felt no pain from scalding water, it became apparent that Father Damian had contracted the disease.

What would make a person do what he did? Certainly not Darwinism. Why do most of us honor his efforts? Certainly not because of the value we place on Survival of the Fittest. By that standard, Father Damian made a stupid life decision. The lepers had nothing to offer to society or to anyone else. In evolutionary terms, the merciful thing to do would be to painlessly euthanize them. I recoil at the thought.

The non-violence that Jesus stood for extends beyond the faith. Gandhi was not a Christian, but through non-violence, he overcame the British Empire. Even Gandhi did not go as far as Jesus. When asked if he could forgive the English, he responded metaphorically, "You still have my pen." In other words, forgiveness was possible only after India fully recovered from the period of British Imperialism.

---

[29] Ibid., 161-162.

Nelson Mandela, who is almost universally accepted to have been a Christian, goes further than Gandhi. He spent more than twenty years in prison, and then through non-violence, he ended apartheid and rose to power. He forgave his captors and brought reconciliation to his nation. His quote, "Until I changed myself, I could not change others," is a profound expression of Christian living.

Martin Luther King was another Christian. Though he paid with his life, his non-violent approach led to significant civil rights victories. William Wilberforce strove for years to peacefully overcome slavery in England. Aleksandr Solzhenitsyn documented the tyranny of the Soviet Union's Marxist government and by many, he was credited with the eventual crumbling of that totalitarian system.[30] Non-violence takes patience, great personal risk, sometimes generations, but in the end, it can win. This is the opposite of evolution, which has no patience, but always favors short-term advantage. Nonviolence is opposite to the greedy algorithm described by natural selection.

Cultures often view themselves as morally superior over their predecessors. We like to say that twenty-first-century society has an improved, mature moral framework. Is this true? Going against natural biological tendencies is hard. We humans still inflict genocides on each other every decade or so. The most recent example is the ISIS beheading Christians, Yazidis, Mandaeans, and so-called apostate Muslims who wished their opponents no harm. They simply believed different things.

Oppression still exists around the globe. The movies we watch glorify the violent superhero. Internet pornography that degrades women is rampant. Sex trafficking is hugely profitable and widespread. Do you think we would reinstitute slavery if we did not have machines? Our violent roots are alive and well, and not likely to change any time soon.

We don't have the excuses that ancient peoples could claim. They didn't have as long a history to help them grow in their insights. We have that history. The horror of Hitler and the Holocaust caused the Darwinist theories to retreat to the back rooms, but they still exist, ready to emerge again at the right time. All that is needed is for the powerful to change the language. Transformed phrases can make a bad thing to sound good, even benevolent.

---

[30] Solzhenitsyn, *The Gulag Archipelago*, (1973).

Consider Peter Singer, for example, who is an Australian moral philosopher, a Professor of Bioethics at Princeton University, and a Laureate Professor at the Centre for Applied Philosophy and Public Ethics at the University of Melbourne. He supports extending the "right to choose" to legalize the killing of newborns. During a thirty-day window, a parent could legally, after giving birth, do away with a child. Supporters of this position claim that anyone who cannot survive without their mother's assistance is not yet a person. It is all about the words we use. These things are snapshots displaying what we can expect from Darwinism if we fall back into that mode of behavior. If morality is simply an evolved characteristic, there is no absolute standard to apply. We can redefine, without recourse, accepted behavior to suit the whims of culture.

I am convinced that if we eliminate Jesus' teachings from society, humanity will not progress, but will slide backwards. Of course, I do not mean that one cannot live a good life apart from Christ. I do mean that our species as a whole will gradually revert to its natural inclinations.

That world that I envision is one where sex, instead of being a sacred intimacy between two adults, degenerates into the satisfaction of biological impulses without regard to the other person. Marriage degenerates from a lifelong bond to a legal contract to be broken whenever the emotions wear thin. Wars, justified by perceived threats, are guaranteed to repeat endlessly. Respect for others is reduced to gross, personal attacks without empathy, especially when hiding behind the anonymity of the Internet. Some seek power not from a desire to serve, but for self-serving interests. Political opponents become mortal enemies that must be destroyed by any means, even if it includes lies, exaggerations, and slander.

I didn't attempt to prove the existence of God in this section. Rather, I hope that I've demonstrated that embracing Darwinism is not the answer for our species. I don't see much hope if it is. Nuclear weapons will kill millions. Chemical weapons will add to the misery. The environment will be destroyed beyond repair. At some point, before it is too late, perhaps humanity will come to understand clearly the light of Jesus' teachings. Perhaps after every alternative is exhausted, his principles will finally reign. I hope so, because otherwise, in my opinion, humanity is rapidly marching down the road towards destruction.

The Supernatural

There once were two crabs; let's call them Rob and Bob. They lived in a watery area at the bottom of a large underground cave, which they called Grotto. These were scientific crabs; they wanted to learn everything about their environment and they developed sophisticated crab technologies to help them in their pursuit. Rob believed that it was possible to know everything there was to know about Grotto using their existing crab technology and that which they would develop in the future. In time, they would know everything that there was to know. Bob was skeptical, believing that Grotto was not a closed system; there was a reality beyond the walls.

One day, a laser of light flashed through Grotto. Bob saw it, but Rob did not. They had heated arguments about the experience and devised experiments to see if it might happen again. It didn't. This convinced Rob that it was a crab hallucination. Bob could not forget the experience and held to his belief. Arguments and debates continued, but neither would relent. They stubbornly stood firm.

Then suddenly, the laser flashed again, and this time both Rob and Bob saw it. Bob was pleased that lasers of light were now an established scientific fact. Still, Rob believed that the laser could be described by natural processes originating from complex interactions on Grotto's walls. Bob didn't go for that, convinced that Rob's explanations were insufficient. So, they disagreed. The disagreement was never settled, leading to much conflict. Rob considered Bob to be embracing a primitive crab superstition. Bob was frustrated that he couldn't convince Rob of the obvious. And so it went. On and on it went.

The basic question comes down to this: Is the cosmos a closed system or is there a larger encompassing reality? Is reality nothing but a huge grotto? Does humanity consist of billions of Robs and Bobs who aimlessly argue back in forth? If somehow, we can settle these questions, another one comes to the fore. Can we know anything about an inherent larger reality and then ascertain the impact that is has on how we should live our lives?

There are a number of competing worldviews in the Western world. One of these declares that belief in God or gods is an initial flawed attempt by humanity to explain the cosmos and to find meaning within that reality. It proceeds to assert that modern science and rationalism eliminates the need for such an approach. A counter opinion is that science and rationalism is a flawed attempt to derive meaning out of a worldview of random meaningless. Adherents to either of these positions can easily provide evidence to back up their claims. For example, supernatural superstitions led to many damaging practices which caused significant pain and suffering. These included voodoo curses, magic spells, witch trials, and inquisitions. Similarly, science and rationalism led to the utopian Marxist philosophy that resulted in approximately one-hundred million deaths in the twentieth century.

The charges and counter-charges are not helpful. One cannot conclusively dismiss a belief system because of the worst abuses that such an ideology produces. It certainly is not valid to compare 21st century science to Middle Age religious practices, even if their shadows can still be found. Adherents to each point of view continually refine their positions to hypothesize better approaches.

One cannot be a Christian if they don't believe in a reality beyond the materialistic Universe. This is a reality that includes living conscious entities, namely God and angels. It likely includes other phenomena, of which we have no way of knowing scientifically. But how do we discern whether such a reality exists or not?

There have been double-blind prayer experiments. Sick folk were chosen, along with some volunteers. The question: does prayer have a statistical impact? The results generally are inconclusive, though a few seemed to indicate that prayer helped a bit.[31]

I have problems with the whole thing. Suppose that prayer consistently helped. Wouldn't the researchers still work to find a naturalistic reason? Of course they would. They would not be good scientists if they didn't. What if there were no difference? Some would say that this invalidates the supernatural. But does it? No, it doesn't. What if the supernatural entities, if they exist, just did not want to participate in our stupid games? The experiments cannot rule this out. I think research along these lines is a complete waste of time.

There are other ways for us to evaluate whether the supernatural exists. This requires us to assess the reliability of those that experience

---

[31] John A. Astin, et al. "The Efficacy of "Distant Healing A Systematic Review of Randomized Trials," Annals of International Medicine 132, no. 11 (June 6, 2000): 903-910.

things that are not explainable in naturalistic terms. Let's consider miracles. By a miracle, I do not mean something that overturns the natural laws. I do mean situations where a supernatural agent intervenes in some way. Let me explain.

Suppose a couple of high school students want to test the law of gravity. One of the students climbs to the top of a building with several rocks and proceeds to drop one of them off the roof. The other student has an accurate stopwatch to measure the time it takes for the rock to hit the ground. But just when the rock begins to fall, a fire cracker explodes and they both look to see what happened. When they look back, they notice that the rock never hit the ground; in fact, it completely vanished. What are they to assume? Was the law of gravity overturned? I think not. A more likely explanation is that someone stuck their hand out a window and caught the rock. They intervened. This is how I define miracle. If there are extra-dimensional conscious agents, they can decide when, why, and how they might alter the goings on in our reality.

What miracles can we evaluate? This is a difficult question, and science is not much help. We might subject the one experiencing a miracle to a lie detector test, but even if they pass, opinions will not likely change. Medical records could help somewhat. For example, one day a person has stage four cancer, and a week later the tumor is gone. There are many of these kinds of things recorded, but normally they are racked up to be unexplained anomalies. Again, opinions are not likely to change.

If a person receives a miracle, to that person, the experience is undeniable. It happened; case closed! Nothing can convince them otherwise. To that person's spouse or close friend, it is a bit more difficult to accept. However, if the person never exaggerated, has no reason to deceive, and subsequently changes their entire outlook on life, the spouse or close friend might very well attest that it happened. But what happens when the miracle is later publicized in a movie, a newspaper, or on the Web? Most of us will be skeptical, and as a result, we are apt to dismiss the account.

In my case, I've never witnessed a miracle. I do have one secondhand account that I can share. A close friend of mine was driving from Oregon to Sacramento on route 101, one lane in each direction. When turning around a curve, he encountered a multi-car pileup and no way to avoid a major crash. My friend tells me that at the next instant, he was parked in front of the crash site on the side of the road with the motor off. Something happened that was extraordinary. I believe my friend's account because I never knew him to be other than honest. Could this be explained naturalistically? I don't know, but I doubt it. Now, what do you as the reader think? You don't know me personally and you certainly don't know my friend. Perhaps if you find my writing honest, you might think the account credible. Or maybe you'll dismiss it altogether. I don't blame you if you do.

Another time, my wife was driving with my two younger kids to an amusement park. I wasn't with her because I was on a two-week mission trip to Honduras with my two older children. She told me that she had a flat on the road when a man drove up and offered to change the tire. He did so, and when she turned to thank him, he and his car were gone. Was he an angel? Perhaps. There are many anecdotal accounts like these.

I've read many miracle accounts. Craig Keener wrote a two-volume book documenting lots of these. Tom Doyle wrote a couple of books documenting Muslims having dreams and visions about Christ. These caused them to give up everything (some were even killed), when they, in Muslim countries, converted to Christianity. Eben Alexander M.D., a former atheist, documents in *Proof of Heaven* his near-death experience. During a seven-day period when he had no brain activity, he had a vivid very *more real than real* experience. I've also read other accounts, but these are a sampling. I can't say that every account is authentic, but I'm confident that they are not all fabrications; some of them are real to be sure.

The larger question is whether we can rationally dismiss all supernatural accounts, and there are millions. There are books and journals that document these things. The International Association for Near Death Studies (IANDS) is one of these. This is a peer-reviewed scientific journal that does not document people seeing a light, a tunnel, or visiting with deceased relatives; it documents experiences where an unconscious person heard conversations down the hall, saw actual items on the roof of the building, or other such things that should be impossible. I would not classify these as defying the laws of nature, but they present evidence that there is more to our being than our physical bodies. There is more to reality than the grotto of the Universe.

This raises other questions, assuming the supernatural is real. Why does one person receive a miracle and not another? How often do supernatural events happen? The second question is the easier one. Supernatural events happen infrequently, evidenced by the fact that most of us rarely or never experience them. Perhaps there is some sort of Star Trek prime directive. "Don't interfere unless there is a darn good reason." But then, why one intervention and not another, especially when there seems to be no rhyme or reason to who benefits? Perhaps a supernatural agent happens to be at the right place at the right time. I don't know. We simply don't have enough information available to answer this question with certainty.

I believe there is a supernatural reality. This belief opens me to consider the possibility that the miracles of the New Testament are true and the gospels might just be recording God's intervention into our world.

New Testament Reliability

> Not only do we not have the originals, we don't have the first copies of the originals. We don't even have copies of the copies of the originals, or copies of the copies of the copies of the originals. What we have are copies made later-much later … And these copies all differ from one another, in many thousands of places.[32]
> — Bart Ehrman

> Bruce Metzger is one of the great scholars of modern times, and I dedicated the book to him because he was both my inspiration for going into textual criticism and the person who trained me in the field. I have nothing but respect and admiration for him. And even though we may disagree on important religious questions — he is a firmly committed Christian and I am not — we are in complete agreement on a number of very important historical and textual questions. If he and I were put in a room and asked to hammer out a consensus statement

---

[32] Bart Ehrman, *Misquoting Jesus*, 10.

on what we think the original text of the New Testament probably looked like, there would be very few points of disagreement — maybe one or two dozen places out of many thousands. The position I argue for in 'Misquoting Jesus' does not actually stand at odds with Prof. Metzger's position that the essential Christian beliefs are not affected by textual variants in the manuscript tradition of the New Testament.[33] — Bart Ehrman

Bart Ehrman and Bruce Metzger are first-rate scholars of textual criticism. Bart is an agnostic, somewhat hostile to Christianity. Bruce, who passed in 2007, was a committed Christian. How do two eminent scholars look at the same data and then come to opposite conclusions?

It turns out that Bart, at one time, was an evangelical Christian. Then through the decades he journeyed away from his Christian faith. I never knew or spoke to him, so my opinion comes from interview footage that aired. It appears that Bart cannot reconcile the evil in the world with the existence of a loving all-powerful God. I've heard Bart say something to the effect, "If there is a God, it most certainly is not the god of the Bible." This tells me that Bart cannot relate to the Old Testament God of love, who is also a God of wrath and vengeance.

Bart is on his own journey, so I'm not going to argue *but this* and *but that* to try to convince everyone that he is wrong. I've walked through a similar journey myself. There was a period of about five years where my wife Vivian and I could not bear to set foot in a Christian church. I've seen others walk similar journeys, including family members. Some found their way back to faith; some did not. This is a major reason I've decided to write this book. Its purpose is not to convince, but perhaps to encourage those on similar journeys. It is an entirely normal and healthy process for one to wrestle with their faith.

A near insurmountable obstacle to faith occurs when one observes evil in the world coming from believers. I think this issue is worth a few paragraphs to provide examples. I'll get back to the issue of New Testament reliability shortly. My wife Viv was raised in a missionary setting. She was born in Ivory Coast West Africa. Her parents were

---

[33] Ibid., 252.

pioneer missionaries, and many of the indigenous people in their area had never previously seen a white person; they would sometimes try to wipe off the whiteness from the skin. At the age of five, Viv was sent to a boarding school, Mamou Alliance Academy. This complex was over a thousand miles away from her parent's station. It was in the neighboring country of Guinea. Each year she was separated from her parents for nine months. That was her life till she was a preteen; then, through high school, she was housed in US boarding schools. At Mamou, there was extensive physical and sexual abuse. A movie called *All God's Children* documents the details. For many years Viv never mentioned her experiences to me. It wasn't till after our children were grown that all the gory details spilled out. It was a hard time.

For the last ten years, I worked to develop freeware software to assist indigenous American tribes in their efforts to restore language and culture. During this time, Viv and I visited various reservations and learned a great deal. Until the 1980s in Canada and the 1960s in the US and Australia, the mantra was, "Kill the Indian and save the man." Children, by government edict, were kidnapped, separated from their parents, and forced into Christian boarding schools. At those schools, children were subjected to all kinds of abuse. The movie *Rabbit Proof Fence* based on real events in aboriginal Australia, gives one example of this era in our history. Many books are also available.

The experiences suffered by Native Americans served as the catalyst for Viv to face her own experiences; painful memories could no longer be pushed down. It was a slow, difficult process for us to find our way back to faith. Even today, Viv has flashbacks. So I get it! I understand how someone would walk away, and I will not in any way try to convince them to come back. This is not my job and it is not my goal for writing this book. I am simply documenting reasons for why I still believe in God in general, and particularly in Jesus.

If you are still reading, let's get back to the subject at hand. Is the New Testament reliable? The question itself is invalid for a couple of reasons. First, the New Testament is not a single book; it is twenty-seven separate and largely independent source documents. Some scholars suspect that Second Corinthians is not a single Pauline letter, but an amalgam of several. This would mean that the New Testament consists of more than twenty-seven books. I don't want to spend pages and pages analyzing each book; that would be boring. For the sake of discussion, I'll treat the New Testament as a single whole.

The next question is: "What do we mean by reliable?" There can be many answers to this question. For example, have the documents significantly changed since their original publication? Were they written by the authors named in our Bible translations? Do the writings reflect the views of the earliest disciples? How long after the crucifixion were the original documents written? I'll discuss these in the following paragraphs. Please bear with me if this gets too technical. The discussion is not meant to be a comprehensive presentation of all the arguments and rebuttals. There are lots of good books available for further research, if you are into that. I'll keep the discussion short.

The earliest complete manuscripts that we have (Codex Vaticanus and Codex Sinaiticus) are dated nearly three hundred years after the crucifixion. So far, not so good. Fortunately, we have a document, Papyrus Bodmer (P75), dated at least one hundred years earlier. It contains most of the gospels of Luke and John. This document closely aligns with Vaticanus, though, according to scholars, both were copied from an even earlier source, perhaps fifty years earlier (as early as 150AD). Apparently, Christians were carefully copying the scriptures by AD 200, and likely even earlier. This brings us to a date of roughly a hundred years after the original writings.

The original published New Testament documents were almost certainly written on papyrus. According to ancient authors,[34] papyrus documents last between one-hundred and three-hundred years. Tertullian, a church father whose writings date between AD 190 and AD 223 implies that the originals were still extant in his time.

> Come now, you who would indulge a better curiosity, if you would apply it to the business of your salvation, run over the apostolic churches, in which the very thrones of the apostles are still pre-eminent in their places, in which their own authentic writings are read, uttering the voice, and representing the face of each of them severally. Achaia is very near you, (in which) you find Corinth. Since you are not far from Macedonia, you have Philippi; (and there too) you have the Thessalonians. Since you can cross to Asia, you get Ephesus. Since, moreover, you are close upon Italy,

---

[34] Lewis, *Papyrus in Classical Antiquity* (1974): 60-61.

> you have Rome, from which there comes even into our own hands the very authority of apostles themselves.[35]
> —Tertullian

If we believe Tertullian, Vaticanus could very well be copied either from the original, or even from a copy of the original. This, to me, indicates that there may be errors, minor discrepancies, and a few additions, but no doctrines are affected, and the writings represent the intent of the original authors.

Now, let's turn to dating those original New Testament documents. I won't address Paul's letters, since there is little controversy concerning them. Scholars date them between fifteen and thirty years after the crucifixion and consider at least seven of them to be authentic. Most of the controversy concerns Acts and the four gospels.

Luke's gospel is typically dated to the AD 70s (or even the 80s). I never understood this late date, even before I took the time to investigate this issue in more detail. It is true that the three synoptic gospels (Mathew, Mark, and Luke) document Jesus predicting that the Jewish temple would be destroyed, and this did happen in AD 70 (approximately 40 years after the crucifixion).

I don't see how this prediction required any supernatural advance knowledge. During the first century AD, tensions between the Romans and Jews were quickly rising to a boiling point. As early as 4BC, for example, Judas the Galilean (Acts 5:37) and his followers rose up in revolt to found the party of the zealots. By the time of Jesus, Roman control over Judea was becoming increasingly tenuous. The people clearly remembered when the Maccabees defeated and expelled the Greeks. Plenty of Jews therefore were eager to follow any messiah that promised liberation. It didn't take much foresight to envision Jerusalem going the way of complete destruction, as did Carthage previously. The Romans were not known to show mercy when challenged.

It is well-known that the events described in the Book of Acts ends at AD 62 with Paul under house arrest. Why does the book stop there? The author doesn't even mention the outcome of Paul's trial. According to church father writings, Paul was released, continued to teach, and eventually was beheaded under Nero.

---

[35] Tertullian, *Prescription Against Heretics*, Chapter 36.

Both Luke and Acts were addressed to Theophilus (Luke 1 and Acts 1), and the author indicates that Acts was written second. This means the gospel of Luke precedes Acts. Perhaps Luke was preparing a legal brief in preparation for Paul's trial when he wrote Acts. It is also interesting to note that the author of Acts goes from third person (they) to first person (we) in the later chapters. It appears that he was an eyewitness to some of Paul's travels. I see no reason to date Acts after AD 62 and Luke after AD 61.

Most scholars believe that Luke used Mark to compose his gospel. This sounds reasonable to me, especially since Luke himself states that he performed a careful investigation into the matter. It seems likely that Mark's gospel was available to him. This would put Mark earlier than AD 61, possibly in the late 50s, or even earlier.

The early church fathers, and modern scholars, are unanimous in placing John last. A quote from the Muratorian Fragment (dated AD 170) perhaps can shed some light:

> In the same night, it was revealed to Andrew of the apostles, that John should write down all things in his own name while all of them should review it.[36] — Muratorian Fragment

This quote implies that some the disciples were still alive when John's gospel was written. If true, its publication date cannot be later than the mid-60s.

Finally, what do we do with the gospel of Matthew? The church fathers seem to indicate that the original, very early version was written in the Jewish dialect. Eusebius, quoting Papias, states that Matthew "wrote the **logia** in Hebrew."[37] Mathew was a tax collector, so it is reasonable to suspect that he was literate in Hebrew and Aramaic. Perhaps Papias was referring to Q, the suspected precursor to the later gospels when he referred to "the logia." If this is the case, Matthew could very well have been recording events and sayings while Jesus was still alive. Yet there is no way to know this with certainty. The following 2nd century quote provides some support to

---

[36] *Muratorian Fragment*, (AD 170): Verses 13-16.
[37] Eusebius, *Ecclesiastical History*, 3.39, verses 15-16.

the premise that Hebrew (or possibly Aramaic) was the original language of Matthew's gospel.

> Matthew also issued a written gospel among the Hebrews in their own dialect while Peter and Paul were preaching at Rome and laying the foundations of the church."[38] —Irenaeus

Nehemia Gordon, a Karaite Jew who assisted in the translations of the Dead Sea Scrolls, back-translated Matthew to Hebrew. He asserts that based on the sentence structure and the naturalness of the Hebrew, it is likely that the gospel of Matthew was originally written in Hebrew and then later translated to Greek. Most scholars would disagree with this premise, but whether true or not, I don't see any reason to date the Greek version of Matthew later than the early 60s.

To summarize, the dating of the four gospels and the Book of Acts is important. There is significant disagreement among scholars on this issue, although nearly all of them place the origins within 50 years after the crucifixion. The dates that I proposed in the above discussion are within this range, though the majority of modern scholars propose dates closer to the end of that range. In any case, it is certainly possibility that the authors of the four gospels and acts either were eyewitnesses, or they received firsthand information from them. It increases the likelihood that the accounts are credible.

Now, let's consider the issue of authorship. I'll comment first a bit on the fourth gospel. Some scholars speculate that John was not the author. The argument goes: "John was an illiterate fisherman. The author of the fourth gospel was highly educated and his use of Greek is very sophisticated. There is no way that the peasant, John, could be the author."

I'll present a scenario where this could be an incorrect assessment. Jesus chose Nathanael, "an Israelite without guile" to be a disciple. Nathanael responded, "How do you know me?" Jesus replied, "I saw you under the fig tree." *Under the fig tree* is a well-known Jewish idiom. It means someone who is a student of Torah. From this, it is reasonable to infer that Nathanael, as well as Matthew, the tax collector was literate. Suppose that Nathanael tutored the other

---

[38] Irenaeus, *Against Heresies*, 3.1.19.

disciples; maybe that is why Jesus chose him in the first place. Regardless, we know that the disciples were, in part, educated, and we know they lived and worked in close quarters, influencing one another as members of a community.

I could see this influence going over Peter's head; maybe he learned some, but probably not much. But John, in the gospels, the one *leaning on Jesus' breast,* is one who soaks it all in. He wants to learn everything there is to learn.

How old was he at the time? According to Matthew 4 and Mark 1, James and John, while mending their father's fishing nets, immediately left their task to follow Jesus. This is not the behavior of experienced fishermen. Likely, the brothers were quite young. Tradition tells us that John lived at least till the end of the first century. If true, this puts his age to be in the late teens or early twenties during Jesus' ministry.

There is no reason to assume that John didn't become the scholar who wrote the fourth gospel. Some Jewish sages did the same. Hillel was poor, so he worked as a woodcutter to support himself while he studied Torah. Today, Jews recognize him as one of the most learned sages of all time. I don't accept that because John started out as a fisherman, he couldn't have written the fourth gospel.

In any case, the church fathers from various geographic areas state that Matthew (a disciple), Mark (Peter's scribe), Luke (a Physician accompanying Paul), and John (a disciple) were the actual authors.

- Irenaeus, AD 175-185, Against Heresies 3.1.1-2
- Tertullian, AD 197-220, Against Marcion 4.2.1-2
- Papias of Hierapolus, AD 110-140, quoted by Eusebius Ecclesiastical History 3.39.15-16
- Clement of Alexandria, AD 180-202, Adumbrationes in Epistolas Canonicas 5:13

It comes down to whether we believe these early witnesses. I admittedly have a bias. But unless there are compelling arguments otherwise, I go with the church fathers. They were much closer to the events and had other sources available to them than we have, some two-thousand years later.

A final question that one could raise is: Can documents written thirty or so years after the fact accurately record the events? When I consider thirty-some years in my past, I come to Ronald Reagan's presidency. I'll state some things I remember about the assassination attempt on his life. It is possible that some of my recollections are wrong, but I don't think so. You, the reader, can check out if my memory is still functioning up-to-par. I'm not cheating by looking up the facts on the Web; I promise.

I remember Hinkley shooting the president and his assistant, Brady. I think it was while Reagan was about to get into a vehicle near the White House. Brady's injuries from being shot in the head were far worse than those suffered by Reagan. He and his wife, from then on, were active in campaigning for gun control legislation. The media initially reported that Reagan's injuries were not life threatening. I remember that he had a collapsed lung and when arriving at the hospital showed good humor by joking with the doctors. Later, years later, we found out that those injuries were far more critical than first reported. They were indeed life threatening. Hinkley spent many years in a mental institution and later went through a period of out-patient visits to his family; he eventually was released. I remember that Reagan was the first president to break a twenty-year curse put on President Harrison (in the 1820s I think) by a Native American chief (Tecumseh I think). He told Harrison that he would become president, but would not survive his term of office. According to the curse, every subsequent president, on even twenty-year intervals, would die in office.

So, how did I do? I hope okay. I'm a follower of the news, but it is not my life's passion. Reagan's assassination attempt sticks in my mind, but it isn't something that had a major impact on my life. What if he was someone who mentored me daily for three years? What if he rose from the dead, and after that ate a fish dinner with me? That would be something!

But one might ask, "Do you remember the actual things that were said?" No I don't. However, I don't live in the ancient world. That was one where the literacy rate was approximately ten to fifteen percent. Today we can simply look something up. People in the ancient world relied on oral transmission and memory. There are some modern counterparts to this. In Muslim areas, it is common for children to memorize the sounds of the entire Koran, even if they don't speak

Arabic. With this in mind, I find it very reasonable that Jesus' words could be remembered and transmitted verbatim in a world where memorization was an essential part of life.

The Resurrection

Philosopher Karl Popper arrived at Cambridge to present a paper called "Are There Philosophical Problems?" Ludwig Wittgenstein chaired the seminar. After the presentation, a passionate ten-minute contentious, intellectual debate ensued. As the argument escalated, Wittgenstein, for emphasis, waved and gestured erratically with a fireplace poker. Finally, Wittgenstein challenged Popper, "State an example of a moral rule." Popper presumably replied, "Not to threaten visiting lecturers with pokers." Wittgenstein, utterly frustrated, stormed out of the room. The fireplace poker silently remained behind.

There were many eyewitnesses, but they could not agree. Was Popper physically threatened? Did Popper lie later? Exactly what did happen?[39]

In the gospel of Matthew, Jesus said that before the rooster crowed, Peter would deny him three times. Later, in the same chapter, it happened exactly as predicted. Mark's account is different. Jesus told Peter, "Before a cock crows twice, you will deny me three times." Sure enough, Mark records that the rooster crowed twice. Luke's and John's gospel agree with Matthew; the rooster will not crow till Peter denies Jesus three times. We have an apparent contradiction. Skeptics are happy to latch on to this and many other similar discrepancies. They say: "The passion accounts are riddled with hopeless contradictions. They tell us nothing of historical value."

I wonder what Popper and Wittgenstein would say. We know that the two philosophers were at the seminar at Cambridge University. We know that they had an intense argument. We know that the famous fireplace poker played a central role. Yet, there are some details that, despite many eye witnesses, are in doubt. Only the fireplace poker knows for sure what happened. Returning to the gospel accounts of the

---

[39] Summarized from: Edmonds and Eidinou, *Wittgenstein's Poker: The Story of a Ten-Minute Argument Between Two Great Philosophers*, (2002).

crucifixion, how many times did the rooster crow? How many roosters were there? Only God and the roosters know for sure.

I don't consider discrepancies in the passion accounts to be invalidations. Rather, they strengthen the argument for their reliability. The New Testament authors each did their best to present the events accurately. In the decades that followed, the gospel writers easily could have communicated to iron out the differences. They didn't; they recorded events as they recalled them. J. Warner Wallace is a professional criminal investigator who wrote *Cold-Case Christianity.* He states that these discrepancies are the very things that convinced him to change his worldview. He was an atheist; now he's a Christian.

The Resurrection is the central doctrine in Christianity. Paul states emphatically:

> Now if Christ is proclaimed as raised from the dead, how can some of you say there is no resurrection of the dead? If there is no resurrection of the dead, then Christ has not been raised; and if Christ has not been raised, then our proclamation has been in vain and your faith has been in vain. We are even found to be misrepresenting God, because we testified of God that he raised Christ—whom he did not raise if it is true that the dead are not raised. For if the dead are not raised, then Christ has not been raised. If Christ has not been raised, your faith is futile, and you are still in your sins. (1 Cor. 15:12-17)

In other words, if the Resurrection did not happen, Christianity is a false religion and it has nothing to offer. It should then be thrown to the trash heap of history. We can easily connect with a lodge or grange to engage with a community of like-minded people who regularly meet together. We can participate in an activity center to enjoy the company of others in friendly competitions. We can stay in contact with our high-school or college buddies. There are many secular non-profits that do-good work. If Jesus did not rise from the dead, simply put: Christianity is not needed. As Paul said, "If for this life only we have hoped in Christ, we are of all people most to be pitied (1 Cor. 15:19)."

From a historical point of view, the idea that one would physically rise from the dead is a hard thing to believe. If Jesus rose from the dead, it was a one-time event. Guess what? People of Jesus' time knew very well that dead people stay dead. For us now, and for those who lived in the first century, the evidence needs to be compelling.

Homer's Iliad and Odyssey provides the Greco-Roman framework for ancient life after death expectations. That mythology declares that the dead go to Hades, a gloomy place. It is a one-way trip, there is no coming back. Plato evolved this expectation somewhat to give people some hope. The evil people would experience ongoing distress, but the fate of the honorable would be some kind of eternal bliss. Immortality also could be achieved by leaving behind a respected legacy. Some thought that the dead go to live with the gods among the stars. In no case would a dead person return. That would be terrible. It would not be a good thing to return again in a physical body to this world of suffering.

It is true that there were some who believed in reincarnation or transmigration of the soul from one person to another. This could explain why Herod thought that Jesus was John the Baptist resurrected (Luke 9:7). Nevertheless, there was no concept of a literal physical resurrection in the New Testament sense.

Egyptians believed that the dead were alive in some way. They buried the dead with food supplies to assist in the journey to the world beyond. Never would they imagine that the dead would return and resume their life.

From the Jewish context, the Pharisees believed in the hope for a physical resurrection. However, this was to be at the end of the age, not in the middle. Yes, Jesus did physically raise several people from the dead in his ministry. These were resuscitated, not resurrected. The distinction is significant.

One might ask, "What about the Matthew gospel account where the dead (Matt. 27:53) came out of the graves and went into the city?" I view this account similar to UFO appearances which many people witness. Strange, unexplainable things happened when Jesus was crucified and thereafter. The historian Josephus documents some of these. I believe that Matthew is simply putting to words those things to which people testified. In any case, the dead didn't buy houses, plot fields, and resume their lives. They mysteriously appeared, and then they were gone. Did this really happen? You decide.

What about Jesus' resurrection? Over a forty-day period, he appeared many times, sometimes to large groups. He was physical, eating meals and engaging in conversations. He was not simply resuscitated; his new body had additional, enhanced capabilities. Where did this belief come from? It was certainly not expected, either from Jewish or from Greco-Roman belief systems. There were no precedents for it. The traditions had no framework for one coming back to life in a physical body, one that could be touched, could eat, but could also go through walls and appear and disappear at will.

The Jews were looking for a charismatic commander who would kick out the Romans, encourage Jews around the empire to come home, and bring an era of unending peace. Jesus was not this; he was the opposite in fact. The disciples had a dead messiah who suffered a humiliating death on a cross between two criminals. He was one of thousands of Jews who were crucified in the first century. Why would a largely uneducated group of Galileans claim that this dead messiah had conquered death, coming back physically? Where did they come up with this weird story? Even stranger, why did it take root? Why was it believed?

Ancient people understood tales of ghosts and spirits, which I believe led to the gnostic movement: the one that taught that Jesus either never was human, or rose again as a spirit. The Christian message didn't make sense to either Jew or Gentile, yet it spread rapidly throughout the Roman world. Why? These questions call for a plausible explanation before we can rationally dismiss the accounts.

The first possible explanation that comes to mind is that the stories were made up. It was all a fabrication. The gospel accounts themselves refute this possibility. The first ones to see Jesus resurrected were women. In the patriarchal, ancient society of the Middle East, nobody would ever fabricate a story like this. The testimonies of women were not considered credible. Luke 24:11 illustrates this point. The apostles thought that the first reports of the empty tomb seemed like nonsense, and the women were hesitant to report it. Celsus, around AD 20 mocks Christians for this very reason.

> After death he rose again and showed the marks of his punishment and how his hands had been pierced. But who saw this? A hysterical female, as you say, and

perhaps some other one of those who were deluded by the same sorcery.[40]

In First Corinthians 15 where Paul provides a list of the witnesses who saw the resurrected Christ during the 40 days that followed the crucifixion, some of whom were still alive at the time. This list contains only men. Apparently, Paul thought that his argument would be less convincing if he included women in the list.

Fabricated stories typically do not have verifiable details like persons (Pilate and Caiaphas), places (Nazareth and the Pool of Siloam), and events (deaths of John the Baptist and Jesus' brother James). Additionally, the gospel narratives present the apostles in an unflattering light. During Jesus' ministry they appear unsophisticated, frequently saying and doing the wrong things. After Jesus' death they come across as weak and afraid, not quite knowing what to do. The accounts present Jesus, the Lord of the world, in very human terms, weeping over Jerusalem and in despair as he faced death. These things argue against a made-up story. We would expect Jesus and the apostles to be far more exalted than what we read. Finally, why don't the authors embellish the moment when Jesus comes forth from the grave. One would expect triumphant accounts where the conquering hero emerges in dramatic fashion. Yet none of this occurs; the gospels do not even provide direct eye-witnesses to this event, which is central to the Christian faith.

Consider the following quote from Will Durant, who was a historian, but not a Christian. His comments strongly argue against the possibility of a contrived, fabricated story.

> It is clear that there are many contradictions between one gospel and another … All this granted, much remains. The contradictions are of minutiae, not substance; in essentials the synoptic gospels agree remarkably well, and form a consistent portrait of Christ. In the enthusiasm of its discoveries the Higher Criticism has applied to the New Testament tests of authenticity so severe that by them a hundred ancient worthies, for example Hammurabi, David, Socrates—

---

[40] Origen, *Contra Celsum*, Cambridge University Press (1965): 109.

would fade into legend. Despite the prejudices and theological preconceptions of the evangelists, they record many incidents that mere inventors would have concealed—the competition of the apostles for high places in the Kingdom, their flight after Jesus' arrest, Peter's denial, the failure of Christ to work miracles in Galilee, the references of some auditors to his possible insanity, his early uncertainty as to his mission, his confessions of ignorance as to the future, his moments of bitterness, his despairing cry on the cross; no one reading these scenes can doubt the reality of the figure behind them. That a few simple men should in one generation have invented so powerful and appealing a personality, so lofty an ethic and so inspiring a vision of human brotherhood, would be a miracle far more incredible than any recorded in the Gospel. After two centuries of Higher Criticism the outlines of the life, character, and teaching of Christ, remain reasonably clear, and constitute the most fascinating feature of the history of Western man."[41]

Other facts argue against a made-up story. The Jews in the centuries both before and after Christ followed other messiahs. These were military commanders. When one messiah died, their followers scattered, and then they either disbanded or looked to find another. That is not what happened in Christianity.

Perhaps the strongest case against the fabrication hypothesis is Paul's conversion. He had nothing to do with the original gospel accounts. Why would he who in his own words was a Pharisee of Pharisees, switch from chief enemy to apostle? He had nothing to gain, and in the end, was beheaded under Nero for his faith. Why?

A second possible hypothesis is the legend theory. Couldn't the whole thing be a myth that evolved over time? This explanation also fails. Christianity spread very fast, without organization. The earliest followers might not have figured out all of its implications, but they were united about several basic points. Jesus was physically resurrected. God's new kingdom was present. Jesus was the true Lord

---

[41] Will Durant, *The Story of Civilization, Vol III: Caesar and Christ*, 557

of the world, not Caesar. The original disciples and their followers were willing to die rather than deny these things.

An extra-biblical look at the early faith comes from Pliny the Younger, writing to the Emperor Trajan. Pliny was governor of Pontus/Bithynia from AD 111-113 and Trajan ruled from AD 97-117. We can confidently date this letter to within eighty years of the crucifixion. Excerpts from his letter follow:

> It is my practice, my lord, to refer to you all matters concerning which I am in doubt. For who can better give guidance to my hesitation or inform my ignorance? I have never participated in trials of Christians. I therefore do not know what offenses it is the practice to punish or investigate, and to what extent. And I have been not a little hesitant as to whether there should be any distinction on account of age or no difference between the very young and the more mature; whether pardon is to be granted for repentance, or, if a man has once been a Christian, it does him no good to have ceased to be one; whether the name itself, even without offenses, or only the offenses associated with the name are to be punished.
>
> In the case of those who were denounced to me as Christians, I have observed the following procedure: I interrogated these as to whether they were Christians; those who confessed I interrogated a second and a third time, threatening them with punishment; those who persisted I ordered executed. ... Soon accusations spread, as usually happens, because of the proceedings going on, and several incidents occurred. An anonymous document was published containing the names of many persons. Those who denied that they were or had been Christians, when they invoked the gods in words dictated by me, offered prayer with incense and wine to your image, ... and moreover cursed Christ—none of which those who are really Christians, it is said, can be forced to do—these I thought should be discharged. Others named by the informer declared that they were Christians, but then

denied it, asserting that they had been but had ceased to be, some three years before, others many years, some as much as twenty-five years. They all worshipped your image and the statues of the gods, and cursed Christ. ...

They asserted, however, that the sum and substance of their fault or error had been that they were accustomed to meet on a fixed day before dawn and sing responsively a hymn to Christ as to a god, and to bind themselves by oath, not to some crime, but not to commit fraud, theft, or adultery, not falsify their trust, nor to refuse to return a trust when called upon to do so. When this was over, it was their custom to depart and to assemble again to partake of food—but ordinary and innocent food. ... I judged it more necessary to find out what the truth was by torturing two female slaves who were called deaconesses. But I discovered nothing else but depraved, excessive superstition. ...

Many persons of every age, every rank, and of both sexes are and will be endangered. For the contagion of this superstition has spread not only to the cities but also to the villages and farms. But it seems possible to check and cure it.[42]

This letter shows that within the short span of eighty years, Christianity was spreading rapidly. When subjected to Roman threats, some recanted, but others accepted execution and torture. The worship exhorted followers to live honorably and sing hymns responsively to Christ as God.

Is there a way to know the content of the hymns to which Pliny the Younger refers, which were sung responsively? The answer to this is yes. Some of these are still sung today (e.g. The Oxyrhychus hymn sung by the Eastern Orthodox church[43]). There are several of these hymns included in the New Testament. Traces survive in the Luke,

---

[42] Paul Halsall, "Ancient History Sourcebook," https://sourcebooks.fordham.edu/halsall/ancient/pliny-trajan1.asp.

[43] "hymn–Papyrus 1786" (AD 260), https://earlychurchhistory.org/arts/oldest-known-christian-hymn.

John, and in the Pauline letters, that were translated from their original Aramaic versions. We'll consider one of these from Philippians 2. The following is a reconstruction of the original hymn:[44]

    (a) Who, though he bore the stamp of the divine Image,
    (b) Did not use equality with God as a gain to be exploited;

    (a) But surrendered His rank,
    (b) And took the role of a servant;

    (a) Accepting a human-like guise,
    (b) And appearing on earth as the Man;

    (a) He humbled Himself,
    (b) In an obedience which went as far as to die.

    (a) For this, God raised Him to the highest honor,
    (b) And conferred upon Him the highest rank of all;

    (a) That, at Jesus' name, every knee should bow,
    (b) And every tongue should own that 'Jesus Christ is Lord'.

Paul was likely quoting a well-known hymn of the time.[45] It affirms Christ as God, along with his death and resurrection. Recent scholarship dates the Philippians letter to AD 52-54. From analyzing Paul's letter to the Galatians, scholars date this hymn even earlier, as early as the first few years or even months after the crucifixion. It is rhythmic, its structure is similar to that of Aramaic poetry, and it is internally coherent. This proves to me that the original Christian message did not evolve over time but originated with the disciples right from the beginning.

The burden of proof is high for the resurrection. For one to deny its occurrence, they only need to put forth a reasonable counter argument that addresses the following questions. Why was the tomb empty?

---

[44] Tyndale Bulletin, 19 (1968): 106.
[45] R. P. Martin, "Carmen Christi: Philippians ii. 5-11 in Recent Interpretation and in the Setting of Early Christian Worship," (Cambridge University Press 1967): xii, 364 55s.

How do we explain the disciples and hundreds of others seeing a physically resurrected Jesus with enhanced abilities? Why did the passion accounts hinge on women testimonies, considered to be unreliable in that day? Why did the followers almost immediately worship Jesus as divine? Why would a group of illiterate Jewish fishermen reinterpret and restructure their faith tradition? Why did Christianity rapidly take root in spite of Roman opposition? Why did Paul and James convert?

The early Christians were severely persecuted, tortured, and killed. Yet, they would not deny Jesus. Why do this if there was no resurrection? They could've avoided the hardships by simply assimilating into Roman culture. If they were Jews, they could've remained Jews, avoiding the loss of friends and family. Or, for Gentiles, they could've remained as they were, remaining connected to their local traditions.

This resurrection truth claim is unique to Christianity. One can believe other faith traditions, but those beliefs are entirely based on faith. There is no way to use reason to verify them. For example, the Quran states that Jesus was not crucified; it only appeared so. How does one know if that claim is true? By faith and faith alone. There are no historical data to back it up.

In the New Testament, Jesus, quoting Deuteronomy 6:5, tells us: You shall love the Lord your God with all your heart, and with all your soul, and with all your mind. If you look up that Old Testament verse, you find that Jesus intentionally added the word, *mind*. The Christian religion requires faith, but also employs reason. In scientific terms, Christianity is falsifiable.

Let's move on. Who were the disciples? Peter, Andrew, James, and John were fishermen. Matthew was a tax collector working with the Romans, and Simon was a zealot hating them. Judas Iscariot had experience handling funds, happy to keep some for himself. Strange bedfellows indeed.

We don't know Phillip's occupation, but he was from Bethsaida, where Andrew and Peter also lived. Some speculate that, because of this, Phillip was also a fisherman. Phillip found Nathanael (Bartholomew) to announce, "We found the messiah." Since Jesus saw Nathanael "under the fig tree," we know that he was a student of Torah. I think he was anticipating the imminent coming of the messiah.

We don't know the occupations of Thomas, James the son of Alpheus, and Thaddeus.

Does this motley crew sound like a group that would change the world with a new religion? I don't think so. The inside four were fisherman from Galilee, a respected trade, but they were very likely to be illiterate. No one would expect this bunch to establish a new religion. Why would they want to? They were second temple period Jews, enmeshed in their tradition.

I've observed the practices of some recent cults. Invariably, they center around a charismatic leader, who exercises tight control over all activities. Christianity started with a crucified messiah and spread organically, haphazardly without any central organization. Cult leaders tend to be narcissistic; the apostles were not this. Furthermore, the apostles never recanted their faith, and most were killed in terrible ways.

Finally, we come to Paul. Why would he, a Pharisee and Roman citizen of high status, convert to this sect that he hated? What did he gain? Not much. He was beaten, stoned, and jailed. Unlike today's TV get-rich evangelists, Paul did not enjoy financial gain. He wound up beheaded. What is the best explanation for this? By his account, he saw Christ resurrected. It changed his life.

Even scholars (e.g. E. P. Sanders) who don't believe in miracles struggle to find reasonable explanations for the rise of Christianity. Most scholars acknowledge that Jesus was crucified, the burial tomb was found empty on the following Sunday morning, and his followers truly believed that he appeared to them alive multiple times afterward. Since I'm open to the existence of the supernatural, I believe it happened. My belief is a rational one, not emotional. It is not blind faith. If the resurrection did indeed happen, then other lesser miracles, like the virgin birth, walking on water, healings, and exorcisms become plausible. If true, the rest of Jesus's teachings are important to consider.

I just presented, in a condensed few pages, the historical facts that convince me that Jesus really did rise from the dead. Naturalistically, this makes no sense. I get that. But no other explanation makes sense either, at least not to me. The alternatives make even less sense.

There are a multitude of books written on this topic. They delve into the historicity of the resurrection with far more detail than what I presented here. I'll end this section providing a sampling. Check them out for yourself.

- *There is a God*, Anthony Flew and Roy Varghese, Appendix B
- *Gunning for God,* John Lennox, Chapter 8
- *The Case for Christ*, Lee Strobel
- *Cold Case Christianity*, J. Warner Wallace
- *The Resurrection of the Son of God,* N.T. Wright
- *Dethroning Jesus: Exposing Popular Culture's Quest to Unseat the Biblical Christ*, Darrell Bock, and Dan Wallace
- *The Case for the Resurrection*, Gary Habermas, and Mike Licona
- *The Resurrection of Jesus*: A New Historiographical Approach, Mike Licona

The Enlightenment

In the previous section, I presented the reasons why I believe that it is rational to accept that the Resurrection of Jesus was a real historical event. This being said, there are more questions to ask. The first is: "Okay, so what does this have to do with me?" In this section, I'm going to contrast the teachings of Jesus with the Enlightenment—the Western ideology which asserts that reason and individualism supersedes religious traditions.

We are children of the Enlightenment, the age of reason. Some say that this period began in 1620 at the beginning of the scientific revolution. Others pin its origin to the early 1700s. Its popularity faded in the first part of the 19th century, yet much of its philosophy lives on to this day.

The two main enemies of the Enlightenment were the divine right of kings and the dominance of the Church. Much of this is understandable. Kings used their power to indiscriminately oppress the masses. Religious wars persisted for over a hundred years after the Reformation. People were fed up. Enlightened thought proclaimed that science and reason contain the answers needed to birth a new age for humanity. All that was required was for the West to spread principles of freedom and democracy to the ends of the earth. A new global world order was in view. This philosophy embodies the myth of progress;

humanity is on an upward journey to the ultimate utopia that is just over the horizon.

In this new age, the supernatural is irrelevant. God is likely off creating other universes, leaving us here with the natural order to handle things ourselves. God is unnecessary, or more recently, Darwin shows that God doesn't exist. Immanuel Kant states in *The Critique of Pure Reason*, "I had to deny knowledge in order to make room for faith."

The Enlightenment's central tenet holds that humanity is maturing. The age of superstition and blind faith is over. Humanity is growing up; it is coming of age. The Enlightenment is the foundation of modern Western political and intellectual thought.

> Enlightenment is man's release from his self-incurred tutelage. Tutelage is man's inability to make use of his understanding without direction from another. Self-incurred is this tutelage when its cause lies not in lack of reason but in lack of resolution and courage to use it without direction from another ... Have courage to use your own reason!'- that is the motto of enlightenment.[46]
> —Immanuel Kant

This new age of reason had profound effects upon the entire world and not all of these were good. It led to the Age of Discovery where major Western powers subdued, enslaved, conquered, and killed millions of indigenous peoples. It was also the time when the Christian message went truly global. Sometimes, to their credit, missionaries attempted to restrain the evils that followed. I'm sorry to say that all too often, they supported and participated in the worst of the atrocities.[47] Some would use these facts to discredit Christianity entirely. This is unfair in my opinion. One cannot reasonably attribute the sins of imperialism to the teachings of Jesus. It is more accurate to state that this was the inevitable consequence of the enlightenment philosophy itself.

For example, Adam Smith, a leading Enlightenment figure, wrote, "The colony of a civilized nation which takes possession, either of a waste country, or of one so thinly inhabited, that the natives easily give

---

[46] Immanuel Kant, "An Answer to the Question: What is Enlightenment?".
[47] *American Holocaust,* David E. Stannard.

place to the new settlers, advances more rapidly to wealth and greatness than any other human society."[48] This quote reminds me of a short dialogue I once posted to an indigenous forum.

> We will play tag. Why will we play tag? You are *IT*. Why am I *IT*? The game says so and because your feet look funny. I don't want to play. Catch us if you can. I can't! We say that you are *IT*!
>
> They are *IT*. Why are they *IT*? They are not like us. They don't want to be *IT*. Everyone says they are *IT*. Everyone? Something is wrong with them. What is that? Look at them, their feet look funny. We say that they are *IT*!
>
> We can take what *IT* has. Why? They have land they don't use. They live there! They have things they don't need. What things? They have gold and don't know it. So? They are stupid, and their feet look funny. They did nothing wrong. We say that they are *IT*!
>
> Let's kill *IT*. Why? They might kill us. They never have. They will defend themselves. Shouldn't they? They are less than human. What? They are animals whose feet look funny. We say that they are *IT*!
>
> Oh my God?? What have you done? Nothing. You abused and killed so many. It never happened. It did happen. You must be an *IT* lover. I hear children screaming. It was their fault. What? They deserved it. Why? Because their feet look funny. They were *IT*.
>
> Oh my God, what has happened? It was *THEY* that did it. Was it? Don't say that again, it wasn't that bad. Wasn't it? Don't keep saying that, good people wouldn't do that. Wouldn't they? *THEY* did it, not me.

---

[48] Adam Smith, *The Wealth of Nations*, 4.7.2.

> Are you sure? There were so few *IT*s anyway. We are good people.
>
> I don't want to play tag. Why not? Because someday I will be *IT*. It is just a game of tag. It is more than a game. It will be fun. Please don't make me *IT*.[49]

The Enlightenment was a period of arrogance. Distant peoples were considered inferior to civilized countries, and because of this, it was okay to take over their territories and violently stamp out any resistance. Consider the following quote spoken by Teddy Roosevelt in 1886, about fifteen years before becoming America's 26th president.

> I suppose I should be ashamed to say that I take the western view of the Indian. I don't go so far as to think that the only good Indian is the dead Indian, but I believe nine out of every ten are, and I shouldn't like to inquire too closely into the case of the tenth. The most vicious cowboy has more moral principle than the average Indian.[50] —Theodore Roosevelt

After the colonial period, the twentieth century witnessed two great wars with unspeakable violence. We experienced the Holocaust and multiple genocides (for example, Armenia, Bosnia, Cambodia, and Rwanda). Stalin and Mao murdered close to one-hundred million. Worst of all, much of this happened in the very heart of the West. What happened? Has man really come of age? If so, what kind of age is this? The myth of progress has no answer for the inherent evil in the world.

As we enter the postmodern era, but what will come next? Despair is on the rise, often resulting from poverty, but also from a general lack of purpose and hope. These things lead people to addictions and suicide. In my small city in the Pacific Northwest, one of five children do not have a permanent residence; six out of ten live in single parent families; 18% seriously consider suicide by the eleventh grade.[51] Throughout the world, streams of fanaticism are leading to extreme

---

[49] Dan Harvey, "Let's Play Tag," Our Daily Frybread (Feb 14 2007 12:00AM).

[50] *Roosevelt in the Bad Lands,* Hermann Hagedorn (Boston, 1921): 354-356.

[51] Samaritan Health Services Community Health Assessment (2014).

ideologies. There are threats of an imminent third great war like nothing ever experienced in human history. The long-term consequences of rapid and radical cultural shifts are yet unknown.

Christianity tells a different story. Humanity did not come of age in the 1700s. The new age began when Jesus was crucified. It shook the cosmos and established the foundation of a new creation. For two millennia, imperfectly and sometimes destructively, it has made significant impacts on the order of things. Societal assumptions regarding human rights, care for the disabled, family values, etc. were very different in the Roman empire.

The new creation declares that love, not reason, will raise humanity to a new level. Unfortunately, we are a stubborn lot. There have been glimpses, to be sure. The early Christians, Gandhi, Martin Luther King, and Nelson Mandela show that it is possible. Non-profits in our time continue to bear witness by looking after those in the worst places with nothing to gain for themselves. These are not publicized, but they do exist, and in large numbers.

Humans are built to attach themselves to something. We are like vine branches that connect to others. Those could be political leaders that we hope will set everything right. It could be an athlete with incredible abilities. It could be a famous movie actor or performer. It might even be a political philosophy. There are problems with this. We wind up with lots of limbs connected to each other, but where is the root? If the source is not grounded, then the whole thing dies.

Jesus made an outrageous statement. He said, "I am the vine and you are the branches. Without me you can do nothing." Is it possible that he is correct? It is something to consider. When we ask, "What can save civilization from repetitions of violence, oppression, and death," the answer just might be embodied in the lessons of Jesus.

How should those of us who are Christian interact with political systems? How do we react to disturbing culture trends? In the West, we live in a secular system. Its structure is able to pass whatever laws it wants. It can redefine morality in whatever ways that the population demands. The early Christians were not primarily concerned with prayer in schools, abortion, or gay marriage. They did not impact society with political power. They demonstrated a good news message, which was irresistible and attractive to an oppressive pagan world.

By the time politicians' rule, it is generally too late. Universities, news outlets, social media, Hollywood, and tech-firms lead by manipulating public opinion; politicians simply follow. If Christianity be true, our job is to simply trust God, and allow him to burn away those things that destroy our souls. At some point in the process, we'll be ready to happily respond to God's invitation to participate in whatever he has going on, whether big or small. Then perhaps collectively, the Church can be a mirror that reflects the Father's love back to the culture.

Conclusion

There are many evidences for the existence of God and for the truth of Christianity. Some of these, by themselves, admittedly, do not settle the issue. The presence of the moral framework that is embedded within us is one example. Though its reality is easily seen and is widely accepted, its origin can reasonably be questioned.

Some arguments can be more persuasive than others, at least for me. The manifestation of the supernatural is one of these. In this case, theists and skeptics fall into the Rob and Bob crab categories (see above). The Robs of the world insist that there is nothing outside of the physical Universe, whereas the Bobs insist that there is a larger reality beyond the materialistic. So again, the issue of God's existence is up for debate. Besides this, even if there is a supernatural, the nature of that realm is difficult to discern.

For me, the historicity of Jesus' resurrection and the uniqueness of his message settles the issue. The conversion of Paul, a former persecutor of the faith, is of particular importance. In his own words, he summarizes his experience and invites his audience to investigate:

> For I handed on to you as of first importance what I in turn had received: that Christ died for our sins in accordance with the scriptures, and that he was buried, and that he was raised on the third day in accordance with the scriptures, and that he appeared to Cephas, then to the twelve. Then he appeared to more than five hundred brothers and sisters at one time, most of whom are still alive, though some have died. Then he

appeared to James, then to all the apostles. Last of all, as to one untimely born, he appeared also to me. For I am the least of the apostles, unfit to be called an apostle, because I persecuted the church of God. But by the grace of God I am what I am, and his grace toward me has not been in vain. On the contrary, I worked harder than any of them—though it was not I, but the grace of God that is with me. Whether then it was I or they, so we proclaim and so you have come to believe. (1 Cor. 15:3-11)

PART 2

Sacred Scripture

> It ain't those parts of the Bible that I can't understand that bother me, it's the parts that I do understand. — Mark Twain

The Bible is a complex library of books written by many authors over a period of a couple thousand years. During that time, the culture, language, and people's understandings of God evolved dramatically. How do we interpret such a collection? In the hands of the irresponsible, the Bible can be used to support almost any ideology, and this can justify anything, no matter how evil. There is almost nothing that can more quickly push a person away from faith than when the Bible is used as a weapon for religious intolerance and bigotry.

It is said that the Bible reveals the full revelation of God. Yet we still see darkly as through a clouded mirror.[52] Even after receiving and understanding sound teaching, it is easy to walk away and ignore what was taught.[53] Scripture is important, but so is the Holy Spirit[54], the God-given wisdom received by the church Fathers, and a community of believers to keep us accountable. Otherwise we are likely to stray using private interpretations and justifications.

Is the Bible inerrant and infallible? How do we apply these ancient texts to the modern world? How do we distinguish between the genres and fit the writings into their cultural contexts? Is the world really 6,000 years old? Was there a literal, global flood? Why are there so many denominational divisions within the Church? Can we make sense of any of it? These are questions that I plan to address in the following chapters

.

---

[52] 1 Cor 13:12.
[53] Jas. 1:21-22.
[54] 2 Cor 3:12-18.

Chapter 4

Authority of Scripture

> As a child abuse and neglect therapist I do battle daily with Christians enamored of the Old Testament phrase "Spare the rod and spoil the child." No matter how far I stretch my imagination, it does not stretch far enough to include the image of a cool dude like Jesus taking a rod to a kid.[55] — Chris Crutcher

Even if we consider the scriptures to be the final authority for issues of life, we still wrestle with interpretation. Consider the above quotation. In past generations, "Spare the rod and spoil the child" was taken literally by most believers. Parents would therefore use rods, belts, or other such instruments to discipline their children. In our generation, the majority of parents read this command symbolically as: "Correct your child when they do wrong, but understand that harsh modes of discipline have the potential to cause permanent psychological damage." So what does it mean when we say that the bible is authoritative? Interpretation is in the mind of the reader. Is all scripture equally authoritative? What about the Old Testament?

The Jewish Scriptures

On November 28, 2007, CNN-YouTube conducted a presidential debate hosting eight Republican presidential candidates. The questions presented were those raised by ordinary citizens. Joseph Dearing from Dallas, Texas asked: "How you answer this question will tell us everything we need to know about you?" He then raised a Bible and added, "Do you believe every word of this book? And I mean the book that I'm holding in my hand. Do you believe this book?"

Three of the candidates did their best to answer the question. Mayor Giuliani said he believes it, and reads it often, but then says that some parts are allegorical and not meant to be taken literally. Governor Romney stated: "I believe the Bible is the word of God." He then

---

[55] Chris Crutcher, *King of the Mild Frontier: An Ill-Advised Autobiography.*

qualified his statement by saying: "I might interpret it differently than you." Finally, Governor Huckabee who has a divinity degree, gave his answer. "The Bible is the word of revelation from God himself." He followed that with qualifications: "Some parts are allegorical. No one believes that we should pluck our eyes out. We should focus on loving our neighbor and not on those parts that are difficult."

I was not surprised by their answers. They are what I would expect from politicians running for office. Let's speculate for a bit. What if one of the candidates answered: "I believe that Jesus rose from the dead and is Lord. I have real difficulties with the violence and genocide described in the Old Testament." Would this be an acceptable answer to Joseph Dearing? I can't know for sure, but I suspect that it would not.

What should we do with the Old Testament, the Tanakh, the thirty-nine books at the front of the Bible? Why do those of us who are Christian care about them? Eliminating those books would save us a lot of grief when working out responses to attacks by skeptics. Almost from the beginning, some Christians did want to do just this. The Old Testament contains passages that, by today's standards, are awful to say the least.

So why do Christians care? I can think of several reasons. First, we get to understand the whole drama of redemption. We see how God, from the beginning, planned to restore all of creation. We learn how, through Israel, the Messiah would seed the Gospel that was destined to spread throughout all of the world. We observe how God patiently worked with an ancient tribal group of people to accomplish his purposes. We experience the whole drama.

Second, all of the New Testament authors quote the Old Testament. For this reason, it is useful to read those Old Testament sections in context. It is particularly revealing how the disciples and Paul reinterpret the plain meaning of earlier Old Testament verses. We find an example of this in First John chapter 4 where Jesus is called God's only begotten son (literally: only born, *monogenes* in Greek). But, Exodus 4 declares Israel not Jesus, to be God's firstborn son. John is not mistaken but is contrasting the birth of Israel as a nation with the physical birth of the Messiah. Where Israel fell short in its mission to bless all of the nations, Jesus, representing Israel, succeeds.

Finally, Jesus tells us in Luke 24:44 that the Law and the Prophets speak about him. It is thought-provoking to ponder how this can be.

Christians often incorrectly interpret the Old Testament. It is wise to remember that Jewish rabbis do not read the 39 books literally. Rather, it is the starting point for debates. They read it filtered using the insights of scholars and sages. The intent is to determine what is appropriate within the framework of contemporary society. Jews consider their Bible to be sacred and holy, not because of what it literally says, but how it can apply to latter generations. After millennia of study, subtleties are still being uncovered. Jews are not really concerned with questions of infallibility or inerrancy. Rabbi Richard Hirsh, director of the Reconstructionist Rabbinical Association, once responded to the question, "Do you believe every word?" with the answer: "That is a goyish question. Jews don't 'believe' in the Torah. We try to live by it as it is interpreted and applied."[56]

Infallibly Inerrant

> All scripture is inspired by God and is useful for teaching, for reproof, for correction, and for training in righteousness, so that everyone who belongs to God may be proficient, equipped for every good work. (2 Tim. 3:16-17)

Since the time of the Protestant Reformation, Christian denominations disagreed over the importance of the written words of scripture as compared to church tradition. Most evangelical protestant churches place a lower value on tradition and, because of this, they assert the infallibility and inerrancy of scripture in their doctrinal statements. Let's consider those words for a bit.

The year was 1741 when one of the great composers thought to give his last public performance. His health was failing; he was hopelessly in debt and terribly depressed. Debtors' prison awaited. But then, unexpectedly, a Dublin charity commissioned him to compose a musical piece for a benefit performance. Subsequently, he hid himself away in a room of his small house, and for 24 days ate almost nothing. The result was hundreds of pages of near-perfect music. Sir Newman Flower wrote, "Considering the immensity of the work, and the short

---

[56] Andrew Silow-Carroll, "What Jews Believe," *Jerusalem Post* (Dec 8, 2007).

time involved, it will remain, perhaps forever, the greatest feat in the whole history of musical composition." The composer himself reflected, "I did think I did see all heaven before me, and the great God Himself." To a friend, he commented, "Whether I was in the body, or out of the body when I wrote it, I know not."

The result: Enough money was raised at the benefit performance to free over a hundred people from debtor's prison. It remains today as one of our most beloved compositions. The person is George Frederic Handel. The piece he composed is simply named *Messiah*.

As I reflect on this account, 2 Timothy 3:16-17 (quoted above) comes to mind. Was Handel inspired? I would answer, "No doubt." Was Handel's *Messiah* God breathed? Yes, I believe it was. What about infallible? If you mean that it could not fail to impact millions and become so well known, I suppose it was. What about inerrant? If by inerrant, you mean that every stanza is exactly as it should be, then yes.

Nevertheless, I would not refer to Handel's Messiah as infallible and inerrant. To do so would detract from, and even possibly destroy the life of the composition. Someone would undoubtedly come along and say, "It is not inerrant, because this or that part could be improved." They could also say, "I don't like the words of that verse; they contradict the words sung later." Another could say, "It is not infallible; I've heard better." As a result, we would dissect the composition to the point where its meaning and its impact were totally lost.

The same issue comes to mind when I reflect on the Bible. I don't like to argue about how many times the rooster crowed before Peter's betrayal. Similarly, arguing about whether there was one or two Gerasene demoniacs is a futile exercise. I certainly don't want to waste my time coming up with convoluted arguments that attempt to harmonize discrepancies in the different passion accounts. These things are the very reasons that often convince those trained in Criminal Science (like Lee Strobel and J. Warner Wallace) to believe. It convinces them that the accounts are those of authentic eye witnesses, and as such, they expect discrepancies, even contradictions.

Similarly, I don't want to waste time arguing why God chose Moses to deliver his people from the oppression of Egypt and shortly after, sought to kill him. Yes, we need explanations to interpret these and many other biblical difficulties, but applying the labels "infallible" and "inerrant" cloud the issue. I accept that the Bible is an inspired, even "God breathed," collection of writings, which will accomplish its purpose to transform humanity away from violence and revenge towards love and peace through Jesus. I see the Bible as infallibly able to point us to the inerrant Word, that being Jesus. I see the Bible depicting a drama that transforms Man's image of God away from that of anger and wrath, requiring human and animal sacrifice, to one of love and grace.

Can the original New Testament authors shed some light on the issue? In second Timothy, the author quotes from the Septuagint (the ancient Greek translation of the Old Testament). Does this mean that he considers the Septuagint to be an infallible and inerrant source? It is a translation, not the original Hebrew scripture.

Following my work writing computer software to revitalize indigenous languages, I can no longer pass over the alterations that translations bring to a text. There isn't a one-to-one correspondence between concepts of different languages. Some words in one language cannot accurately be translated to another; the concept might not even exist. For example, you would think that a basic word like *love* would exist in every language. It does not. Wess Stafford, former president of Compassion International, pondered this in his book, *Too Small to Ignore*. Try translating the New Testament without using this word. We could even argue that *love* in its first-century sense no longer exists in English. That word is so overused in our day that it has largely lost its meaning. It originally was a word of action; now it connotates vague, temporary emotions and feelings.

Languages reflect the land and cultures where they are used. For example, Jesus makes the statement that a fool builds his house on the sand, but the wise man builds his house on a rock. That may be okay in Israel, but not so in Bangladesh. In that area, which is subject to annual floods, houses are built on stilts. If one tries to build a house on a rock, it will wash away. Another example is where Jesus is called the Lion of Judah. In some African tribes, lions are feared and are considered enemies. The Lion metaphor does not work. A final example concerns one Native American tribe, I forget which one, when first encountering a missionary. That missionary was insistent in referring to our messiah by the name Jesus Christ. When he did that, the tribe laughed and walked away. Those syllables in their language meant: *He pees*.

Another issue concerns individuals within the same culture. I think something; my brain fires a bunch of neurons. My mouth starts moving. Sound emerges. It goes through the air. The sound waves enter a listening person's ears. Neurons fire. The brain translates. The listener perceives the meaning of what was said. In speech recognition, this is known as the noisy channel. What makes us think that we all hear the same thing in the same way? There is good evidence to say that we don't.

Different languages have many special idioms and distinct cultural practices. Is it possible for us to fully understand these things today? For example, there is a phrase recorded in the New Testament where Jesus cries in Aramaic, "My God, My God why have you forsaken me?" This puzzled commentators for hundreds of years. How can God forsake God? Of course, Jesus is simply asking a question, not making a statement. In that moment, he didn't feel the Father's presence. He is quoting Psalm 22, and if we read further into that Psalm, we find that the Father is present and does not, in fact, despise nor turn away from the afflicted. But there is another twist on this cry that I discovered when reading James Lamsas' writings. He is a Bible translator who published the Peshitta version of the New Testament, and whose first language is Aramaic. He states that Jesus' cry is an Aramaic idiom that is still used today. It means, "This is my destiny, for this I was born."

Languages change with time. One indigenous North American language was documented by missionaries in the 1700s. That language was entirely different one generation later. When a later linguist inquired, some of the younger tribal members responded, "That is the way the old people spoke."

Metaphors that made sense in the first century don't in our time. Say *step on it* a thousand years from now: Do you think people will know that it means *speed up*? How about saying to the apostles: "I'm going to google it"? What about: "I'm in a pickle"? That would surely be confusing.

In a previous section, I've presented why I believe the New Testament texts are reliable. But what about the Old Testament? Can we know who the original authors were and guarantee that their writings were not modified over time? The Dead Sea scrolls prove that these documents were carefully preserved from well before the time of Christ. We have no way to know for sure what happened before that. For example, scholars use patterns of language to date portions of the Old Testament. Certain phraseology used in the first temple period would not be expected at the time of Moses. This enables researchers to identify areas of potential refinements.

This is not a criticism. Prophets had the authority to do this. So, for example, let's suppose that one like Ezra merged the sources extant to him to produce what we have today. This would be considered perfectly acceptable to second temple Jews. When I read the Book of Leviticus, for example, I notice phrases throughout like: "The Lord spoke to Moses, saying, 'Speak to the people of Israel saying.'" Perhaps a prophet somewhere along the line, used this third person expression to add additional weight to the commands. This would be like an authorized person in a corporation stamping a document with the official corporate seal. That person would have the authority to speak for the corporation even though they were not the CEO. In times where Israel was falling into idolatry, it would make sense for a prophet to want to give extra weight to the Mosaic laws.

Even if the Bible is infallible and inerrant, interpretation is not. Each sermon is an interpretation. Pastors like to say that they are preaching the whole oracle of God. They like to say, "I'm teaching the Word," or "the Bible says," or "If God be true, my words are true." Unfortunately, they are teaching their interpretation. There are tens of thousands of pastors who *teach the word*, yet they disagree significantly. What we have is Bible plus.

The Bible itself is a debate. The prophets and Jesus challenge aspects of the Law of Moses. There are different explanations for the tragedies that Israel faced. There is the voice claiming that God is angry and violent; there is the voice claiming that he is long-suffering and merciful. The Bible is wonderfully complex.

I'm sure that God is well aware of the difficulties of transmitting his eternal message in words. Language is a limited medium. I'm sure he is well aware of the human flaws of those whom he entrusted to deliver and preserve the message. Does it need to be infallible and inerrant in the traditional sense? No. Is it sufficient to enable us to understand the nature of God and his plan for the world? Yes. Is it exactly what it should be? Yes.

Interpretation

Article XIX.
WE AFFIRM that a confession of the full authority, infallibility, and inerrancy of Scripture is vital to a sound understanding of the whole of the Christian faith. We further affirm that such confession should lead to increasing conformity to the image of Christ.

WE DENY that such confession is necessary for salvation. However, we further deny that inerrancy can be rejected without grave consequences, both to the individual and to the Church.[57]

Almost three hundred evangelical leaders affirmed article XIX along with the other preceding 18 articles. The idea is that if you don't accept them all, you won't be included within the evangelical umbrella. Yet, despite the consensus, there are thousands of independent evangelical splinter groups in the United States alone. Their disagreements are significant enough that many a Christian would not feel comfortable or be accepted within these congregations. As a result, if they attend, they would need to either shut up or leave. Why do you suppose this is?

It all comes down to interpretation. Churches tend to emphasize and favor some sections of scripture, while ignoring or down playing others.

Consider Phinehas. I've not heard many expository sermons on this Old Testament figure. Yet, besides Abraham, Phinehas is the only person in the Bible who was accounted as righteous (Ps. 106). Who is he? He shows up several times in the Old Testament. The first appearance is in Numbers, where he runs a spear through an Israelite and his Midianite companion who were having sexual relations in a tent. Some say it happened in the tabernacle area, but this is unclear. Somehow, Phinehas's action appeased the angry god and stopped a plague of some kind. If Phinehas did this today, he would be guilty of a double homicide. His actions are not any different than those of ISIS who kill because their version of Allah commands it.

---

[57] International Summit Conference of evangelical leaders (Fall 1978).

I googled this issue, but I didn't find much in the way of alternative interpretations, only a few preachers defending Phinehas for his zeal and asserting that he was justified. They say that God's wrath had to be assuaged or the entire congregation would be held to account. Sorry! For me, this explanation doesn't cut it. Let's bring the account to our times. Many churches have a welcome area with chairs and couches. Suppose, one Sunday there was a person who while waiting for the service to start was sitting on one of these couches watching pornography on their cell phone. Would that church be in danger of experiencing a plague? Would it be justified for a zealous deacon to kill that person? How is this hypothetical situation different than the Phinehas account?

Abraham was counted righteous because he believed that God would provide him an heir through which his descendants would be uncountably numerous. Phinehas was counted righteous because he ran a spear through two unsuspecting individuals, a Hebrew and a Midianite. Zipporah, Moses' wife, was also a Midianite. Apparently, a Midianite woman was okay for Moses, but not for that poor soul who died in a most undignified way.

Phinehas shows up later, in the Book of Joshua. The Israelites had established themselves in the promised land. The three tribes of Manasseh, Gad, and Rueben were free to return home to their allotted land on the Jordan's west bank. But then, they built an altar to God. Phinehas and other leaders went to inquire. They were seriously considering going to war and slaughtering the three tribes that just finished helping them in their recent battles. Fortunately, the war didn't happen. The leaders of Manasseh, Gad, and Rueben talked their way out of it by claiming that the altar was never intended to be for sacrifice. Why was building an altar a problem anyhow? Abraham built altars, as did Isaac and Jacob. Before the temple was built, the prophet Samuel sacrificed regularly at three sites. Altars at different places were not an issue till Solomon's temple was built. Yet Phinehas and his friends were ready to go to war over this issue.

There is one more appearance of this Phinehas. It occurs in the Book of Judges when eleven tribes almost wiped out the tribe of Benjamin. Before the war, the leaders prayed and asked God, "Should we attack?" God said, "yes"; they attacked and lost more than 20,000 in the effort. They prayed again; same result. Phinehas prayed a third time, but this time they changed their military strategy, and won, committing genocide in the process. In the 21st century, these are war crimes.

The account is not over. The warring tribes felt guilty when they realized that they went too far. So, to appease their guilt, they agreed to provide brides for the four hundred men that were still alive. Virgins were kidnapped from a village that refused to participate in the slaughter, and then the Israelites destroyed that village. Phinehas was in the center of all of these things.

I can see why few pastors mention Phinehas in their sermons. Yet after all these gory details, I can't ignore this part of the biblical narrative. There are lessons for us in these verses. Just because some Old Testament person prays and hears something, we don't have to assume that it is from God. If God approved the battle against the Benjaminites, why did he allow more than 40,000 to be killed before the final victory? One Psalmist accounted Phinehas as righteous, this is true. But another thought it blessed to smash their enemy's children against rocks (Ps. 137:9). Various psalms contain important, accurate revelations. Others contain imprecatory, emotional prayers of people in distress. It is important to understand the various accounts in context. I agree that Phinehas most certainly had zeal, but so did Saul, in the Book of Acts before he converted to Christianity, when he approved the of stoning Stephen (an early Jesus follower).

There is a danger when we internalize verses like those just mentioned. With a view of a god who considered Phinehas to be righteous, Christians frequently imitate that god and commit atrocities. There are many examples that I could cite. One of these is a 1689 sermon by the Puritan preacher Cotton Mather. He applied the passage where Moses commanded the Israelites to blot Amalek from under heaven[58] to Native Americans and called for their extermination.[59]

My point is this. Any Christian who places a high value on the authority of scripture must deal with violence in the Old Testament head on. Before 9/11 and ISIS, we could downplay or even ignore troubling verses, but no more. The upcoming generation will not stand for it. Without good interpretations, even long-term Christians will walk away from the faith. It is not good enough to excuse these things

---

[58] Deut. 25:19
[59] Roland Bainton, *Christian Attitudes Towards War and Peace* (1979), 167-169

Authority of Scripture

by attributing them to the culture of the times. Diverting and showing the many places in the Old Testament where God is compassionate and merciful also doesn't work. It especially doesn't work to say that God has the right to do whatever he wants because he is God. The worst thing a Christian can do is to try to justify these things or just get angry and shut down the conversation. Atrocities in the Old Testament are wrong; it's as simple as that. Our job is to establish a consistent, reasonable method of interpretation to explain why these verses exist in scripture and explain how they apply to us today.

Jesus and the Old Testament

> No one defended the inerrancy of the Scriptures more than Jesus. He quoted biblical passages in responding to His disciples (Mt 16:21), His critics (Mt 22) and the devil himself (Mt 4:4,7,10). He referred to almost every controversial story in the Old Testament including: Noah, Jonah, Elijah, Elisha, Isaiah, and Daniel. He emphasized technical details of interpretation (Ps 110:1) and dared to claim the entire Old Testament message was all about Him (Lk 24:44). We are ultimately left with one of two choices: poor dumb Jesus or poor dumb scholars. I'll stick with Jesus every time.[60]

The above quote is representative of the arguments presented by some religious leaders to defend the concept of biblical inerrancy. This one was composed by a dean and professor of religion. For the sake of this discussion, I'll call him the Professor. It is easy to quickly post something without thinking it through, so I'll not mention his name.

According to the Professor, it all comes down to a binary choice: either poor dumb Jesus or poor dumb scholars. It is interesting that the Professor, a dean and distinguished professor of religion, puts down his own area of expertise. I guess he wants to shame us poor dumb Christians to choose Jesus; certainly, we cannot choose those poor

---

[60] Dean and Professor of Religion, http://defendinginerrancy.com/inerrancy-quotes/ Accessed 7/27/2017.

dumb scholars. If we stop here, there is nothing left to be said; no dialogue possible. Please excuse my sarcasm, though. The Professor's basic defense of the concept of inerrancy deserves a reasoned response.

In his one short paragraph, I note numerous examples of the *hasty generalization* logical fallacy. If I state that I like one of the Beatle's songs, can you safely conclude that I like all of them? Maybe that conclusion is true; maybe it is not. There is simply not enough information to be certain. It is true that Jesus referred to many miracle accounts of the Old Testament, such as those associated with Noah, Jonah, Elijah, Elisha, Isaiah, and Daniel. I don't intend to argue whether these things are historical at this point, but instead expose the fallacies in The Professor's reasoning.

Utilizing the lore of the day in a presentation says nothing about inerrancy, one way or the other. Peter (2 Pet. 2:4) refers to Tartarus, a Greek mythological version of hell. It imprisons Cyclops, guarded by Hecatoncheires, a super strong creature with a hundred hands and fifty heads. Here Sisyphus, founder of Corinth, had to repeatedly roll a huge stone up a steep hill only to watch it roll down. The Danaides, a group of girls who murdered their cousins, had to fill a jar full of holes with water. Another poor occupant was tied to a wheel spinning round and round forever. The Book of Enoch, a Jewish writing contemporary to the first century portrays the archangel Uriel guarding Tartarus where 200 fallen Watchers are imprisoned.

I doubt that Peter or even the Romans and Greeks believed in these things any more than we now believe in Star Wars. Yet Peter, loosely referring to the apocryphal Book of Enoch, tells us that God threw the fallen angels there. By the Professor's logic, Peter was affirming, under the inspiration of the Holy Spirit, that the Greek mythological Tartarus was a real place, and the Book of Enoch was equal to scripture. I don't buy either of these conclusions, and I'm confident that the Professor doesn't either.

Paul often quotes Greek philosophers in his letters, sometimes confusing even Peter, an unschooled fisherman.

> So also, our beloved brother Paul wrote to you according to the wisdom given him, speaking of this as he does in all his letters. There are some things in them hard to understand, which the ignorant and unstable

twist to their own destruction, as they do the other scriptures. (2 Pet. 3:15-16)

A clear example of Paul's philosophical prowess is clearly revealed in Acts 17. Paul encounters some Epicurean and Stoic philosophers, who challenge him: "What does this babbler want to say?" and: "Can we know what this new teaching is that you are presenting? It sounds rather strange to us, so we would like to know what it means."

Paul didn't miss a beat. He responded by referring to the inscription of the unknown god and then, from memory, he banged out a series of quotes from Seneca and other renowned philosophers. Paul was no babbler, but one well-schooled in the philosophies of the day. He capped off his presentation by quoting from the poet, Aratus, "for we are his offspring."[61]

Paul's Acts 17 quotes follow:

1. **Plutarch:** God dwelleth not in temples made with hands (On Stoic self-contradiction, 1034B).
2. **Seneca:** And he is not served by human hands, as if he needed anything. Rather, he himself gives everyone life and breath and everything else (Moral Epistles 95.48).
3. **Seneca:** God is at hand everywhere and to all men (Moral Epistles 41:1, 95:47-50).
4. **Epimenides:** In him we live and move and have our being (Minos).

There are more examples of Greek Philosophers that Paul quotes in his letters. If you are familiar with these letters, you'll recognize those that follow. There are other examples as well, but I believe that these are sufficient to prove the point.

1. **Menander:** Evil communications corrupt good manners (From the play *Thais*).
2. **Epimenides:** The Cretans are always liars, evil beasts, slow bellies (*Cretica*, 6th century BC).
3. **Aristotle:** Against such there is no law, for they themselves are a law (*Politics*, III. 13, 1284a, 10-14).

---

[61] Aratus, *Phaenomena* (3rd century BC).

4. **Plato:** There is a war against ourselves — going on in every individual of us (*Laws*, I. 626).
5. **Plato:** Now if death is like this, I say that to die is gain (Plato, *Phaedo*).
6. **Socrates**: To begin with, our several natures are not all alike but different. One man is naturally fitted for one task, and another for another (Plato, Republic, II. 370a7-b2).
7. **Socrates:** Just as the features of a face do, and the parts make the whole, but each serves a different purpose; the eye is not like the ear nor has it the same function (Plato, *Protagoras, 329b-330b*).
8. **Socrates**: If the finger of one of us is wounded, the entire community of bodily connections stretching to the soul for 'integration' with the dominant part is made aware, and all of it feels the pain as a whole (Plato, *Republic,* V. 462d).

Paul was not averse to using Greek philosophy to advance the Good News into Gentile areas, and he was brilliant in his ability to do so. This does not at all imply that Paul, a Jew, accepted the entirety of Greek and Roman teachings. He spoke in a way that the people could understand, and he used metaphors that were well-known. Do we not do the same thing today as we present the gospel to a new generation? If not, Paul's example demonstrates that we should.

A strong point in the Professor's defense of inerrancy is his reference to Luke 24, where Jesus tells his disciples, "Everything written about me in the law of Moses, the prophets, and the psalms must be fulfilled (Luke 22:37)." The question here is to define those areas in the Law, the Prophets, and the Psalms that speak about Jesus. Jesus doesn't say which ones he means. Does he mean all of the Law, the Prophets, and the Psalms, or only some of them? Does Psalm 137 speak of Jesus where it blesses those who throw children against the stones? I think not. Certainly not the law where a woman must consume bitter water to prove she is not an adulteress.[62] How about the law where a slave owner can keep the family of a slave when that slave is eligible for freedom?[63] Not that law, I hope. Jesus is careful indeed to qualify his statement. He is referring only to those parts that

---

[62] Num. 5:12-31
[63] Exod. 21:2-4

speak of him, not the entire Old Testament. Biblical scholars work hard to discern which parts apply.

The Professor's other Bible references are even less convincing. One can safely assume that during his temptations in the wilderness, Jesus considered certain verses authoritative. It is a *hasty generalization* to conclude that this means that he accepted every verse this way.

The Professor references Matthew 16:21 and Psalm 110:1. The former verse loosely refers to various prophecies, but it is not even a direct Old Testament quotation. Jesus directly quotes Psalm 110:1, but this verse has nothing to do with inerrancy or a method of interpretation.

This brings us to the key question. Why is the Professor and other evangelical leaders so concerned about inerrancy? The answer is another logical fallacy, the *slippery slope*. If we back away even a little from inerrancy, the entire Christian faith is in jeopardy. I understand this to a degree. There is some historical basis for the fear. During the early part of the Enlightenment, many scholars were deists. They believed that some sort of creator got things started, but then walked away to concentrate on other things. As a result, those scholars were skeptical of any of the miraculous accounts in the Bible. When evolutionary theories came along, skeptics gave themselves permission to discount or reject significant parts of the Bible, or even all of it. Some mainstream denominations wanted to appear modern and scientific, and so they went along with the cultural trends, causing a crisis within the Protestant tradition. If biblical authority is gone, there is no foundation, and the entire faith disappears into quicksand. Still, this *slippery slope* is not a given. We can be rational and learned, and still hold the Bible in high regard. Many recent biblical scholars prove this to be true.

Chapter 5

Reading the Bible

> But to the wicked God says, "What right have you to recite my statutes, or take my covenant on your lips? For you hate discipline, and you cast my words behind you. You make friends with a thief when you see one, and you keep company with adulterers. You give your mouth free rein for evil, and your tongue frames deceit. You sit and speak against your kin; you slander your own mother's child. These things you have done, and I have been silent; you thought that I was one just like yourself. But now I rebuke you and lay the charge before you. Mark this, then, you who forget God, or I will tear you apart, and there will be no one to deliver. (Ps. 50:16-21)

The above quote was directed to those who considered themselves to be righteous. People read the Bible in different ways. Sometimes, people find verses to justify things that they know in their hearts are wrong. Even when this is not the case, it is so easy to use scripture to confirm our presuppositions. Verses can be found to agree with almost anything. It is much harder to meditate on those teachings that challenge us, cut to the heart, and bring us to repentance. Maybe this is the meaning of the phrase, the Bible is a two-edged sword. When Jesus came into the world, the *faithful* were expecting a warrior messiah that would defeat the Romans and set up an everlasting Davidic kingdom. There were plenty of verses to confirm their view. Today American Christians seek the Lion of Judah to rapture them out of here and then conquer, just like what was expected in the first century. The mantra, *first like a lamb and then like a lion*, is prevalent in many churches. But wouldn't this undermine the purpose of Jesus' first coming? If it takes violence and power to bring order out of chaos, wouldn't that detract from the teachings of Jesus? Can love win over violence or, in the end, is violence the only way?

The same Bible has been used to promote slavery and to fight for its elimination. It has been used to justify wars and to speak out against them. It sometimes has been used to support oppression and other times to proclaim the evils of oppression. As I said above, if we read scripture improperly, we will find a god who agrees with us regardless of our position. In a sense, that god is us.

The Geneva translation published in AD 1557 was the first English translation which cut up the Bible into chapters and verses. Since then, people have stopped reading the text; they select isolated verses out of context. This hides the overall message under a maze of conflicting statements. We wouldn't do this to any other writing.

I see the Bible as a drama. It is the four-thousand-year-old story of the Jewish people. When Jesus appeared, its impact expanded. It is now the drama of humanity. Like any drama, it is messy. It has suspense. It has highs and lows. It has victories and defeats. Its heroes are amazing and yet flawed. David, the man after God's own heart, composes deeply-impacting psalms. The same man has a loyal friend killed so he can steal his wife. He forcibly takes a woman away from her husband who follows along weeping. Subsequently, he leaves her barren because of an insult. He has a practice in killing everyone in towns that he attacks. The Bible tells it like it is.

The Bible has many voices. It presents God as a merciless warrior. It presents the same God as seeking justice for the orphan and widow; as one who takes no pleasure in the death of the wicked. This only makes sense when we understand that the Bible is a drama. It contains many actors with different voices and differing roles.

The Bible is a love story. Humanity turned from God, and then God, in unfathomable love, pursues us for thousands of years. The goal from the beginning is restoration; for a new heaven and earth and a new kingdom to arrive. The goal is to reconcile all things to himself.

The pinnacle of the story is Jesus. He is not the one expected. His message subverts many of the previous interpretations. According to John's gospel, Jesus is the living Word, not the Bible, which is the pointer to Jesus. Jesus' message is so unexpected, so different, and so foolish that, if true, it can only be from an external source; from God if you will. Who can imagine that a world run by power and force could really be conquered by love? Yet this is the overall message.

How should we read the Bible? In my opinion, we should always give voice to the victim. This is what Jesus did, and so should we. For many years, as I read the books of Judges, Samuel, and Kings, I sided with the Israelites. A cognitive dissonance arose in me that caused me to be completely unaware of the victim's plight. I sometimes thought, "They were evil, they deserved it." Other times, "God must have known what he was doing." I don't read scripture like this anymore. This, in my opinion, is the wrong way to read the Bible. When I read about the destruction of one of the ancient cities, I think of the families there. I visualize the panic that sets in when the Israelites come shouting, "Jehovah is great!" I see Jesus saying, "No, not like this!"

A recent movie, *The Last of the Dogmen*, has a quote that pertains to the winning of the West and it rings true. Professor Lillian Stone states: "What happened was inevitable. The way it happened was unconscionable."

There are many biblical accounts that are appalling. Consider the hypocrisy of doing evil things for the sake of honoring a vow. Jephthah, when returning from a military victory, pledged to sacrifice the first one that came out of his house. As expected, it was his daughter who wanted to greet her father in celebration. Jephthah then blames his daughter for this, and she faithfully submits after negotiating a two month stay of execution. Apparently, the Israelites of the time considered honoring a vow to be more important than preserving human life. No wonder Jesus said, "Let what you say be simply 'Yes' or 'No'; anything more than this comes from evil."

Reading the Bible critically is liberating. It enables me to examine the Old Testament texts with clear eyes, not with eyes that seek strained explanations to defend the indefensible. I guess what I am saying is that to properly evaluate the Old Testament, I need Jesus as a guide. In one of his appearances after the resurrection, Jesus provided this same insight to his disciples:

> Was it not necessary that the Messiah should suffer these things and then enter into his glory? Then beginning with Moses and all the prophets, he **interpreted** to them the things about himself in all the scriptures. (Luke 24:26-27)

There is a poem composed by pastor Brian Zahnd—Word of Life Church—that captures the essence of how to read the Bible. His words are better than mine, so I'll include them below.

Reading the Bible Right (best read aloud)

It's a STORY
We're telling news here
Keeping alive an ancient epic
The grand narrative of paradise lost and paradise regained
The greatest "Once upon a time" tale ever told
The beautiful story which moves relentlessly toward—
"They lived happily ever after"
Never, never, NEVER forget that before it's anything else it's a story
So let the Story live and breathe, enthrall and enchant
Don't rip out its guts and leave it lifeless on the dissecting table
Don't make it something it's really not—
A catalog of wished-for promises
An encyclopedia of God-facts
A law journal of divine edicts
A how-to manual for do-it-yourselfers
Find the promises, learn the facts, heed the laws, live the lessons
But don't forget the Story

Learn to read the Book for what it is—
God's great big wild and wonderful surprise ending love story
Let there be wonder
Let there be mystery
Let there be tragedy
Let there be heartbreak
Let there be suspense
Let there be surprise
Let it be earthy and human
Let it be celestial and divine

Let it be what it is and don't try to make it perfect where it's not
This fantastic story of—
Creation
Alienation
Devastation
Incarnation
Salvation
Restoration

With its cast of thousands, more Tolstoy novel than thousand-page sermon
It's a Story because we are not saved by *ideas* but by *events!*
Here's a plotline for you: Death, Burial, and Resurrection
Yes, it's a story—not a plan, not ology or ism, but a story
And it's an amalgamated patchwork story told in mixed medium
Narration, history, genealogy
Prophecy, poetry, parable
Psalm, song, sermon
Dream and vision
Memoir and letter

So, understand the medium and don't try so hard to miss the point
Try to learn what matters and what doesn't
It's not where and when Job lived
But what Job learned
In his painful odyssey and poetic theodicy
It's not how many cubits of water you need to put Everest under a flood
But why the world was so dirty that it needed such a big bath
Trying to find Noah's ark
Instead of trying to rid the world of violence
Really is an exercise in missing the point
Speaking of missing the point—
It's not did a snake talk?
But what the freakin' thing said!
Because even though I've never met a talking snake
I've sure had serpentine thoughts crawl through my head

Literalism is a kind of escapism
By which you move out of the crosshairs of the probing question
But parable and metaphor have a way of knocking us to the floor
Prose flattened literalism makes the story small, time confined and irrelevant
But poetry and allegory travel through time and space to get in our face
Inert facts are easy enough to set on the shelf
But the Story well told will haunt you

> Ah, the Story well told
> That's what is needed
>
> It's time for the Story to bust out of the cage and take the stage
> And demand a hearing once again
> It's a STORY, I tell you!
> And If you allow the Story to seep into your life
> So that THE STORY begins to weave into *your* story
> That's when, at last, my friend, you're reading the Bible right.[64]

Interpretive License

> I do not want you to be unaware, brothers and sisters, that our ancestors were all under the cloud, and all passed through the sea, and all were baptized into Moses in the cloud and in the sea, and all ate the same spiritual food, and all drank the same spiritual drink. For they drank from the spiritual rock that followed them, and the rock was Christ. (1 Cor. 10:1-4)

A twenty-first-century reader of this passage might wonder, "What is Paul talking about?" If we accept that the Old Testament accounts are authoritative and we read them literally, we find many discrepancies here. No one was baptized into Moses. There was manna, but that was physical, not spiritual. And what was that spiritual drink? I don't remember reading about a spiritual rock bouncing along after the people. I do remember a cloud, but I thought it led the people, so how were they under it? It all seems weird.

The questions are: What do we make of Paul's writings? What do we make of many other examples where New Testament authors creatively cite sections of the Old Testament? We have some choices at our disposal. We can pretend these verses don't exist and just skip over them. We could go to extreme lengths to come up with tortured explanations. We could dismiss them and just conclude that the New Testament can't be trusted. Or, just maybe, we could try to figure out

---

[64] Brian Zahn, *Sinners in the Hands of a Loving God*, 73-75

what is going on. Before providing my take on this, I'm going to set the stage with examples from our time.

My cousin served in the WW2, Korea, and Vietnam wars. He was a colonel in the Eighty-second Airborne Paratrooper Division. Because of his photographic memory, he spent much of his service behind enemy lines. At one point, Hollywood got hold of his resume and decided to make a low budget movie, *Diplomatic Courier*, featuring one of his top-secret assignments. There was some truth in the plot, but much was embellished or simply made up.

Another example is the movie, based on true events, called *Fly Away Home*. It features a pre-teen girl who, after losing her mom in an accident, was taken to Canada to live with her dad. The plot has her raising some geese from hatchlings. When the time came for the geese to migrate, her dad sold his replica of the lunar lander to purchase a slow-flying plane. This plane was then used to lead the geese on a migration path. At the end of the movie, the girl's relationship with her dad was restored, the migration worked, and the geese successfully returned to Canada the next spring. I was disappointed to learn that there was no young girl and no lunar lander; much of the story was simply made up. The truth to it is that there are people in Canada who successfully help endangered birds learn their ancient migration patterns by leading them in flight.

We call this artistic license. The stories still can present lots of truth and move us, stirring our emotions. I'm fine with movies taking real stories and creating a story line around the basic events. Most of us are not reluctant to view such movies, so it is safe to conclude that artistic license is acceptable.

Let's now turn back to first-century Israel. The Greeks and Romans had their tragedies, where everyone dies. They had the comedies where some deity is lowered from above to save the day. Their athletics performed naked in view of approving audiences. They conducted bizarre spectacles where people died. What did the second temple Jews have in terms of artistic license? Of course, some of them modernized and assimilated with Greco-Roman culture. But some did not. You could say that this group learned to dance with their scriptures. This does not just apply to Paul and New Testament authors; it is what many Jews did then and still do today.

Let me explain. The Old Testament accounts are not complete; there are many holes and cryptic events that one could fill in using some creativity and imagination. For example, after Adam and Eve both ate the forbidden fruit, why was only Adam expelled from the garden, not Eve? Why did Abraham and Isaac go up Mount Moriah, and only Abraham come down? Did Sarah die of heartbreak when she found out that Abraham was going to sacrifice her beloved son?

There are more mundane examples. For example, Jews are obligated to daily recite the Shammah, which is a daily declaration of their faith (Deut. 6:4-9, 11:13-21, and Num. 15:37-41). What if one is interrupted in the middle? Does a half Shammah recitation count? Or should it be repeated from the beginning? These and many other issues are discussed in the Talmud, the Jewish oral tradition. When Jews consider these traditions, they to this day, participate in a debate. This makes the Old Testament, not a dead book, but living, and it is applied creatively and differently to each generation. We might call this *interpretive license*.

Let's consider an example in the Book of Matthew. We read: "Jesus told the crowds all these things in parables; without a parable he told them nothing. This was to fulfill what had been spoken through the prophet: 'I will open my mouth to speak in parables; I will proclaim what has been hidden from the foundation of the world (Matt. 13:35).'" The commentaries indicate that Matthew is referring to a Psalm which reads: "I will open my mouth in a parable; I will utter dark sayings of old, which we have heard and known, and our fathers have told us (Ps. 78:2-3)." It is not at all obvious that the Psalmist is talking about Jesus in this passage, and few categorize this Psalm among those considered messianic. Furthermore, Matthew's tells us that the parables were hidden from the foundation of the world, but the Psalmist indicates that these dark saying were heard, known, and taught from times old. What is going on?

Matthew, a first-century Jew, wrote to a Jewish audience. He used his interpretive license to tie Jesus to this Old Testament scripture. Jesus speaking in parables was sufficient to connect him to Psalms 78. Matthew intentionally changed the wording; it was not a mistake. The dark sayings (mysterious truths), though they were long taught and heard, were not understood. It took Jesus to reveal their deeper meanings. In this way, they were hidden from the foundation of the world.

Matthew is not unique. Rabbi Akiba, a leading Jewish sage who was instrumental in putting the Jewish oral tradition to writing, did the same. He proclaimed Bar Kokhba (meaning Son of the Star) to be King Messiah by alluding to Numbers 24:17: "I see him, but not now; I behold him, but not near—a star shall come out of Jacob, and a scepter shall rise out of Israel; it shall crush the borderlands of Moab (Num. 24:17)."

Let's now consider Paul's paragraph cited above. He is doing the same thing. The spiritual food and drink to which he refers is that which God provides by spiritual means. Under the cloud means under God's care. Crossing the sea and being baptized to Moses is a way to express that the Jews were beginning a new covenantal relationship with their creator. When we publicly declare our relationship to Jesus in baptism, we do the same. The water is a common symbol of cleansing used in each case; all is made new.

But what about Jesus being the rock following along during the wilderness period? Paul is alluding to a first-century oral tradition. There are two incidents in the Torah where Moses struck the rock and water emerged. One was in Exodus at the beginning of the journey (Exod. 17:6); the other was in Numbers (Num. 20:11) near the end. Didn't they need water in the intervening time? If so, where did it come from? The oral tradition's answer: It was the same rock that Moses struck, and it travelled with them on the journey.[65]

Paul extends this interpretation a bit further. The Old Testament indicates that God is the rock of our salvation (Ps. 89:26). Jesus declares that he is the stone that the builders rejected (Mk. 12:10). Jesus also declares to the Samaritan woman that he is the source of living water (Jn. 4:10). Hence, Jesus is the rock in the wilderness that provided water, enabling ancient Israel to live during the forty years in the desert.

You could say that Mathew, Paul, and Rabbi Akiba all dance with their scripture. Perhaps we could learn from them. Instead of dogmatically saying *the Bible says*, we might give each other some interpretive license and dance a bit.

---

[65] "Targum Onqelos to Numbers 21:16-20," *Tosephta Sukka* 3.11, *Pseudo-Philo's Book of Biblical Antiquities* 10:7; 11:15; 20:8.

Midrash

The Lord was wondering how he could know which of His servants serve Him out of fear and which of them serve Him out of love. He devised a method that would discover this knowledge. He built a room four by four, a four-square room with only one small peep hole of four by four spans. The Lord put all His servants into this room. Those servants who served Him out of fear stood in that "four by four" room and said, "If the Lord had wanted us to break out of this room, he would not have built it and put us into it." The servants who loved the Lord said, "We want to break out of this room and join the Lord in the outside in the wide-open spaces." However, the little peep hole was too small, and they had to make themselves suffer and lose much weight to be able to fit through the small peep hole in the door and join the Lord in the wide-open spaces. They loved the Lord so much that they could not stay closed in the "four by four" room even knowing that the Lord had built it and placed them there. They wanted to "break out" by force and violence from the "four by four" room and join the Lord who was sitting on His throne in the wide-open spaces.

Biblical basis for the above Jewish parable: I will surely gather all of you, O Jacob, I will gather the survivors of Israel; I will set them together like sheep in a fold, like a flock in its pasture; it will resound with people. The one who breaks out will go up before them; they will break through and pass the gate, going out by it. Their king will pass on before them, the LORD at their head.[66] (Mic. 2:12-13)

---

[66] Tana Debi Eliyahu, Ish-Shalom Edition, 82.

The above quote illustrates an example of Midrash. The Midrashic method of interpretation embodies four different levels of meaning. These are:

1) **Peshat**: The plain, simple meaning of a text
2) **Remez**: deep or implied or hinted meanings
3) **Derash**: Using metaphors, similes, analogies to expose different, but relevant meanings.
4) **Sod**: Infer hidden, secret, mysterious, or philosophical meanings.

Matthew, in his gospel, applies this Jewish technique of interpretation. Consider his verses having phrases similar to the following, "This is fulfilled that which was spoken of the LORD by the prophet." For many years, I took Matthew's word for it and kept reading. Recently though, I decided to look up what the prophets said and was befuddled. "What is going on? That isn't what the prophet said." Sometimes the context doesn't even match. One example of this appears in Matthew 2:15, referring to Hos 11:1.

> **Matthew:** and he [Joseph] remained there until the death of Herod. This was to fulfill what had been spoken by the Lord through the prophet, Out of Egypt I have called my son.
>
> **Hosea:** When Israel was a child, I loved him and out of Egypt I called my son.

This kind of thing is quite disconcerting when first noticed. Many complain with reason, that the New Testament writers abused the Old Testament scriptures, contriving interpretations that fit their theology.

My first discovery helping me through this dilemma occurred when I looked the Greek word translated *fulfilled*. It does not always convey foretelling the future. It can also mean *to complete*. Matthew, in this context, is not claiming that Hosea was thinking of Jesus when he wrote his book. Hosea clearly wrote about the Israel nation. Matthew was drawing out a deeper meaning. Because Israel failed to achieve God's full purposes, it took Jesus, the true Israelite, to bring things to fruition.

To understand what Matthew was thinking, let's take a trip back to the first century. Jesus was crucified, he rose from the dead, and then he physically appeared many times to his disciples. The risen Jesus told and instructed them how the Old Testament prophets spoke of him (Luke 24:44). The logical thing for Matthew to do was to continue poring through the sacred scriptures to find those verses that point to Jesus. I'm sure I would have done the same thing if I were in his place. If Jesus never rose from the dead, Matthew would never have thought to do this. Why would he? Matthew did not believe that Jesus is Lord because of Hosea; he believed because he saw Jesus alive after he was crucified. In my opinion, the Old Testament doesn't necessarily foretell and prove who Jesus is; the Old Testament confirms Jesus in hindsight.

As the disciples searched through the Old Testament, I'm sure they quickly found the obvious references pointing to Jesus, like Isaiah 53, Daniel 9, and a few Psalms. Then, digging deeper, they found many others using the same methods of interpretation employed by the rabbis. How could the rabbis argue? The disciples were doing what the rabbis do. Paul, for example, in dozens of places compares Jesus to David using Old Testament verses that clearly reference the latter. As David is the king of Israel, Jesus is the ruler over God's kingdom, a fair Midrashic comparison. And so, because of Matthew, Paul, and the other authors' efforts, these subtle references are available to us today in our Bible translations. They add a richness that otherwise would be absent.

Some modern rabbis cry foul. They say that Christians, especially Protestants, cannot appropriately use this method of interpretation. The rabbis argue that since Christians hold to *Bible alone*, it only allows peshat interpretation (the plain meanings of a passage). There is a simple answer to this charge; Matthew and Paul were not modern Christians, and they certainly were not Protestants. They lived and died as first-century Jews. Of course, they could use rabbinic modes of interpretation.

Misquotes and Reinterpretations

A common charge is that made by skeptics who assert that the New Testament scriptures are unreliable. They assert: "New Testament writers misquote Old Testament passages." An example of this is Matthew 1:23 quoting Isaiah 7:14: "Behold, the virgin shall conceive in her womb, and will bear a son. And they will call His name Emmanuel" where the Hebrew Masoretic text reads *young maiden* and not virgin. The argument goes: Hebrew and Greek have a word that clearly means virgin. It pertains to sexual history, and Isaiah used that word many times. The word for young maiden signifies age and gender; it has nothing to do with sexual history.

Yes, all of this is correct. Still, Matthew didn't misquote the verse; he used the Septuagint version of the Old Testament, written a couple centuries before Christ. The Septuagint uses the Greek word for virgin, not the word for young maiden. Before Jesus, many expected the messiah to be conceived miraculously, including the Septuagint translators. Furthermore, the New Testament writers mostly quoted from the Greek Septuagint; they did not retranslate the Hebrew scriptures. No deception here. Many of the other supposed New Testament misquotes can be explained this same way.

Of course, one could argue, why didn't the writers use the original Hebrew scriptures and instead use a translation that scholars today consider to be inferior? There are times when they did. Generally, this was when the Septuagint's translation strayed too far from the Hebrew. But why use the Septuagint at all? We could counter: "Why do pastors today still use the King James, which is based on the Septuagint? Are there any perfect translations? Are they all equally good?"

In the first-century, many Greek speaking Jews were not fluent in Hebrew. For them, the Septuagint was the only scripture available. It wasn't until a few centuries later that Jewish rabbis created another Greek translation to replace it. The gospel writers were careful to convey truth based on the familiar Septuagint where possible, and the Masoretic where necessary.

Note also, the Dead Sea Scrolls reveal competing versions of the Old Testament; some of the scrolls agree with the Septuagint, not the Masoretic Hebrew text. The gospel writers clearly believed that Jesus' birth was miraculous and therefore agreed with the Septuagint translators use of the word *virgin*.

There are other charges against the writers of the New Testament. Some of these, I find humorous. For example, Paul says that no one has seen God. Critics pounce and say that Jacob saw God face to face, so Paul was wrong. This particular example reminds me of a movie I saw, called *The Freedom Writers*. In that movie, Andre, a high school student, wrote in a journal, "My mom thinks I'm going to wind up in jail like my brother. She doesn't see me." Later, Andre's teacher confronts him for missing classes. She says while looking intently into his eyes, "I see you! Do you understand? I see YOU!" Of course, she is not talking about vision.

Another similar criticism is the apparent conflict between Paul's statement "For as in Adam all die, even so in Christ shall all be made alive," compared to: "The fathers shall not be put to death for the children, neither shall the children be put to death for the fathers; every man shall be put to death for his own sin." The first quote states that we die because of Adam's original sin. The second implies that we, Adam's descendants, cannot be held accountable for what Adam did. The critic has not taken the time to consider Paul's intent. He refers to Adam as an archetype. In other words, we are all Adam; as he sinned, so do we all. This is the nature of humanity. Who can argue with that?

In a few cases, the writers of the New Testament stated things that were wrong. In Acts 7, Steven (an early believer) indicates that seventy-five of Jacob's family went down to Egypt. According to Genesis, the correct number is seventy. I don't see a problem here. The author of Acts was accurately reporting what Steven said in his speech. Additionally, Steven was quoting from the Septuagint, which includes the five sons of Manasseh and Ephraim in the count. So, were Steven and the Septuagint wrong? For me, it doesn't matter. Ancient writers did not record or interpret history using modern standards.

Another example comes from Matt 27: 9-10 where Matthew cites Jeremiah instead of Zechariah. I agree; Matthew's citation was wrong. Critics then say, "This proves that the New Testament is not inspired." I disagree. It might weaken the case for inerrancy, but this is different from saying the New Testament is not inspired. God in my opinion, inspired and trusted his followers to tell the story. They did an incredible job. Regarding Matt 27:9-10, we could argue that this mistake strengthens the case for the gospel. One would expect a scribe somewhere along the line to alter the text and correct the citation. Yet they didn't. This gives me confidence that our scripture is true to what the original authors wrote, discrepancies and all.

There are many other attacks, like taking a phrase or even a word, and then finding some contradictory way that phrase or word is used elsewhere. I wonder why people don't do this to Harry Potter books.

Even if they do, who takes them seriously? It is far better to read texts in context to ascertain the authors intent than to treat them as long, puzzling lists of interrelated phrases.

There are challenges saying that New Testament authors don't quote verses exactly, word for word. Why do they have to? What is wrong with a paraphrase, or even making a statement that brings a couple of verses together? Why is it wrong to change the wording for emphasis? I don't see a problem.

In my opinion, most of the criticisms just discussed are a lot about nothing. But there are a few that deserve a serious look. Those are the ones where New Testament writers intentionally misquote Old Testament verses to make a point or to bring a new interpretation. Let's look at a few instances.

At the start of his ministry, Jesus is handed a scroll. He reads a famous passage from the Book of Isaiah, apparently from the Septuagint.[67] This passage promises deliverance from oppression and announces the initiation of a new eternal kingdom of peace centered in Jerusalem.

> The Spirit of the Lord is upon me, because he has anointed me; he has sent me to preach glad tidings to the poor, to heal the broken in heart, to proclaim liberty to the captives, and **recovery of sight to the blind;** to declare the acceptable year of the Lord, **and the day of recompense.** (Isa. 61:1-2 Brenton translation of the Septuagint)

Jesus declares two things in his reading. First, he declares that the prophecy is fulfilled in their presence. This means that he is the messiah for whom the Jews are waiting. Second, he intentionally leaves out "the day of recompense (Septuagint)" or "day of vengeance of our God (NRSV)." Why does he do this?

The people listening were confused. How could this person who they knew all his life make such a claim? Then, Jesus answers:

> But the truth is, there were many widows in Israel in the time of Elijah, when the heaven was shut up three

---

[67] Luke 4:17-21

> years and six months, and there was a severe famine over all the land; yet Elijah was sent to none of them except to a widow at Zarephath in Sidon. There were also many lepers in Israel in the time of the prophet Elisha, and none of them was cleansed except Naaman the Syrian." (Luke 4: 25-27)

I can imagine the reaction from the crowd: "What? Not only does he claim to be the messiah, he now tells us about times when Gentiles, not Jews, received deliverance."

The Jews were waiting for a messiah that would free them from the yoke of Rome and restore the Davidic kingdom. Jesus makes it clear that he is not that. There would not be a day of vengeance. He also implies that there would be deliverance for Gentiles. The audience was enraged. Those present subsequently attempted to throw him off a cliff. They neither expected nor wanted a messiah of this kind.

A second example concerns doubts by John the Baptist after he was arrested by Herod. John told his disciples to ask Jesus: "Are you the Messiah or should we expect another?" Jesus responds:

> Go and tell John what you hear and see: the blind receive their sight, the lame walk, the lepers are cleansed, the deaf hear, the dead are raised, and the poor have good news brought to them. And blessed is anyone who takes no offense at me. (Matt. 11:4-6)

It is understandable why John was having doubts. Why wasn't Jesus taking control as the Davidic warrior? That was the kind of messiah who John and others were expecting. Jesus paraphrases several Old Testament passages, including Isaiah 60:1-2, and Isa 29:18-20, purposely leaving off the violent parts. He sums up his response by blessing those who accept his message of good news and peace without requiring a conquering hero.

At the end of his ministry, Jesus is betrayed and brought for interrogation by the high priest. Note the following portion of the trial.

> But he was silent and did not answer. Again, the high priest asked him, "Are you the Messiah, the Son of the Blessed One?" Jesus said, "I am; and 'you will see the

> Son of Man seated at the right hand of the Power', and 'coming with the clouds of heaven.'" Then the high priest tore his clothes and said, "Why do we still need witnesses? [64] You have heard his blasphemy! What is your decision?" All of them condemned him as deserving death. (Mk. 14:61-64)

He was the messiah, and the Kingdom of God was at hand. Coming in the clouds is a metaphor used to indicate vindication. Jesus was alluding to the same wording in Daniel chapter 7.

> As I watched in the night visions, I saw one like a human being coming with the clouds of heaven. And he came to the Ancient One and was presented before him. To him was given dominion and glory and kingship, that all peoples, nations, and languages should serve him. His dominion is an everlasting dominion that shall not pass away, and his kingship is one that shall never be destroyed. (Dan. 7:13-14)

There are other instances where Jesus brings light to verses of the Old Testament. A series of these concern the Old Testament law. These are interesting, at least for me. They provide insights into the minds of the authors and reveal something of the heart of God. I'll discuss this topic in a later chapter.

Chapter 6

Myth or History

> Mythology is not a lie, mythology is poetry, it is metaphorical. It has been well said that mythology is the penultimate truth—penultimate because the ultimate cannot be put into words. It is beyond words.[68]
> — Joseph Campbell

Joseph Campbell and other scholars place a high value on expressing things in mythological terms. As he states in the above quote, sometimes there is not a better way to express truth. At the same time, we do not want to automatically assume that ancient texts are non-historical. When we consider the book of Genesis, we need to ask, "Is it mythology?" and, "Is it history?" "Is it a God-given revelation?" and, "Is it a combination of all of these?" I'll explore these questions in this chapter.

Origins

> In the beginning, there was a great explosion producing time, space, matter, and energy as biproducts. As the natural laws established themselves, intense chemical reactions ensued, with great heat and flashes of light. The Universe stretched out, constellations condensed, and planets like Earth formed. The light, which we call Day, overcame the darkness, which we call the Night. The creative power of natural law hovered throughout the cosmos. It was the beginning of order, the first day. It was all good.
>   On earth, condensation commenced, dividing the waters from the waters. And so, there was an expanse, which we call heavens, separating the waters below from the clouds above. And it was so. Order was coming to the earth, the second day. It was all good.

---

[68] Joseph Campbell, *The Power of Myth*, 206.

The waters receded into what we call Seas. Solid ground, which we call earth, appeared; and it was so. Through a series of complex pre-biotic chemical reaction, first life appeared, and through cell-division, the earth brought forth tender sprouts. Various herbs, trees, and fruits began to self-replicate after their kind; and it was so. It was the end of a lifeless planet, the third day. It was all good.

The thick, dark atmosphere became translucent, causing heavenly lights to become visible and to shine on the earth. They separated the day from the night and would become signs for measuring seasons, days, and years. The two greatest lights were particularly important, the Sun to rule the day and the Moon to rule the night. And there also were a multitude of stars. Earth's atmosphere could now support complex life, the fourth day. It was all good.

More life forms appeared in the waters, which swarmed with complex creatures. New phyla appeared, including birds that fly over the earth in the sky. Huge sea creatures, things that creep, and winged organisms reproduced after their kind. Life was established, filling the earth and the seas. Complex life forms were now everywhere, the fifth day. It was all good.

The earth brought forth various living creatures, including cattle, creepers, and the beasts of the earth, reproducing after their kind; and it was so. Humanity arrived on the scene, with the ability to reason, to create, and ponder how the cosmos came to be. The human species rapidly established dominion over the fish of the sea, over the fowl of the air, over the cattle, over all the creeping things on the earth, over the entire planet.

Humans, both men and women, had superior intellect to all other creatures and they were blessed by the plentiful resources that were now available. They were fruitful, and they multiplied rapidly. Humanity began to dominate the entire environment. Available to them for sustenance was every herb bearing seed, all fruit trees, and greenery. There were sufficient food sources to sustain all life on the planet. Humanity was here, the sixth day. Everything was very good.

So, through the power of natural law, everything was in place. Earth was now teeming with life and the human species was in charge. Everything was established for the drama that was to come.

When I was a pre-teen, I saw a TV interview that I vaguely remember. The journalist asked his guest why he thought the Bible was false. The guest responded, "If you can't trust even the first sentence of the Bible, you cannot trust anything that follows." I'm not sure why that interview sticks in my mind. I have no memory of who the journalist was, who the guest was, what program it was, or even which channel I was watching. Yet I clearly remember the question and the response.

Now, many years later, we could get equally sarcastic, if we wanted. Since the *Big Bang* genesis of space and time is an established fact verified by science, we could say: "If science was incorrect about something as basic as the origin of the Universe, why should we trust any scientific proposition?" Of course, like the guest's answer, that would also be an equally foolish logical fallacy. If this is the first thing my hypothetical friend Mr. Bill's says to me, then I could ignore everything else Mr. Bill says for his entire life. Poor Mr. Bill! Marginalized because of one false statement.

It is clear that the above scientific version of the Genesis account that I just offered differs little from that of the Bible, other than removing God from the equation. The steady-state Universe is a false hypothesis that no longer stands up to the evidence. There are alternative theories, but none of those are falsifiable, so they are simply hypothetical guesses, not true science.

More recently, I listened to a debate between a Christian and a skeptic. The skeptic challenged the Christian with a question, "What was God doing before making the Universe? Wasn't he bored?" I was surprised to learn that St. Augustine in his Confessions, chapter 10.30, written some seventeen-hundred years ago, addresses this exact question.

> **Question:** Lo, are they not full of their ancient way, who say to us, "What was God doing before he made heaven and earth? For if," say they, "He were unoccupied, and did nothing, why does he not forever also, and from now on, cease from working, as he did in times past?"
>
> **Answer:** But if before heaven and earth there was no time, why is it asked, "What did you do then?" For there was no *then* when time was not.

I find Augustine's answer amazing. Here was someone with no modern scientific training. He had no telescopes, and none of the modern technologies. Yet, his answer is profound. It took science nearly two millennia to catch up. We now know that time had a beginning.

Some Christians read the Genesis accounts literally and ascribe exactly twenty-four hours to each creation day. In my opinion, this is unfortunate. Day six, for example, included the creation of various animal species, of Adam, his naming of the animals, of Eve, and finally, the instruction for humanity to fill the earth. This could not all have happened in one literal day. Furthermore, we are still in day seven, and this seventh day is set to continue for a long period (maybe a thousand years after Jesus returns). The lengths of days 6 and 7 therefore are obviously much greater than twenty-four hours. Why would we assume, then, that the other five days of creation are literal lengths? This doesn't make sense.

A Christian once told me that if the days in Genesis are not literal, and if Darwinism proves to be true, then God is a liar and no longer credible. What he is really saying is, "I won't believe in a God who doesn't agree with my interpretation." Perhaps this kind of reasoning is grounds for the existence of many thousands of Christian denominations. We fight over things that are unimportant and then look ridiculous to those on the outside. In my opinion, the twenty-four-hour position raises barriers where none is needed. I have no problem interpreting the days of creation as long periods of time. It is a non-issue.

From my limited reading on the subject, I accept that carbon-14 and other dating methods are reliable. If I were to be in a conversation with scientists whose expertise relates to dating methods, there is no way that I would want to challenge their competence. If I tried, I would immediately be dismissed as ignorant, and this over an unimportant issue. I'm aware of some Ph.D. scientists who hold to the literal six-day interpretation. Good for them! Do your research, get your results published, and then, perhaps, prevailing opinions will change.

Adam, Eve, and the Snake

> *If he had brought us out from Egypt* and had not carried out judgments against them. Dayenu!
>
> *If he had carried out judgments against them* and not against their idols. Dayenu!
>
> *If he had destroyed their idols* and had not smitten their firstborn. Dayenu!
>
> *If he had smitten their firstborn* and had not given us their wealth. Dayenu!
>
> *If he had given us their wealth* and had not split the sea for us. Dayenu!
>
> *If he had split the sea for us* and had not taken us through it on dry land. Dayenu!
>
> *If he had taken us through the sea on dry land* and had not drowned our oppressors in it. Dayenu!
>
> *If he had drowned our oppressors in it* and had not supplied our needs for forty years. Dayenu!
>
> *If he had supplied our needs for forty years* and had not fed us the manna. Dayenu!
>
> *If he had fed us the manna* and had not given us the Shabbat. Dayenu!

If he had given us the Shabbat and had not brought us before Mount Sinai. Dayenu!

If he had brought us before Mount Sinai and had not given us the Torah. Dayenu!

If he had given us the Torah and had not brought us into the land of Israel. Dayenu!

If he had brought us into the land of Israel and had not built for us the Temple. Dayenu![69]

There are many parallels between this passover song and the genesis account, which involve the Jewish word *dayenu*. Like many Hebrew, Greek, or Yiddish words, there is no direct corresponding English word. A rough translation is *it would have been enough*. But even this translation is not quite correct. There is a sense of restlessness, a tinge of longing, behind the meaning. It should be enough, but it is not; we don't know why, we should be grateful, but we want more. Consider the Exodus account. God delivered us with a mighty hand from Egypt, dayenu. It sure would be nice if we could leave the wilderness.

I'll return to this dayenu concept later in this section, but first let's set the stage. Were there a literal Adam and a literal Eve? When? Did the snake really speak words? Why did God subject them to a test that he knew they would fail and then punish them for it?

I'm not going to argue either for or against the historicity of the Adam and Eve Genesis account in this section. This, I believe misses the point (despite some recent scientific support for the hypothesis that we all descended from a single ancestral pair, namely Y Chromosomal Adam and Mitochondrial Eve). There simply are no compelling arguments that I know, which will conclusively settle the issue. The real questions that I want to consider are: Why are the Adam and Eve accounts included in scripture? What lessons do they teach?

Western culture has advanced in many ways, but we have lost the art of orally telling a story in a community setting. We have campfire stories, but these normally describe a fearful creature or spiritual being that could appear at any moment. Such an experience succeeds when

---

[69] Jewish Passover Song, "Dayenu."

everyone is shaking in their boots. We tell stories in novels and movies, but these mostly are concerned with murder investigations or romance. There are action adventures, but these generally focus on stopping the bad guy from pursuing the goal of mass destruction.

Ancient and indigenous stories serve a much more important purpose. They connect a community with each other and with those who came before; they teach about the various rituals, their meaning, and why they, as a people, exist. They connect a people to their common culture and values. The lack of these things leads to disintegration. In America, for the last decade or so, we seem to be struggling to find common roots that bind us together. A society connected by Starbucks, iPhones, and Football is on loose footing.

Typically, in the West, we think a mythical story has no value and dismiss it out of hand. Early missionaries to North America happily shared the Genesis accounts of Adam and Eve, and the native people undoubtedly were very impressed. Then, the local tribal leaders would reciprocate and begin to share one of their own stories. The missionaries typically mocked and ridiculed them with comments as: "That's absurd." Yet, many of those indigenous myths live on into the twenty-first century. They are valuable and interesting, containing valid life lessons. They help us understand and learn from cultures different from our own.

Storytelling requires us to suspend our rational minds, engage the imagination, and enter the world portrayed. Do we not do this when we go to see movies such as Star Wars, Avatar, or Wonder Woman? Isn't the same true when we read a novel?

The early chapters of Genesis are examples of age-old accounts from prehistory. Tribal storytellers are trained from youth to exactly preserve every detail as they act out one of their traditional indigenous myths. Because of this, oral traditions can survive unchanged for many thousands of years.

Throughout Genesis chapter 1, Elohim is the name used for God. He created the heavens and the earth, separated light from darkness, created the plants and the animals, and finally said, "Let us make man in our image, to have stewardship over all the earth." He blessed them and saw that everything was very good. We get a high-level overview describing how everything came to be. We see a God who is different from other ancient gods; not fighting but creating by speaking. He did not need to gather together things that already existed but made the cosmos from nothing. This deity is super-powerful, creates what he wants, and has no covenantal obligations. He is distant and impersonal; He is fully within his rights to create or destroy as he sees fit. The Universe is like a painting that is manipulated at the will of the artist. An argument cannot be presented to this God; he has the final word on every matter.

A major point of the Adam/Eve account is: God is personal and involved.

Yahweh is the God of Genesis 2, starting at verse 8 and going through chapter 3; Elohim disappears. This account presents a different side of the Creator. He takes man, places him in the paradise garden, gives him a wife, and fellowships with them on a close personal level. This Creator is involved intimately with his creation. Humanity throughout history sometimes perceives Elohim, at other times perceives Yahweh, and there are those who perceive no god at all.

I enjoy listening to various Rabbinic and Christian interpretations of the Genesis Adam and Eve account and have constructed a combined interpretation. Bear with me on this as I explain.

The word Dayenu is implied all through the Adam and Eve narrative.

> If God would just have given me life. *Dayenu!*
>
> If God would just have put me into a perfect garden. *Dayenu!*
>
> If God would just have given me something to do in this perfect garden. *Dayenu!*
>
> If God would just have given me wonderful things to eat. *Dayenu!*
>
> If God would just have communicated to me personally. *Dayenu!*
>
> If God would have just have given me a partner. *Dayenu!*

> If God would just have given me rules and burdens
> that were easy. *Dayenu!*

According to Genesis, Adam and Eve lived in a paradise, yet they willingly gave it up. Maybe they did not consider the sheltered garden to be as great as we might think. It is true that human nature yearns for the abstract concept of a perfect utopia. Unfortunately, there is good evidence to believe that if ever it were achieved, humanity would immediately seek to destroy it. We seem to like the process of progressing towards some outcome, but when we get there, we are left restless and bored.

I can envision Adam at the end of the garden looking out and longing for the excitement of exploring the other side. I could see him looking at that tree of knowledge and wanting to know and experience more. He wanted to decide for himself those things that were good and those that were evil. The chaos of the unknown was more attractive than the stability of the known.

In this scenario, Adam was the first to say *dayenu*. He thought: "If God gave me paradise, it should have been enough." He fully appreciated it, but he wanted to experience more. My guess is that he saw that special tree as something that Yahweh was withholding from him. Maybe he did not want to be in the protected, perfect environment. He longed to be outside where it was wild and unpredictable. Yes, there were earthquakes, floods, and volcanoes, but there was so much going on out there, and it was exciting. A quest was awaiting, and he was convinced that he could subdue the unknown and prevail. He wanted to use his free will to make his own independent decisions. He wanted the power to judge, even if the cost was to give up immortality for the privilege. Of course, judgment was not imminent. He did not have to take that final step of disobedience. Nevertheless, the seeds of defiance were likely already flowering in his heart. The snake was simply the catalyst who opportunistically provided the temptation when the desire was ripe.

Often, we get the picture of Yahweh as one who planted that tree, just so he could say: "Ah, hah! Got ya; you die today!" This is not the picture of the God of love that I see taught in scripture. Perhaps the tree of knowledge was like an expensive Porsche bought for a thirteen-year old son. It would be his when he was old enough to handle the responsibility. He had much to learn, and Yahweh was there to teach.

But one day, the keys were left on the table, and the son took a joy ride. Exciting? Yes! But there are always consequences. And, of course, God was well-aware of what would happen.

Adam and Eve were ashamed when they ate of the tree, and for the first-time they experienced vulnerability, self-consciousness, and fear. No longer did they possess a childlike innocence. They were encountering chaos. They were experiencing reality. They recognized that there were such things as good and evil, but did not have the ability or insight to distinguish between them. Reality is very complicated. They were on their own and would have to discern for themselves: "This is good and that is evil." They were to be the ultimate arbiters, not God.

What would Yahweh do? How would he react? Adam and Eve were afraid. This is how we react to God even to this day. When we are on the right track, our relationship is strong, and as John says, "Perfect love casts out fear." When we are on the wrong track, we hide and turn away. Fear and shame replace love. Scripture tells us that "Fear is the beginning of wisdom." But this is just the starting point. When we internalize Yahweh's perfect love there is no more fear, only love. I don't believe Yahweh wants us to walk around cowering in fear; He wants us to love him, love each other, and act responsibly.

How did Yahweh respond? I find it quite interesting how in this role, God acts as a loving mom. She calls: "Adam what did you do?" Adam says, "Eve, who YOU gave me, made me do it; it was her fault." Adam blames both God and Eve, he takes no responsibility. She, God, then turns to Eve to hear her explanation. Eve says: "The snake tricked me and then ate my homework."

The teenage kids were growing up, and She (as a mom), as moms must, had to let them go, and experience the consequences that life's trials would surely bring. She made them some clothes, probably packed some food, gave instructions as to how to survive in the difficult, unforgiving world outside the garden. She gave them an eternal promise that things would turn out okay in the end and sent them on their way. Note that a careful read tells us that Adam was ushered out of the garden, not Eve. Interesting, isn't it? Sin originated with Adam. He was the one who was warned not to consume the fruit from the tree of knowledge, not Eve (who was tricked). Apparently, Eve followed and left the garden by choice.

What about the curses? I see these as observations. Adam will have to work. Of course, this is true. One cannot tame the chaos of the unknown without effort. The forces of nature along with humanity's propensity for evil guarantee lives of difficulty and suffering. The task is to find meaning within these certainties.

Eve will experience pain in childbirth, as the large brain size of our species guarantees. She will follow after her husband because women in the ancient world were most vulnerable after giving birth.

What about that snake, the symbol of evil? It will slither in the darkness. It will have its hour, wounding God's good creation and causing much destruction. But in the end, God the messiah will enter creation, evil and death will be destroyed, and everything will be set right.

In the next chapters of Genesis, we see Yahweh observing, seeing what happens. Unfortunately, the offspring of Adam and Eve crashed the Porsche. The picture of God I get here is one who has the capacity to feel, to be disappointed, to love like the prodigal son's father. God longed for that close relationship with his children to be restored. I see a God who willingly limits his power. If there is one story consistent throughout scripture, it is God longing for humanity to choose to come home, not by force, but by choice. It is not God who separates himself from humanity; it is humanity that separates itself from God.

The picture I get in the first chapter of Genesis is Elohim the all-powerful, distant, detached, and above-it-all God. Yahweh, on the other hand is intimately and personally involved with His creation, and willing to do anything to restore the broken relationship with humanity. The distinction is quite clear.

Let's apply this to account to ourselves in the twenty-first century. If we were put in a garden of paradise today, would eat the forbidden fruit? Would we be looking to see what is on the outside of the garden? Would we want to decide for ourselves what is good and what is evil? Would we give up immortality for temporary adventure? Would we be tempted to destroy paradise? I bet we would. You could say that Adam is an archetype; he is each one of us. In this sense, the original sins are the ones we all commit. The Genesis account reminds us of this.

What makes us think that the nebulous concept of paradise would be enough for us now? Perhaps this is the reason *turn and burn* messages can be so effective. If you can't sell them on how great paradise is, it sure beats the alternative. What kind of place is heaven?

What will the restored new earth be like? Most of us cling to a vague, blissful hope, a kind of land of milk and honey. But when Israel reached the Promised Land, their difficulties did not end. What makes us think that if we fight and war among ourselves now that things will be any different in the restored new creation? Humanity is well able to destroy the most beautiful paradise.

In the new creation, will we still have a desire to sin? If not, why not? Maybe God will change our personalities. But this implies that we will lose the ability to freely choose. If so, what does that prove? Restore the free will, and sin will return. Another possible answer that I've heard is that in the new life, we will see reality clearly so sinful temptations will not exist. But what if our understandings were clouded; would our behaviors darken again? The only way that paradise can remain paradise is if all who go there transform from the inside out. As Ezekiel states, the dry bones need to raise up and the stony hearts be replaced with a heart of flesh. This is not an easy transformation, and we must be willing participants. The path is difficult and many are reluctant to take the journey.

It is easy to see God as Elohim who withholds things from us, not providing what we desire. I wonder how the story would have played out if Adam and Eve saw the Tree of Knowledge of good and evil, not as a test, but as the Porsche that would be theirs when they were ready. What if they saw Yahweh as trusting them so much that he gave them the keys for safe keeping? Would that be a better story? Or does the drama of history have a goodness of its own that will lead to an even better reconciliation in the future?

Now let's turn our attention to the famous account of Noah's flood.

The Flood

> **Africa (Tanzania)**: The rivers began flooding. God told two men to go into a ship, taking with them all sorts of seed and animals. The flood rose, covering the mountains. Later, to check whether the waters had dried up, the man sent out a dove, and it came back to the ship. He waited and sent out a hawk, which did not

return because the waters had dried. The men then disembarked with the animals and seeds.[70]

North America (Cherokee): Day after day, a dog stood at the river bank and howled piteously. Rebuked by his master, the dog said a flood was coming, and he must build and provision a boat. Furthermore, the dog said, he must throw him, the dog, into the water. For a sign that he spoke the truth, the dog showed the back of his neck, which was raw and bare with flesh and bone showing. The man followed directions, and he and his family survived; from them, the present population is descended.[71]

South America (Arawak): Since its creation, the world has been destroyed twice, once by fire and once by flood, by the great god Aiomun Kondi because of the wickedness of mankind. The pious and wise chief Marerewana was informed of the coming of the flood and saved himself and his family in a large canoe. He tied the canoe to a tree with a long cable of bush rope to prevent drifting too far from his old home.[72]

Asia (Eastern Siberia) A flood covered the whole land in the early days of the world. A few people saved themselves on rafts made from bound-together tree trunks. They carried their property and provisions and used stones tied to straps as anchors to prevent being swept out to sea. They were left stranded on mountains when the waters receded.[73]

Europe (Welsh): The lake of Lion burst, flooding all lands. Dwyfan and Dwyfach escaped in a mastless ship

---

[70] Theodor H. Gaster, *Myth, Legend, and Custom in the Old Testament*, 120-121.
[71] Ibid. 116-117.
[72] Ibid. 126.
[73] Ibid. 100.

with pairs of every sort of living creature. They landed in Prydain and repopulated the world.[74]

Pacific Islands (New Guinea): The wife of a very good man saw a very big fish. She called her husband, but he couldn't see it until he hid behind a banana tree and peeked through its leaves. When he finally saw it, he was horribly afraid and forbade his family to catch and eat the fish. But other people caught the fish and, heedless of the man's warning, ate it. When the good man saw that, he hastily drove a pair of all kinds of animals into trees and climbed into a coconut tree with his family. As soon as the wicked men ate the fish, water violently burst from the ground and drowned everyone on it. As soon as the water reached the treetops, it sank rapidly, and the good man and his family came down and laid out new plantations.[75]

When I read the flood account of Genesis, the first question I must ask myself is, "What was the author trying to convey?" Then other questions come to mind: What genre is this? Is it mythological, or is it history? If it is a myth, then what are the lessons that we are to learn? If it is entirely mythological, why does it contain specific details regarding the dimensions of the ark (or more accurately, the Barge[76]) that turns out to be sea-worthy? If historical, was the flood local or global? Why would a loving God wipe out all those people? Then there is the question: why is this account in the Bible at all?

I am convinced that there is a historical aspect to the flood account. This being said, even if it is mythological, there are important lessons embedded in the account. For example, if disaster is imminent, and warnings appear that we don't want to hear, we must never ignore them. Prepare. Another lesson is this: Evil tends to multiply and, if left unchecked, it will lead to total destruction.

---

[74] Ibid. 92-93.
[75] Ibid. 105.
[76] Scholars comparing the flood account with its Sumerian counterpart frequently refer to Noah's boat as a barge.

The strongest evidence for a literal flood is not scientific, it is anthropological. Hundreds of diverse people groups from all around the world have flood legends. I don't buy the explanation that this is because all of the indigenous peoples experienced local floods. Consider the common aspects of many of the stories. These include God being angry, people being bad, a warning, and a boat. If these aspects were centered around the Middle East, I could see how a single legend could spread with these common features. I doubt it could have spread to the Americas or to the Far East Pacific Islands, so that explanation doesn't wash. These reasons convince me that a large flood occurred early in human prehistory.

Given that there was a flood, was it global or local? I tend to side with those who think it was local. I've listened to speculations supporting the global position, but I don't find them convincing. Global proposals hypothesize that Earth's climate was once uniform, evidenced by large trees and wildlife buried near the poles. They also hypothesize that there were major geological upheavals resulting because of the flood, evidenced by fossils on top of the largest mountains.

Some say that a comet of ice hit the atmosphere, split into pieces, struck near the North Pole, altered Earth's orientation relative to the sun, instantly froze the grazing Mammoths, split the earth's crust, and triggered the flood. There are too many ifs in that scenario for me. Plus, the Antarctic ice cores reveal no sudden geological upheavals or changes in climate. Mammoths quickly freezing could simply be the result of the poor creatures falling down a crevice and getting stuck. Their suffocating could result from stuff that fell on them after they fell. Large trees in northern areas can easily be explained by plate tectonics. These can also explain sea fossils at high altitudes.

I'm also suspicious of those who are ready to make war with science every time a verse or two seems to contradict a scientific finding. Perhaps it is healthier to first see if there might just be an alternative interpretation. Most Christians now acknowledge that the Psalmist writing that the earth sits on a solid foundation that can never be moved does not mean that our planet can't freely rotate around the Sun (Ps. 104:5).

So, how do I read the verses in Genesis that seem to imply that the flood must be global? Well, there are other verses in the Bible that refer to everything under heaven, or the whole earth. These, in context, never refer to the Inuit people of the Artic. For example, in Colossians 1:23, Paul states that the gospel was already preached in all creation under heaven. If that meant the Inuit, Paul was a lot more well-traveled than I thought. It is true that Genesis 7:19 says that "all the high mountains were covered." This, to me, implies that Noah only saw water when he looked out, no land. Noah had no concept that Mt. Everest existed outside his field of vision. A local flood the size of Lake Superior would be sufficient for Noah to make this statement, if he was in the middle of it.

This brings us to the next question. Why would God do such a thing? There is one explanation that is historical, in the sense that early Christians and Jews held to it. The clue comes in Genesis 6.

> When people began to multiply on the face of the ground, and daughters were born to them, the sons of God saw that they were fair; and they took wives for themselves of all that they chose. Then the LORD said, "My spirit shall not abide in mortals forever, for they are flesh; their days shall be one hundred twenty years."
>
> The Nephilim were on the earth in those days—and also afterward—when the sons of God went in to the daughters of humans, who bore children to them. These were the heroes that were of old, warriors of renown. The LORD saw that the wickedness of humankind was great in the earth, and that every inclination of the thoughts of their hearts was only evil continually. (Gen. 6:1-6)

Early Christians and Jews believed that fallen angels procreated with men and animals (refer to the apocryphal Book of Enoch for details). In modern terminology, human and animal genomes were manipulated by this unnatural intermarriage, and God put a stop to it. Of course, if one doesn't believe that inter-dimensional beings like angels can exist, they will immediately dismiss this explanation. I get that. I'm not committed to this interpretation, but I suppose that it is a possibility.

The Genesis account indicates: "Yahweh saw that the wickedness of man was great in the earth, and that every intention of the thoughts of his heart was only evil continually. And Yahweh was sorry that he had made man on the earth, and it grieved him to his heart. So Yahweh said, 'I will blot out man whom I have created from the face of the land, man and animals and creeping things and birds of the heavens, for I am sorry that I have made them (Gen. 6:5-7).'"

I understand the wickedness part of the above quote and how it would cause God to grieve. The part I question is whether God was sorry that he created man. Is that true? Or was that Noah's perception? Consider Job 16:9 where Job perceives God to be assaulting and tearing him apart in his anger. Was that true? It cannot be. The entire context of this poem is Job's innocence. When we read the Bible, it is important to discern whether the account is God or if it is man's perception of God. In the flood account, it is obvious to me that much of the writing reflects human perceptions.

The next question to address is whether there are lessons to be learned in the flood account. I think there are. The major one, I think, is that God tolerates evil only so long, and then allows us to face the consequences. He lifts his protection and things take their natural course. Isn't this what we do as parents? We might tolerate some complaining, back-biting and bad behavior in our children. But there comes a point where we say, "That's it; no more."

Another lesson concerns the suddenness of the judgment. If our kids are getting loud and rowdy, they are not even considering that mom and dad might be at the point where they appear and step in. The same is true for humanity. If we, as a species get more and more violent and evil over time, God will eventually act. It would be well to consider that.

A third lesson relates to what would happen if God does not step in. Very likely, we, the human species, would destroy ourselves. With the massive weapons at our disposal, humanity may very well be at a critical point even now. A full-scale nuclear war could very well trigger a mass extinction. Suppose an experimental biological organism got loose. No one knows what consequences that would bring.

Finally, God is patient. He waits till the last minute and does not step in until there is no other choice. This sometimes leads many of us to ask, "Why God, did you let this happen?" Perhaps a better question is to ask, "Why humans, do you let things get so bad that he must?"

An interesting feature of the Genesis flood verses is that they contain two interleaved self-contained accounts. Richard Elliott

Friedman makes a compelling case for this in his book, *Who Wrote the Bible*.

The first flood account refers to God, Elohim, throughout; the second refers to God, Yahweh. The first was probably handed down through the Northern Tribes of Israel who saw God as Elohim; the second through the Southern Tribes, Judah-Benjamin, who related to God as Yahweh. The similarities in the two versions give evidence that they both could have originated from the same source.

Scholars hypothesize that the merging took place at the time when the Northern Kingdom was conquered by the Assyrian empire.[77] At that time, many from the northern ten tribes fled south. A prophet, perhaps Isaiah, would be reluctant to alter the traditions of the north, so he simply merged them with those of the south producing a unified account.

In the Yahweh version, God regrets, feels, smells the animal sacrifice, and personally closes the door to the ark. The Elohim version portrays the powerful, in-charge, all-knowing God. The Yahweh version contains an animal sacrifice; the Elohim version does not. The Yahweh version tells the story from Noah's perspective; the Elohim version tells the story from God's perspective. Both versions follow below, using Richard Elliot Friedman's translation.

Yahweh version

Gen 6:5 Yahweh saw that the wickedness of man was great in the earth, and that every intention of the thoughts of his heart was only evil continually.

Gen 6:6 And Yahweh was sorry that he had made man on the earth, and it grieved him to his heart.

---

[77] Some scholars favor a later date. The books of Kings cite the chronicles of the kings of Israel and Judah, which in my opinion, were annals destroyed by the Babylonians. The Chronicler transfers these citations to 1 and 2 Chronicles, but I believe the documents were already lost at that time. For these reasons, I favor an earlier date.

Myth or History

Gen 6:7 So Yahweh said, "I will blot out man whom I have created from the face of the land, man and animals and creeping things and birds of the heavens, for I am sorry that I have made them."

Gen 6:8 But Noah found favor in the eyes of Yahweh.

Gen 7:1 Then Yahweh said to Noah, "Go into the ark, you and all your household, for I have seen that you are righteous before me in this generation.

Gen 7:2 Take with you seven pairs of all clean animals, the male and his mate, and a pair of the animals that are not clean, the male and his mate,

Gen 7:3 and seven pairs of the birds of the heavens also, male and female, to keep their offspring alive on the face of all the earth.

Gen 7:4 For in seven days I will send rain on the earth forty days and forty nights, and every living thing that I have made I will blot out from the face of the ground."

Gen 7:5 And Noah did all that Yahweh had commanded him.

Gen 7:7 And Noah and his sons and his wife and his sons' wives with him went into the ark to escape the waters of the flood.

Gen 7:10 And after seven days the waters of the flood came upon the earth.

Gen 7:12 And rain fell upon the earth forty days and forty nights.

Gen 7:16 And Yahweh shut him in.

Gen 7:17 The flood continued forty days on the earth. The waters increased and bore up the ark, and it rose high above the earth.

Gen 7:18 The waters prevailed and increased greatly on the earth, and the ark floated on the face of the waters.

Gen 7:19 And the waters prevailed so mightily on the earth that all the high mountains under the whole heaven were covered.

Gen 7:20 The waters prevailed above the mountains, covering them fifteen cubits deep.

Gen 7:22 Everything on the dry land in whose nostrils was the breath of life died.

Gen 7:23 He blotted out every living thing that was on the face of the ground, man and animals and creeping things and birds of the heavens. They were blotted out from the earth. Only Noah was left, and those who were with him in the ark.

Gen 8:6 At the end of forty days Noah opened the window of the ark that he had made

Gen 8:8 Then he sent forth a dove from him, to see if the waters had subsided from the face of the ground.

Gen 8:9 But the dove found no place to set her foot, and she returned to him to the ark, for the waters were still on the face of the whole earth. So, he put out his hand and took her and brought her into the ark with him.

Gen 8:10 He waited another seven days, and again he sent forth the dove out of the ark.

Gen 8:11 And the dove came back to him in the evening, and behold, in her mouth was a freshly plucked olive leaf. So, Noah knew that the waters had subsided from the earth.

Gen 8:12 Then he waited another seven days and sent forth the dove, and she did not return to him anymore.

Gen 8:13 And Noah removed the covering of the ark and looked, and behold, the face of the ground was dry.

Gen 8:20 Then Noah built an altar to Yahweh and took some of every clean animal and some of every clean bird and offered burnt offerings on the altar.

Gen 8:21 And when Yahweh smelled the pleasing aroma, Yahweh said in his heart, "I will never again curse the ground because of man, for the intention of man's heart is evil from his youth. Neither will I ever again strike down every living creature as I have done.

Gen 8:22 While the earth remains, seedtime and harvest, cold and heat, summer and winter, day and night, shall not cease."

Elohim version

Gen 6:9 These are the generations of Noah. Noah was a righteous man, blameless in his generation. Noah walked with Elohim.

Gen 6:10 And Noah had three sons, Shem, Ham, and Japheth.

Gen 6:11 Now the earth was corrupt in Elohim's sight, and the earth was filled with violence.

Gen 6:12 And Elohim saw the earth, and behold, it was corrupt, for all flesh had corrupted their way on the earth.

Gen 6:13 And Elohim said to Noah, "I have determined to make an end of all flesh, for the earth is filled with violence through them. Behold, I will destroy them with the earth.

Gen 6:14 Make yourself an arc of gopher wood. Make rooms in the ark, and cover it inside and out with pitch.

Gen 6:15 This is how you are to make it: the length of the ark 300 cubits, its breadth 50 cubits, and its height 30 cubits.

Gen 6:16 Make a roof for the ark, and finish it to a cubit above, and set the door of the ark in its side. Make it with lower, second, and third decks.

Gen 6:17 For behold, I will bring a flood of waters upon the earth to destroy all flesh in which is the breath of life under heaven. Everything that is on the earth shall die.

Gen 6:18 But I will establish my covenant with you, and you shall come into the ark, you, your sons, your wife, and your sons' wives with you.

Gen 6:19 And of every living thing of all flesh, you shall bring two of every sort into the ark to keep them alive with you. They shall be male and female.

Gen 6:20 Of the birds according to their kinds, and of the animals according to their kinds, of every creeping thing of the ground, according to its kind, two of every sort shall come in to you to keep them alive.

Gen 6:21 Also take with you every sort of food that is eaten, and store it up. It shall serve as food for you and for them."

Gen 6:22 Noah did this; he did all that Elohim commanded him.

Gen 7:6 Noah was six hundred years old when the flood of waters came upon the earth.

Gen 7:8 Of clean animals, and of animals that are not clean, and of birds, and of everything that creeps on the ground,

Gen 7:9 two and two, male and female, went into the ark with Noah, as God had commanded Noah.

Gen 7:11 In the six hundredth year of Noah's life, in the second month, on the seventeenth day of the month, on that day all the fountains of the great deep burst forth, and the windows of the heavens were opened.

Gen 7:13 On the very same day Noah and his sons, Shem and Ham and Japheth, and Noah's wife and the three wives of his sons with them entered the ark,

Myth or History

Gen 7:14 they and every beast, according to its kind, and all the livestock according to their kinds, and every creeping thing that creeps on the earth, according to its kind, and every bird, according to its kind, every winged creature.

Gen 7:15 They went into the ark with Noah, two and two of all flesh in which there was the breath of life.

Gen 7:16 And those that entered, male and female of all flesh, went in as God had commanded him.

Gen 7:21 And all flesh died that moved on the earth, birds, livestock, beasts, all swarming creatures that swarm on the earth, and all mankind.

Gen 7:24 And the waters prevailed on the earth 150 days.

Gen 8:1 But Elohim remembered Noah and all the beasts and all the livestock that were with him in the ark. And Elohim made a wind blow over the earth, and the waters subsided.

Gen 8:2 The fountains of the deep and the windows of the heavens were closed, the rain from the heavens was restrained,

Gen 8:3 and the waters receded from the earth continually. At the end of 150 days the waters had abated,

Gen 8:4 and in the seventh month, on the seventeenth day of the month, the ark came to rest on the mountains of Ararat.

Gen 8:5 And the waters continued to abate until the tenth month; in the tenth month, on the first day of the month, the tops of the mountains were seen.

Gen 8:7 and sent forth a raven. It went to and fro until the waters were dried up from the earth.

Gen 8:13 In the six hundred and first year, in the first month, the first day of the month, the waters were dried from off the earth.

Gen 8:14 In the second month, on the twenty-seventh day of the month, the earth had dried out.

Gen 8:15 Then Elohim said to Noah,

Gen 8:16 "Go out from the ark, you and your wife, and your sons and your sons' wives with you.

Gen 8:17 Bring out with you every living thing that is with you of all flesh—birds and animals and every creeping thing that creeps on the earth—that they may swarm on the earth and be fruitful and multiply on the earth."

Gen 8:18 So Noah went out, and his sons and his wife and his sons' wives with him.

Gen 8:19 Every beast, every creeping thing, and every bird, everything that moves on the earth, went out by families from the ark.

I'm going to finish this section with my own interpretation. I believe that the flood is an extremely ancient story. Noah and his sons passed the original account down through the generations. In the Elohim version, God says the least amount possible to accomplish his purpose. Basically: "Noah, I'm bringing a flood that it is going to destroy everything. Build a barge to these specific dimensions, and alert everyone that you can." This is consistent with Jewish interpretation, which states that Noah and Methuselah warned the populace for one hundred and twenty years before the disaster. God always gives fair warning.

But why? Perhaps if evil were allowed to continue unchecked, humanity would self-destruct. If this was allowed to happen, God's plan to redeem creation could not succeed.

How did the following generations perceive this? The Yahweh version gives us the answer. Over time, people added commentary. They speculated on Noah's reactions:

> God is angry. There was evil everywhere. No one would listen to me. God regrets that he created mankind and the animals. I'm sure glad that I found

favor; my family must be the only one worth saving. I hope he doesn't do this again. What will happen after things dry out? I better offer a burnt offering sacrifice. That surely will appease his anger.

Therefore, we have the wording of the two flood accounts, merged together. The Elohim version contains God's revelation. The Yahweh version of the flood embodies the human attempt to explain the event. This dichotomy repeats all through the Bible. There are God's revelations contrasted with human perceptions of those revelations. We have mixed voices merged together. Unwinding them is an important key to responsible biblical interpretation.

The first ten chapters of the Book of Genesis describe the creation of the world, the fall of humanity, and the flood of Noah. They contain a complex mixture of history and mythology. Skeptics are quick to attack those parts that seem to conflict with Science. All too often, this puts believers on the defensive, especially when they disregard the important lessons that come from mythological teachings. This leads to Science vs. Religion tensions and arguments.

In this chapter, I hope that I've established a bridge. Yes, there is history, and yes, there is mythology. The history stimulates our minds with compelling facts; the mythology sinks deep into our hearts with transforming life lessons. It is all valuable and good. It is inspired and God-breathed.

Chapter 7

Denominational Divisions

> Four score and seven years ago our fathers brought forth on this continent, a new nation, conceived in Liberty, and dedicated to the proposition that all men are created equal. Now we are engaged in a great civil war, testing whether that nation, or any nation so conceived and so dedicated, can long endure. We are met on a great battle-field of that war. It is rather for us to be here dedicated to the great task remaining before us—that from these honored dead we take increased devotion to that cause for which they gave the last full measure of devotion—that we here highly resolve that these dead shall not have died in vain—that this nation, under God, shall have a new birth of freedom—and that government of the people, by the people, for the people, shall not perish from the earth.[78]

The United States' Declaration of Independence was signed in 1776 with great anticipation and hope. Not long after, in 1787, Washington, Jefferson, Hamilton, Adams, and the other founding fathers came together with a spirit of compromise to produce the American constitution.

All was well; or was it? Only seventy-six years passed from 1787, and the country was engaged in a bloody civil war. To put it into perspective, the Vietnam war took the lives of 153,303 Americans. The Civil War took four times that many when the total population of the United States was only a tenth as large. The cost to eliminate slavery was great when measured in loss of life.

In many ways, we are still fighting the civil war, not with bullets but with words. American Slavery no longer exists, but conflicts related to race seem to again be rising to the surface. Have we taken Lincoln's words in his Gettysburg address seriously? Many today,

---

[78] Abraham Lincoln, "Gettysburg Address," (November 19, 1863) Bliss Copy (for Colonel Alexander Bliss).

don't even know what they were. Did those, both white and black, who fought in the Civil War die in vain? Will a country like America ultimately perish from the earth? The answer is not at all clear.

The birth of Christianity followed a similar pattern. It started with great anticipation and hope, just like the founding of America. Those early believers celebrated the initiation of God's kingdom coming to earth, and there was an early spread of the Good News throughout the provinces of the Roman Empire. Unfortunately, almost immediately, seeds of division crept in, and within a century, this Jewish sect split from its roots and became a separate religion.

Over the following centuries, the Church had to contend with many heresies, and then, because of the Great Schism of 1054, it split in two. The Protestant Reformation led to dozens of fractures. Today we have thousands of splinter denominations. In the midst of all this, there were religious wars and much bloodshed. There was also clergy abuse that was kept hidden and ignored. Can the teachings of Jesus survive amid denominational conflicts like those just described? Will Christianity perish from the earth? Fortunately, the New Testament scripture promises an ultimate victory.

People often have idealistic visions of the past. It is easy to look back to the first decades after the American War of Independence with nostalgic longings. Similarly, amid today's divisions in the Church, many long for the purity of first-century worship and unity. Unfortunately, things are never quite so clear. It is true that we can learn from the past successes and failures, but each generation faces its own set of challenges. We can never return to bygone days; we live now.

As just mentioned, history records many rifts in the Church. In this chapter, I will focus on the first of these, which is documented within the very pages of the New Testament, and then draw some lessons that we can apply to our age.

Peter and the disciples lived and died as first-century Jews. The Way, as they called it, started out as a Jewish sect. Approximately seven weeks after the crucifixion, many thousands of Jews from all around the Roman empire arrived in Jerusalem to celebrate the holiday of Pentecost. We can read chapter two of Acts, but that presents the event from the disciples' point of view. Forgive me, but I would like to imagine for a bit that I'm one of those Jews visiting Jerusalem on that Pentecost.

Suddenly, there was a rushing wind. From a nearby house some Galileans began to speak in my native language. Jerusalem was very crowded that day. I looked around and I noticed Jews from all over, from Mesopotamia, Judea, Asia, and Arabia. They were from all around the world; some were Gentiles and others were recent converts to Judaism. We all heard what these Galileans were saying in our own languages.

This can't happen; after all I'm a *modern* Roman. Yeah, I know, lots of people sacrifice animals to idols, and give homage to Caesar as god, but we know that these things are all ritual. Miracles don't really happen. Yet, here it is, happening before our very eyes. What is going on? Are they drunk?

Next, one of the Galileans gets up and gives a speech. We all still hear it in our native languages. He tells us that this guy, Jesus, performed many miracles even more powerful than this one. He was recently crucified, but conquered death when he was physically raised. How can this be? Dead people don't rise. These Galileans claim that they all witnessed it, saying that he was with them for forty days before being exalted to the right hand of God in honor. His kingdom is being ushered in.

We ask, "What are we supposed to do with this?" They answer, "Repent of the wrong things that you do, believe, and be baptized. Then you will also receive this Holy Spirit." Many of us did. The miracles that occurred in the days that followed were incredible. When we returned to our home towns, we reflected on these things and shared what happened with our family and friends. This is how the Way began.

I can't scientifically confirm the events of that day. They do explain the sudden and rapid growth of Christianity, especially when its leader was a dead messiah. It explains why even those who were not direct witnesses of Jesus' resurrection were willing to sacrifice everything to follow him.

In Acts chapter 10, Peter has a vision where he is instructed to eat unclean foods. I'll paraphrase a bit to set the stage.

Peter complains: "This is crazy. Jews don't do this.".

The voice in the vision responds: "What God has made clean, do not call common."

Three times, the vision repeats. Peter doesn't know what to make of it. While he was still pondering, men were sent from Cornelius, a Roman centurion, to fetch Peter. I find Peter's first words to Cornelius very revealing.

> You yourselves know that it is unlawful for a Jew to associate with or to visit a Gentile; but God has shown me that I should not call anyone profane or unclean. So, when I was sent for, I came without objection. Now may I ask why you sent for me? (Acts 10:28-29)

First-century Jews did not associate with Gentiles; they were unclean and uncircumcised. God, however, had different plans; the Way was to include Gentiles. The works of the Satan were defeated and his power of deception was diminished. Because of this, the Gentiles became open to hear the Good News. All are welcome. Bigotry is no more.

In Peter's words: "Truly I see that God is no respecter of persons; but in every nation *he who fears Him and works righteousness is accepted by Him.*"

Peter's account rings true to me. It would take something like this for first-century Jews to welcome a Gentile into their ranks, especially a Roman centurion. Peter's visit with Cornelius didn't go over well with the other disciples and recent Jewish converts to the Way. They challenged Peter, "You went in to uncircumcised men and ate with them." Fortunately, they accepted Peter's explanation, and backed down. This, however, was only the beginning of the conflict.

The seeds of division were apparent. It is embodied within Peter's very words from the quote above, "he who fears Him and works righteousness is accepted by Him." What was Peter and the disciples' understanding of this? *Work righteousness* means observe Torah.

Along comes Saul, who was determined to stamp out this new heresy. With authorization from the High Priest, he strove to arrest and bring back in chains all Way-followers that he found. However, Jesus got in the way.

> Now as he was going along and approaching Damascus, suddenly a light from heaven flashed around him. He fell to the ground and heard a voice saying to him, "Saul, Saul, why do you persecute me?" He asked, "Who are you, Lord?" The reply came, "I am Jesus, whom you are persecuting." (Acts 9:3-5)

Later a follower of the Way, Ananias, was told in a vision to find Saul:

> Go, for he is an instrument whom I have chosen to bring my name before Gentiles and kings and before the people of Israel; I, myself will show him how much he must suffer for the sake of my name. (From Acts 9:15-16)

From this point on, all New Testament references use Paul, Saul's Roman name. His life was transformed; the Pharisee of Pharisees was now to be the apostle to the Gentiles. As Ananias was told, Paul suffered many things. Eventually he was beheaded during the reign of Nero.

The question at hand was: Does a Gentile need to become Torah-observant to become a follower of the Way? Paul emphatically said: No! Many of the early believing Jews insisted: Yes! The seeds of division erupted and the Way, within a hundred years, evolved into Christianity. Starting from a Jewish sect containing mostly Jews, the movement transformed to a religion of mostly Gentiles. It led to two millennia of hostility between Jews and Christians.

Paul's ministry had the support of the church at Jerusalem. According to his letter to Galatians he visited Peter for fifteen days, three years after his conversion, approximately AD 35, Then fourteen years later, Peter, James, and John entrusted Paul to bring the Good News to the Gentiles. They agreed that they did not need to become Torah-observant; they only had to avoid sacrificing to idols and be sensitive to the needs of the poor. All seemed well; but not so fast.

Many Jewish believers strongly disagreed. The Ebionites, for example, were early Christians that demanded that Gentiles must indeed be Torah-observant and follow *the works of the law.* For a long time, scholars thought that Paul made up the term *works of the law.* Recently, though, a Dead Sea Scroll (4q MMT) proved different. The term actually refers to those requirements that must be satisfied for one to be considered a *true* Jew. These Torah-based Jewish believers and the other sects (Pharisees and Sadducees) followed Paul from place to place, stirring up dissension. They tried to kill him, and eventually succeeded in getting him arrested.

The situation came to a head in Galilee. Apparently, these Jewish teachers arrived and, by emphasizing the works of the law, they threatened to destroy his work. Paul was livid, evidenced by his letter to the Galatians. He challenged Peter face-to-face for acting one way around the Jewish believers and another in the presence of Gentiles. Even Barnabas, his missionary partner, wavered. At one point in his Galatians letter, Paul bluntly asks why "stop at circumcision;" go all the way to castration. He calls the false teachings dung; Paul was not a happy camper.

Next, we come to the Book of Romans. Paul did not establish this church, though there were many persons in the various Roman house churches that Paul knew well. He acknowledges them in chapter 16. Sometimes, lists of names are boring, but not this list. Some of the names are Roman or Greek and others are Jewish; It is a diverse group containing both men and women.

Let's speculate a bit about divisions within the Roman congregations. In AD 49, Claudius issued a decree expelling Jews from Rome. We get a glimpse of the reason from a passing remark by the historian Suetonius.

> Since the Jews constantly made disturbances at the instigation of Chrestus[79], he [the Emperor Claudius] expelled them from Rome.[80]

Evidently, there was dissension and the emperor, Claudius, had enough. Acts chapter 18 corroborates the expulsion. Priscilla and Aquila met up with Paul after leaving Rome and they pursued a

---

[79] This was an alternate spelling of Christ in the early days of Christianity. Irenaeus comments about this in his book *Against Heresies,* 1.XV.2.

[80] Suetonius, *The Lives of the Twelve Caesars,* 25:74).

tentmaking business together. We could ask, "What happened to the Roman house churches after the Jews left?" The answer: The Gentile believers adjusted as they continued to practice Christianity, and life went on.

AD 54 came along. Claudius died, Nero came to power, and so the expulsion order expired. The Jewish believers were free to return, but now, they were no longer in leadership positions. Conflict followed between the returning Jewish believers and the Gentile converts. Could Torah observance be enforced? Probably not. Would the Jewish believers associate, or even break bread with those uncircumcised Gentiles who were unwilling to adhere to the *works of the law*? Probably not.

This brings us to the purpose of Paul's letter to the Romans. A long, difficult, scholarly book written by Douglas Campbell (*The Deliverance of God*) provides some intriguing insights. Hopefully, I can summarize the pertinent points.

As mentioned earlier, Paul was not the founder of the Roman church, and he no longer was headquartered at Antioch. He hoped to travel to Spain to found new churches where other apostles had not yet traveled. He needed support. He was aware of the divisions between Gentile believers and Jews and wanted to get his point of view across before his enemies had a chance to arrive. Perhaps they were already there. He knew that both Jews and Gentiles were attending the house churches, and his desire was that they would join in fellowship without division.

Paul, in the Book of Romans, uses a rhetorical technique called *prosopopoeia*. This was common in the ancient world where the literacy rate was at most ten to fifteen percent. Letters were meant to be read aloud. Prosopopoeia features the author engaging with an imaginary person in a back-and-forth dialogue. It is a specific type of a diatribe. An actor, or reader, simply changes voice when each person is speaking. Much of Romans is not Paul; it is the imaginary person, which I'll label the Teacher for the purposes of this discussion.

Prosopopoeia explains why Paul sent a reader to deliver his letter in person, instead of using the much less expensive route of sending correspondence by ship. The reader was trained to know when each person speaks, and to change voice appropriately. This explains why we can get confused when we read Romans and other Pauline letters.

When we read the whole thing as Paul, he appears to contradict himself repeatedly.

For prosopopoeia to be successful, it must accurately represent the alternative viewpoint, especially if the reading is done in a mixed audience. Otherwise, those opposing the Teacher would object saying, "That's not fair; we don't think like that." The responses must also be accurate or other objections would be raised, and this would lose the audience.

Let's consider Romans chapter 1 in this light. It is well-known that verses 18-32 are a synopsis of anti-Gentile polemics of the first century. Much of it is extracted from the apocryphal book, *The Wisdom of Solomon*, chapters 13 through 15. These verses are not Paul's voice; they are the Teacher's. A Gentile in the audience, hearing this, would think: "There may be some like that, but that is not us. Yeah, we are sinners, but we never did those things." Meanwhile, those agreeing with the Teacher would be thinking, "Preach it brother." But then, unexpectedly, Paul, in chapter 2, turns the table and rebuts the argument. The back-and-forth between Paul and the Teacher continues through the first four chapters.

The following presents these sections of Romans, using the NRSV translation, where Paul's and the Teacher's voices are delineated. It is difficult to decipher the start and end points nearly two thousand years later, but Campbell suggests the demarcations. Since he is a renowned scholar, who has dedicated years to this issue, I'll take his word for it. I believe Campbell is right on. It is unique in that it can revolutionize the way we read Paul's letters.

Paul's Introduction

[14] I am a debtor both to Greeks and to barbarians, both to the wise and to the foolish [15]—hence my eagerness to proclaim the gospel to you also who are in Rome. [16] For I am not ashamed of the gospel; it is the power of God for salvation to everyone who has faith *(Recent scholarship: believes or trusts)*, to the Jew first and also to the Greek. [17] For in it the righteousness of God is revealed through the gospel through faith for faith *(Recent scholarship: 'from faithfulness to faithfulness', meaning God's faithfulness, not ours)*; as it is written, "The one who is righteous will live by faith *(Recent scholarship: trust)*."

Teacher's Introduction

[18] For the wrath of God is revealed from heaven against all ungodliness and wickedness of those who by their wickedness suppress the truth. [19] For what can be known about God is plain to them, because God has shown it to them. [20] Ever since the creation of the world his eternal power and divine nature, invisible though they are, have been understood and seen through the things he has made. So they are without excuse; [21] for though they knew God, they did not honor him as God or give thanks to him, but they became futile in their thinking, and their senseless minds were darkened. [22] Claiming to be wise, they became fools; [23] and they exchanged the glory of the immortal God for images resembling a mortal human being or birds or four-footed animals or reptiles.

[24] Therefore God gave them up in the lusts of their hearts to impurity, to the degrading of their bodies among themselves, [25] because they exchanged the truth about God for a lie and worshiped and served the creature rather than the Creator, who is blessed forever! Amen. [26] For this reason God gave them up to degrading passions. Their women exchanged natural intercourse for unnatural, [27] and in the same way also the men, giving up natural intercourse with women, were consumed with passion for one another. Men committed shameless acts with men and received in their own persons the due penalty for their error.

[28] And since they did not see fit to acknowledge God, God gave them up to a debased mind and to things that should not be done. [29] They were filled with every kind of wickedness, evil, covetousness, malice. Full of envy, murder, strife, deceit, craftiness, they are gossips, [30] slanderers, God-haters, insolent, haughty, boastful, inventors of evil, rebellious toward parents, [31] foolish, faithless, heartless, ruthless. [32] They know God's decree, that those who practice such things deserve to die—yet they not only do them but even applaud others who practice them."

Paul's Rebuttal

2[1] Therefore you have no excuse, whoever you are, when you judge others; for in passing judgment on another you condemn yourself, because you, the judge, are doing the very same things. [2] You say, 'we know that God's judgment on those who do such things is in accordance with truth.' [3] Do you imagine, whoever you are, when you judge those who do such things and yet do them yourself, you will escape the judgment of God? ⁴ Or do you despise the riches of his kindness and forbearance and patience? Do you not realize that God's kindness is meant to lead you to repentance? ⁵ But, by your hard and impenitent heart you are storing up wrath for yourself on the day of wrath, when God's righteous judgment will be revealed.

Teacher's Restatement
⁶ He will repay according to each one's deeds: ⁷ to those who by patiently doing good seek for glory and honor and immortality, he will give eternal life; ⁸ while for those who are self-seeking and who obey not the truth but wickedness, there will be wrath and fury. ⁹ There will be anguish and distress for everyone who does evil, the Jew first and also the Greek, ¹⁰ but glory and honor and peace for everyone who does good, the Jew first and also the Greek. ¹¹ For God shows no partiality. ¹² All who have sinned apart from the law will also perish apart from the law, and all who have sinned under the law will be judged by the law. ¹³ For it is not the hearers of the law who will be righteous in God's sight, but the doers of the law who will be justified.

Paul's Rebuttal
¹⁴ When Gentiles, who do not possess the law, do instinctively what the law requires, these, though not having the law, are a law to themselves; ¹⁵ they show that what the law requires is written on their hearts, to which their own conscience also bears witness; and their conflicting thoughts will accuse or perhaps excuse them ¹⁶ on the day when, according to my gospel, God, through Jesus Christ, will judge the secret thoughts of all.

¹⁷But if you call yourself a Jew and rely on the law and boast of your relation to God ¹⁸ and know his will and determine what is best because you are instructed in the law, ¹⁹ and if you are sure that you are a guide to the blind, a light to those who are in darkness, ²⁰ a corrector of the foolish, a teacher of children, having in the law the embodiment of knowledge and truth, ²¹ you, then, that teach others, will you not teach yourself? While you preach against stealing, do you steal? ²² You that forbid adultery, do you commit adultery? You that abhor idols, do you rob temples? ²³ You that boast in the law, do you dishonor God by breaking the law? ²⁴ For, as it is written, "The name of God is blasphemed among the Gentiles because of you."

²⁵ Circumcision indeed is of value if you obey the law; but if you break the law, your circumcision has become uncircumcision. ²⁶ So, if those who are uncircumcised keep the requirements of the law, will not their uncircumcision be regarded as circumcision? ²⁷ Then those who are physically uncircumcised but keep the law will condemn you that have the written code and circumcision but break the law. ²⁸ For a person is not a Jew who is one outwardly, nor is true circumcision something external and physical. ²⁹ Rather, a person is a Jew who is one inwardly, and real circumcision is a matter of the heart—it is spiritual and not literal. Such a person receives praise not from others but from God.

Dialogue—Paul Questions the Teacher
Paul: **3**¹ Then what advantage has the Jew? Or what is the value of circumcision?
Teacher: ² Much, in every way. For in the first place the Jews were entrusted with the oracles of God.
Paul: ³ What if some were unfaithful? Will their faithlessness nullify the faithfulness of God?
Teacher: ⁴ By no means! Although everyone is a liar, let God be proved true, as it is written, "So that you may be justified in your words, and prevail in your judging."
Paul: ⁵ But if our injustice serves to confirm the justice of God, what should we say? That God is unjust to inflict wrath on us? (I speak in a human way.)
Teacher: ⁶ By no means! For then how could God judge the world?
Paul: ⁷ But if through my falsehood God's truthfulness abounds to his glory, why am I still being condemned as a sinner? ⁸ And why not say (as some people slander us by saying that we say), "Let us do evil so that good may come?"
Teacher: Their condemnation is deserved!

Pauls' Clinching Argument
⁹ What then? Are we any better off? No, not at all; for we have already charged that all, both Jews and Greeks, are under the power of sin, ¹⁰ as it is written:

> "There is no one who is righteous, not even one;

> ¹¹there is no one who has understanding, there is no one who seeks God.
> ¹²All have turned aside, together they have become worthless; there is no one who shows kindness, there is not even one."
> ¹³ "Their throats are opened graves; they use their tongues to deceive."
> "The venom of vipers is under their lips."
> ¹⁴ "Their mouths are full of cursing and bitterness."
> ¹⁵ "Their feet are swift to shed blood;
> ¹⁶ruin and misery are in their paths,
> ¹⁷and the way of peace they have not known."
> ¹⁸ "There is no fear of God before their eyes."

¹⁹Now we know that whatever the law says, it speaks to those who are under the law, so that every mouth may be silenced, and the whole world may be held accountable to God. ²⁰ For "no human being will be justified in his sight" by deeds prescribed by the law, for through the law comes the knowledge of sin. ²¹ But now, apart from law, the righteousness of God has been disclosed, and is attested by the law and the prophets, ²² the righteousness of God through the faith in Jesus Christ *(Recent scholarship: faithfulness of Jesus the Messiah)* for all who believe. For there is no distinction, ²³ since all have sinned and fall short of the glory of God; ²⁴ they are now justified by his grace as a gift, through the redemption that is in Christ Jesus, ²⁵ whom God put forward as a sacrifice of atonement by his blood effective through faith *(Recent scholarship: his faithfulness)*. He did this to show his righteousness, because in his divine forbearance he passed over the sins previously committed; ²⁶ it was to prove at the present time that he himself is righteous and that he justifies the one who has faith in Jesus *(Recent scholarship: trusts in the faithfulness of Jesus)*.

Dialogue — The Teacher Questions Paul
Teacher: ²⁷ Then what becomes of boasting?
Paul: It is excluded.
Teacher: By what law? By that of works?
Paul: No, but by the law of faith. ²⁸ For we hold that a person is justified by faith *(Recent scholarship: God's faithfulness)* apart from works prescribed by the law.
Teacher: ²⁹ Or is God the God of Jews only?

Paul: Is he not the God of Gentiles also?
Teacher: Yes, of Gentiles also.
Paul: ³⁰ Since God is one; and he will justify the circumcised on the ground of faith and the uncircumcised through that same faith.
Teacher: ³¹ Do we then overthrow the law by this faith?
Paul: By no means! On the contrary, we uphold the law.
Teacher: 4¹ What then are we to say was gained by Abraham, our ancestor according to the flesh? ² For if Abraham was justified by works, he has something to boast about.
Paul: But not before God. ³ For what does the scripture say? "Abraham believed God, and it was reckoned to him as righteousness."

Let me provide my summary of the Book of Romans: We, all believers, whether Jew or Gentile, are joined together in one spiritual body. The focus is on the faithfulness of the Messiah, not on our faith. There should be unity in the body of Christ; there should not be dissension between Jew and Gentile believers.

This has application to us in our generation. It is interesting that Christianity has done the exact thing that the Teacher did. For centuries you could not be a Christian and also be Torah-observant. Jewish believers were mocked for attending synagogue or for following kosher laws. I see no problem with Jewish Christians following Torah, if it is to preserve relationships with friends and families or participate with their cultural identity. It is not a sin. It becomes an issue when it becomes compulsory. This goes both ways, Jew to Christian and Christian to Jew.

In the first few centuries of Christianity, Torah-observance was not the only issue. Various groups synchronized Christian teachings with Greco-Roman philosophies. Others introduced *hidden Gnostic* mystical understandings. It is not surprising that inter-denominational disputes are very much with us today. There are fights about the age of the earth, Heaven and Hell, the return of Christ, politics, and many other things. At the same time, major denominations defensively hide perpetrators of sexual crimes, and high-profile evangelists regularly take advantage of vulnerable people for financial gain. The Church cannot be a positive force if these kinds of disputes persist. Divisions are deadly.

We can learn from Campbell's analysis. I see it as ground-breaking; I will never again read Paul with the same lens. I find the Teacher's voice harsh and legalistic. My wife and I recently read the first four chapters of Romans aloud. The different voices were so clear, way more than when I read it silently. It was surprising.

Many of us misunderstand Paul. We often view him as cantankerous, opinionated, contradictory, and narrow-minded. We quickly read past those statements in his letters where he encourages believers to help each other in community and to love one another. Consider this. If he did not live out what he preached, the congregations would have considered him to be a hypocrite. His letters would have been immediately destroyed. They weren't. Instead, they stood the test of time. He was the real-deal. In the face of a life of persecution he remained faithful till the end. At times, as Second Corinthians portrays, he was close to a complete psychological breakdown (2 Cor. 1:8). It was only his life in Christ that carried him through.

Paul was a brilliant scholar, but he didn't normally have the time to carefully craft theses, like Plato or Aristotle. His correspondences were highly-condensed pleas to his various congregations that needed immediate, timely encouragements. He wrote his letters either when he was in prison or on the run. He was well acquainted with all of the leading Greek and Roman philosophies of the day, but he loved his Jewish God and the faith tradition of his forefathers. His passion was to present him through the lens of Jesus. His two primary focuses throughout all of his letters were unity and right-living. It is important to read Paul using this filter.

Consider Philippians chapter 2. This is one example where Paul exquisitely crafts his argument. The first five verses contain a heartfelt persuasive plea for unity. Then comes an early Aramaic Christian hymn describing his Messiah. This is followed by six verses describing how a believer should live. In eighteen versus, we see a clear presentation of the Good News. The chapter is a sandwich. Unity and right-living wraps around Jesus in the center. If only the Church could live out these verses. We might even see God's kingdom come and his will be done. Denominational differences that divide us could soon vanish.

PART 3

The Nature of God

> If this is your God, he's not very impressive. He has so many psychological problems; he's so insecure. He demands worship every seven days. He goes out and creates faulty humans and then blames them for his own mistakes. He's a pretty poor excuse for a Supreme Being. —Gene Roddenberry

Although the above quote is a caricature, over the years, I've found that many Christians do have a harsh view of God, the Father. Theirs is a god who at sometimes is longsuffering and merciful, but other times is angry and wrathful. It is a god who we can never seem to please, one whom Jesus protects us from.

In the next part of this book, I'm going to wrestle with these issues. Why the Levitical laws? What's up with the sacrificial system? Did God really command genocide? Why does the Bible contain so much violence? What does it mean to be at peace with God? Is God a being that we can love with our whole heart?

Chapter 8

Mosaic Laws and Rituals

> These words the LORD spoke with a loud voice to your whole assembly at the mountain, out of the fire, the cloud, and the thick darkness, and he added no more. He wrote them on two stone tablets and gave them to me. When you heard the voice out of the darkness, while the mountain was burning with fire, you approached me, all the heads of your tribes and your elders, and you said, "Look, the LORD our God has shown us his glory and greatness, and we have heard his voice out of the fire. Today we have seen that God may speak to someone and the person may still live. (Deut. 5:22-24)

In this chapter, we will discuss the Mosaic laws and its sacrificial system. These regulations when analyzed out of context are often attacked for being harsh and petty. Is this true? The laws of the Old Testament deserve careful study before we should cast judgment.

Three months after the Exile, Moses and the people reached the wilderness of Sinai. As the above passage from Deuteronomy shows, the people were at first excited after experiencing God's display of power. But fear quickly set in and the tribal leaders said: "You, Moses, speak to us, not God, or we will die." From that point on Moses was the intercessor.

Moses then went up the mountain and God said: "If you obey my voice and keep my covenant, you shall be my treasured possession out of all the peoples ... You shall be for me a priestly kingdom and a holy nation." Shortly after, according to Exodus 31:18, God wrote his covenantal instructions on two stone tablets. Most Biblical theologians identify these as containing the ten commandments. It should have been enough. So where did the complex set of 613 Mosaic laws and the sacrificial system come from?

Moses delayed on one of his journeys up the mountain to meet God. When he did not return as quickly as expected, the people quickly reverted to paganism. As a result, an inferior, more complicated system was required. It was a temporary step, which was all that the people could accept at the time.

The church father, Irenaeus, reflects on this in his book *Against Heresies* (4:16). He states that the Ten Commandments have always been written on the hearts of man, and these are still in effect. Unfortunately, over the course of time, they faded into oblivion. The purpose of the Exodus was God's initial attempt to restore friendship with humanity. Irenaeus elaborates by stating that God needs nothing from us; his only requirement is that we love him and walk in his ways. This is not for God's benefit; it is for ours. Because the people were not ready after the Exodus, additional prohibitions became necessary. These were compatible with ancient customs, but they put the people in bondage and replaced the better covenant of liberty.

The Law

> The LORD spoke to Moses, saying: Speak to the Israelites and say to them: If any man's wife goes astray and is unfaithful to him, if a man has had intercourse with her but it is hidden from her husband, so that she is undetected though she has defiled herself, and there is no witness against her since she was not caught in the act; if a spirit of jealousy comes on him, and he is jealous of his wife who has defiled herself; or if a spirit of jealousy comes on him, and he is jealous of his wife, though she has not defiled herself; then the man shall bring his wife to the priest. And he shall bring the offering required for her, one-tenth of an ephah of barley flour. He shall pour no oil on it and put no frankincense on it, for it is a grain offering of jealousy, a grain offering of remembrance, bringing iniquity to remembrance.
>
> Then the priest shall bring her near, and set her before the LORD; the priest shall take holy water in an earthen vessel, and take some of the dust that is on the floor of the tabernacle and put it into the water. The priest shall set the woman before the LORD, dishevel the woman's hair, and place in her hands the grain

offering of remembrance, which is the grain offering of jealousy. In his own hand the priest shall have the water of bitterness that brings the curse. Then the priest shall make her take an oath, saying: "If no man has lain with you, if you have not turned aside to uncleanness while under your husband's authority, be immune to this water of bitterness that brings the curse." But if you have gone astray while under your husband's authority, if you have defiled yourself and some man other than your husband has had intercourse with you,¯let the priest make the woman take the oath of the curse and say to the woman—"may the LORD make you an execration and an oath among your people, when the LORD makes your uterus drop, your womb discharge; now may this water that brings the curse enter your bowels and make your womb discharge, your uterus drop!" And the woman shall say, "Amen. Amen."

Then the priest shall put these curses in writing, and wash them off into the water of bitterness. He shall make the woman drink the water of bitterness that brings the curse, and the water that brings the curse shall enter her and cause bitter pain. The priest shall take the grain offering of jealousy out of the woman's hand, and shall elevate the grain offering before the LORD and bring it to the altar; and the priest shall take a handful of the grain offering, as its memorial portion, and turn it into smoke on the altar, and afterward shall make the woman drink the water. When he has made her drink the water, then, if she has defiled herself and has been unfaithful to her husband, the water that brings the curse shall enter into her and cause bitter pain, and her womb shall discharge, her uterus will drop, and the woman shall become an execration among her people. But if the woman has not defiled herself and is clean, then she shall be immune and be able to conceive children.

This is the law in cases of jealousy, when a wife, while under her husband's authority, goes astray and defiles herself, or when a spirit of jealousy comes on a man and he is jealous of his wife; then he shall set the woman before the LORD, and the priest shall apply this entire law to her. The man shall be free from iniquity, but the woman shall bear her iniquity.[81] (Trial by Ordeal, also known as the bitter waters ceremony, Num. 5:11-31)

When reading this passage, many of us wonder: "Why is this in the Bible?" I will discuss its implications shortly, but first I want to take some time to discuss the Mosaic laws in general. It is easy to focus on the bad parts and then conclude that the whole thing is rotten. I remember a time when I was working on a project to create a shed. In the process I carelessly stepped on a nail. It went through my shoe and into my foot. My world became my foot. It didn't matter that I was in excellent overall health. The foot was the thing.

We can look at the Laws of Moses in this way. Much of it is amazing and unique, especially in the context of the ancient violent culture of the Middle East. The commands to treat strangers fairly, to care for the widow and orphans, and to love your neighbor as yourself were life changing. Arguably, the Ten Commandments, more than anything else ever written, define the foundational prerequisites for a just and successful civilization. We can forget this when we focus on those laws that should never apply in the twenty-first century.

I once heard a Jewish story about a rabbi. One day he visited a member of his congregation, a bank manager. He, of course, was invited in for dinner. During the meal he was asked, "How is it that are we blessed with your presence?" The rabbi answered, "I would like to tell you, but you wouldn't be able to accept my words at this time." The next week the rabbi returned, followed by the same question and the same answer. Then on the third week, the rabbi visited again. This time he was asked emphatically: "Tell me what is on your mind!" The rabbi answered: "A member of the congregation has fallen on hard times. You should forgive his debt." To this came the answer: "I can't do that. I don't have the authority." The rabbi replied: "See, I told you that you wouldn't be able to hear," and he left. In the weeks that followed, the debt was forgiven.

---

[81] This procedure is also known as the Sotah - Trial by Ordeal.

Jesus uses the phrase many times: "Whoever has ears, let them hear." This is the way I view the Old Testament law. We are dealing with an ancient people who were very set in their customs, which were very much like those of the surrounding peoples.

Some of the Old Testament laws are fine, even by today's standards. Some of it was designed to take a step to wean the people away from idolatry. These included things like prohibiting the practice of trimming beards, forbidding wearing clothes with mixed kinds of cloth (Zeph. 1:8), or rules against tattooing the body. By today's standards, they seem petty. Other laws were geared to healthy living. Still more were designed to limit evil practices. Finally, there are laws meant to separate the Jewish people from the surrounding nations. This was because God intended to use Israel to bless the nations. It was through this ancient people group that the messiah of the world was to come.

The laws to restrain evil did not immediately intend to force the good. They went as far as possible, but not so far that the people would reject them. One example of this is the limitation placed on what to do with women captured in a war. Even today, some ideologies encourage the victors to capture women and immediately make them into sex slaves. The Old Testament law puts restrictions on the practice.

Let's consider the law where a rebellious child should be stoned to death. I struggled with this one for a long time. Recently I heard the Jewish explanation. In many parts of the world, even today, honor killing is an accepted practice. A son or daughter who brings shame to a family can be killed without consequence. As strange as that Old Testament law comes across, it prohibits the practice. The child must be brought before a court. The family is not allowed to take matters into their own hands.

There is another law that sets a price for men and women slaves where women were worth less than men. In ancient Israel, slaves could be bought back and freed for a price. As weird as this law sounds, it prohibits someone from setting a price so high that the slave could never be freed. The maximum price is fixed. The law does not address whether slavery is a good or bad thing, but it does put limits on the practice.

Surprisingly enough, Christians are often more dogmatic about the Old Testament laws than are Jews. The laws, as they were written, were never meant to be permanent. Rabbis, sages, and prophets have the authority to apply the laws to the current generation. They can reinterpret and even overturn them. This allowance is not without limits. A prophet cannot say that murder is okay. They can, however, proclaim that thoughts of murder make one guilty already in their heart. A prophet cannot say that adultery is permitted. They can assert that the punishment of stoning be abolished in favor of mercy. They cannot eliminate the need for atonement for sins. They can teach though, that repentance and prayer replace the need for rituals of animal sacrifice. Prophets, like Isaiah and Jeremiah did these kinds of things, as was their right. As we will see shortly, so did Jesus in many places.

Let's now return to the trial by ordeal (stated above). Could this one fit into the category of limiting evil? I suppose that it is possible, but I've not figured out how. A woman must drink some horrible potion. Then everyone wonders if a miscarriage will come about. Supposedly, this would establish a woman's guilt or innocence. Almost an entire chapter in the Torah is dedicated to the ritual.

Before we judge this ancient text, it is wise to self-reflect. I've seen instances on the Dr. Phil show where a husband brings his wife in front of the nation and accuses her of being unfaithful. An embarrassing lie detection test follows, which involves hours of humiliation. Finally, the results are unsealed on public TV. If I had to choose, I'd drink the dirty water.

What is the origin of this ritual? It turns out that there were many instances of trials by ordeal in the ancient world, and this kind of thing continued well into the middle ages. In the Law of Hammurabi, #132, we read: "If the "finger is pointed" at a man's wife about another man, but she is not caught sleeping with the other man, she shall jump into the river for her husband."[82] I suppose that if she doesn't drown, she is innocent. Or perhaps, the onlookers determine whether she floats or not.

The Talmud documents that the Jews abolished the practice basing their ruling on a passage in Hosea. The Talmud, Seder Nashim, Tractate Sotah; Chapter 9 reads:

> When adulterers became numerous, the bitter waters ceased, and Rabban Yochanan ben Zakkai abolished

---

[82] Eleventh Edition of the Encyclopedia Britannica, (1910-1911).

> them [the waters ceremonies], as it is written (Hosea 4:14) "I will not punish your daughters when they commit harlotry, nor your brides when they commit adultery; for they themselves go aside with harlots, and they sacrifice with cult prostitutes; therefore, the people who do not understand shall fall."

The rabbis argue that since men are unfaithful, and go without punishment, their wives will no longer be subject to this trial by ordeal. As I mentioned above, prophets and rabbis have the authority to overturn a Torah command using justification from the writings of a prophet or sage, in this case, Hosea.

Actually, the trial by ordeal ceased to be enforced very early in Jewish history. The ritual requires that the dust be used from the floor of the tabernacle. There is no evidence that the tabernacle even existed after the time of David and Solomon.

Finally, let's suppose that the procedure worked. If the woman is guilty, a miscarriage would occur. This is tantamount to a divine abortion. The baby is the victim. Perhaps God allowed the ritual because it never did work, and before long, the jealous husbands would hesitate to bring such charges against their wives.

The trial by ordeal is not the only example of problematic laws in Torah. Deuteronomy chapter 25 contains another.

> If men get into a fight with one another, and the wife of one intervenes to rescue her husband from the grip of his opponent by reaching out and seizing his genitals, you shall cut off her hand; show no pity. (Deut. 25:11-12)

There are many tortured explanations that attempt to defend this law. Examples include: The poor man lost his progeny, or the passage was not meant to be taken literal, or the word for hand didn't really mean hand. Sorry, these don't cut it for me. Perhaps God allowed it because it never was likely to happen. I seriously doubt that women ran around grabbing testicles when their husbands got into fights. There are parallels to this law in other ancient law codes.[83] Apparently, hand amputation was considered fair compensation for the taboo and shame resulting from the action.

Another especially difficult law comes from Exodus:

> You shall not delay to make offerings from the fullness of your harvest and from the outflow of your presses. The firstborn of your sons you shall give to me. You shall do the same with your oxen and with your sheep: seven days it shall remain with its mother; on the eighth day you shall give it to me. (Exod. 22:29-30)

In this case, Jehovah is claiming the firstborn sons for a blood sacrifice. It is true that in other passages firstborn sons are bought back, but not in this section. The prophet Ezekiel acknowledged that God permitted laws that were not good, but he claims that they were done to get the Israelites to eventually turn away from them and acknowledge Him (Ezek. 20:25-26). Jeremiah went even further. He, declares that God never did command nor think to command child sacrifice (Jer. 7:31) or animal sacrifice in general (Jer. 7:22-23). This proves that there are Old Testament laws that God allowed, but did not favor.

These are a but a few of the examples of questionable Old Testament laws. As a Christian, what am I to make of them? I'm not going to say something like, "That was for the Jews, it doesn't apply to me." They certainly do apply because they are in our bibles; we cannot ignore them. There must be a better way to interpret these laws. How do we deal with passages like these? I believe that Jesus provides the answer.

> Teacher, which commandment in the law is the greatest? He said to him, "**'You shall love the Lord your God with all your heart, and with all your soul, and with all your mind.'** This is the greatest and first commandment. And a second is like it: **'You shall love**

---

[83] Martha T. Roth ed., *Law Collections from Mesopotamia and Asia Minor*, 2d ed., Society of Biblical Literature Writings from the Ancient World Series (Atlanta: Scholars Press, 1997), 156-157.

> **your neighbor as yourself.' On these two commandments hang all the law** and the prophets." (Matt. 22:36-40)

There are two revolutionary parts of Jesus' statement. The first is the phrase, "with all your mind," and the second is "On these two commandments hang all the Law and the Prophets." Jesus is clearly critiquing the Old Testament law. "Use your mind," was not part of the verse in Deuteronomy to which Jesus refers. He is adding context. Don't just assume that all these laws are good; use your mind. Fortunately, Jesus provides the criteria for evaluation. If a law violates one of those two commandments, reject it.

There are many places in the New Testament where Jesus' comments extend or reinterpret Old Testament laws. For example, in Matthew, we read:

> They said to him, "Why then did Moses command us to give a certificate of dismissal and to divorce her?" He said to them, "It was because you were so hardhearted that Moses allowed you to divorce your wives, but from the beginning it was not so." (Matt. 19:7-8)

Interesting! Moses gave them the divorce law, not God. What other laws came from Moses and not God? Consider the following quotes from Jesus:

> Then do you also fail to understand? Do you not see that whatever goes into a person from outside cannot defile, since it enters not the heart but the stomach, and goes out into the sewer?" (Thus, he declared all foods clean.) And he said, "It is what comes out of a person that defiles. For it is from within, from the human heart, that evil intentions come: fornication, theft, murder, adultery, avarice, wickedness, deceit, licentiousness, envy, slander, pride, folly. All these evil things come from within, and they defile a person. (Mark 7:18-23)

And again:

> Again, you have heard that it was said to those of ancient times, 'You shall not swear falsely, but carry out the vows you have made to the Lord.' But I say to you, "Do not swear at all, either by heaven, for it is the throne of God, or by the earth, for it is his footstool, or by Jerusalem, for it is the city of the great King. And do not swear by your head, for you cannot make one hair white or black. Let your word be 'Yes, yes' or 'No, no;' anything more than this comes from the evil one."
>
> You have heard that it was said, 'An eye for an eye and a tooth for a tooth.' But I say to you, do not resist an evildoer. But if anyone strikes you on the right cheek, turn the other also; and if anyone wants to sue you and take your coat, give your cloak as well; and if anyone forces you to go one mile, go also the second mile. Give to everyone who begs from you, and do not refuse anyone who wants to borrow from you. (Matt. 5:33-42)

And again:

> But I say to you, Love your enemies and pray for those who persecute you, so that you may be children of your Father in heaven; for he makes his sun rise on the evil and on the good, and sends rain on the righteous and on the unrighteous. For if you love those who love you, what reward do you have? Do not even the tax collectors do the same? And if you greet only your brothers and sisters, what more are you doing than others? Do not even the Gentiles do the same? Be perfect, therefore, as your heavenly Father is perfect. (Matt. 5:44-48)

Mosaic Laws and Rituals

Even more dramatic is Jesus saying:

> "The sabbath was made for humankind, and not humankind for the sabbath; so, the Son of Man is lord even of the sabbath." (Mark 2:27-28)

In these very few statements, Jesus reinterprets entire chapters of the Law of Moses.

What then do we say about the repeated statements throughout the Torah: "Jehovah spoke to Moses, saying," or "speak to the sons of Israel and say to them"? Doesn't this prove that the commandments are from God? Even if they were, as I argued above, God permitting a law doesn't mean that God favored it. Reality contains many shades of gray; not everything is black and white.

Furthermore, the Torah used expressions such as "The Lord said," as a stamp of authority, not in the modern sense in which we read these texts. Obey Moses because he is God's spokesman, and he said thus. We hear this kind of thing today from TV evangelists. "Touch not the Lord's anointed. And by the way, that's me." I choose to evaluate Old Testament law using the criteria that Jesus gives. If a command violates either love God or love your neighbor then reject it. It is straightforward; it is easy to apply.

One could challenge my analysis by quoting from Matthew's gospel:

> Do not think that I have come to abolish the law or the prophets; I have come not to abolish but to fulfill. For truly I tell you, until heaven and earth pass away, not one letter, not one stroke of a letter, will pass from the law until all is accomplished. Therefore, whoever breaks one of the least of these commandments, and teaches others to do the same, will be called least in the kingdom of heaven; but whoever does them and teaches them will be called great in the kingdom of heaven. (Matt. 5:17-19)

My first question is this: "What does Jesus mean by 'All things accomplished'?" A second is: "Which commandments are included in the phrase 'these commandments'?" If we think carefully, we discover three possibilities. These are: (1) the oral law of the Pharisees, (2) the entirety of the law of Moses, and (3) the Mosaic laws driven by the two greatest commandments, no matter how insignificant they appear to be. From the gospel narratives, it is obvious that Jesus is not referring to the oral law. From my above discussion, I am convinced that Jesus would not want an innocent woman to be humiliated with the trial by ordeal. This eliminates the whole of the law of Moses as a possibility. Only the third option remains.

Even if we wanted to uphold all of the 613 Mosaic laws, we can't. There are laws in the books of Exodus, Leviticus, Numbers, and Deuteronomy that conflict. For example, Exodus tells us that slave owners must release the slaves after seven years, but the owner can keep a male slave's wife and children if the marriage occurred during the enslavement. This law destroys the sacredness of marriage. In contrast, Deuteronomy presents a different version of the law. It commands a master to provide gifts to the slave upon their freedom; not to leave them empty handed. That law says nothing about keeping the family as a possession. It is unlikely that the owners were allowed to break up families.

Let's contrast the Book of Deuteronomy with the Book of Leviticus. Aaron is a central figure in Leviticus. In Deuteronomy, he is mentioned only three times, twice recalling his death (Deut. 10:6, Deut. 32:50) and once recalling God's anger over the incident of forging a golden calf (Deut. 9:20-21). In Leviticus, entire chapters are dedicated to burnt-offerings; in Deuteronomy, they are mentioned only a few times in passing. Leviticus requires that burnt-offerings be sacrificed at the tent of meeting; Deuteronomy indicates no such requirement, but instead anticipates "The place where God will choose." In fact, Deuteronomy instructs the Israelites to sacrifice on an altar of unhewn stones after crossing the Jordan (Deut. 27:6), not at the tent of meeting. Leviticus requires that all of the animals be burnt up; Deuteronomy indicates that the meat can be eaten (Deut. 12:27). Twice in Deuteronomy, Moses directs that nothing should be added or removed from what he commands as he speaks (Deut. 12:26, 4:2). This seems to imply that the commands given in Deuteronomy take precedence over the other books of Torah. It is apparent that in the time between the writing of Leviticus and Deuteronomy, Israel was evolving.

From what I just presented; the Mosaic laws were not meant to be permanent. Yes, in the books of Moses, there are the phrases: "for all generations," or "this is a permanent statute." These do not pertain to any of the commandments that we discussed in this section. It is interesting that the prophets never complained about the people failing to observe those laws that seem crazy. So, the questions I pose are: "Did God approve or did he tolerate the laws? Did he give Moses some leeway to construct them?" In that case, some of the laws would be from Moses, not from God. Would the ancient people have been able to accept laws that went further in the direction of the Good? Probably not.

All told, I'll not defend those laws that are abhorrent. I'll go with Jesus' approach and use my mind to determine if they comply with the two greatest commandments. The Old Testament contains God's true revelation, as well as the people's understanding of that revelation. Jesus' interpretive approach separates these voices.

The Sacrificial System

> You shall lay your hand on the head of the burnt offering, and it shall be acceptable in your behalf as atonement for you. The bull shall be slaughtered before the LORD; and Aaron's sons the priests shall offer the blood, dashing the blood against all sides of the altar that is at the entrance of the tent of meeting. The burnt offering shall be flayed and cut up into its parts. The sons of the priest Aaron shall put fire on the altar and arrange wood on the fire. Aaron's sons the priests shall arrange the parts, with the head and the suet, on the wood that is on the fire on the altar; but its entrails and its legs shall be washed with water. Then the priest shall turn the whole into smoke on the altar as a burnt offering, an offering by fire of pleasing odor to the LORD. (Lev. 1:4-9)

As we consider the sacrificial system and the detailed procedures related to animal sacrifice, it is important to understand the Bible's central message. It is the drama in which God intends to restore his good creation, working through imperfect, sinful people. The Old Testament is the inspired book that points to the true and living Word, that being Jesus. It is told through the lens of an ancient, primitive, violent people, doing the best they could to understand the living God who created the Universe. The Old Testament reflects the Word; it is not itself the Word.

Let me illustrate. Abraham was promised that his descendants would occupy the land of Canaan. Those descendants, freed from Egypt, fully expected this dream to be quickly realized. Unfortunately for them, the dream led to much bloodshed and resulted only in partial victories.

This compelled an explanation. Why? Either God lied to them, he delayed for some reason, or it was their fault. We get mixed answers.

Deuteronomy promised that God would drive out the tribes living in Canaan before them. The picture I get is that they thought they would stroll into the promised land and the inhabitants would simply run away. It was to be easy. But this was not to be. In another place we are then told that the process would be slow. God would drive the Canaanites out, but it would take time. This way there wouldn't be so many wild animals that would put the Israelites in danger (Exod. 24). Then there was a warning. If the Israelites didn't drive the people out, their enemies would be a constant thorn in their side. Make no treaties; peace is not an option. Disobedience means that God would do to the Israelites what he planned to do to the other tribes (Num. 24). In this passage, driving out switched from God's promise to the Israelites' responsibility. Joshua 15 describes how they tried, but the Jebusites were too entrenched. Joshua 17 reports that though God was with Judah, they couldn't win in the valley. Their opponents possessed iron chariots. Then, Joshua 24 puts all this behind, and celebrates the victories they did achieve. He gives credit to God who fulfilled all his promises. Then, in the second chapter of Judges: God becomes angry. He will no longer drive the indigenous tribes away. The Israelites disobeyed; they failed to destroy all the altars to foreign gods. An alternative explanation emerges later, in chapter three. We are told that God left those opposing tribes to determine if the Israelites would remain faithful.

There are mixed voices, which often are difficult to untangle. Sometimes God appears angry; other times he appears longsuffering and merciful. The Book of Judges is a sequence of battles won and battles lost. Times of oppression imply God's disfavor. Then, a charismatic, flawed leader rises and wins, thereby proving God's support. These leaders don't at all seem godly; often they often come across as just the opposite.

Later accounts in Kings and Chronicles contain similar conflicts. The authors of those books add editorial comments. This king is good; that king is bad. Yet, these statements do not seem to correlate with the fate of the country or even the fate of the king. Manasseh was bad, but he ruled for more than fifty years. Saul was bad, but he reigned a long time after Samuel prophesied that David would be his successor. We are told that the future breakup of the kingdom was because Solomon worshipped other gods late in his reign. Other kings were worse, but they didn't experience the same judgment. Bad prophecies were given to the good kings, like Hezekiah and Josiah. Judgment was proclaimed on the good king Jehoshaphat for being friendly with Israel. Rehoboam was told that Israel were kin and not to hurt them. God was present throughout, but not in the ways expected by those recording the events.

I understand that one can come up with scenarios to harmonize these different accounts. This is not the point. It is important to recognize that there are different voices present. One might ask, what was God's role during this time? I believe he had the long view in mind. He was preparing for the fullness of time when he would directly enter history, reveal his true nature, and save humanity from its violent disposition. In the meantime, little by little, he would reveal that which could be heard. To their credit, or more likely because of inspiration, the ancient authors did not attempt to reconcile the conflicting voices. They did not delete or alter what came before. As a result, we get to view a wonderfully complex drama as we travel through history. We live thousands of years later, but we get to read all the accounts and view this drama for ourselves. In this way, the Bible is a unique, living book, one which deserves to be preserved and studied.

With this in mind, let's turn our attention to the *sacrificial system.* Before considering the biblical teachings about this, I think it useful to discuss its origins. In the ancient world, humans sought to answer the same questions that we do in our time. Why am I here? What is my purpose? How did the cosmos originate? People sought to make sense of tragedy as we do. Why was there a drought? Why did that earthquake or flood devastate our village? Why did my son die? These are very natural questions. The ancients did not have access to modern science or modern technology, and even if they did, their cultural framework was very different from ours. In any case, their answer to tragedy was, "The gods were not happy."

It was understandable for our ancestors to believe in many gods, one for the Sun, another for the weather, and so on. It was natural to conceive of powerful beings populating the heavens. So if a bad thing happened, it was either because the gods were fighting with each other or they were mad at us. These gods tended to be understood in our image. They were unpredictable: angry one moment, and beneficent the next. They were warlike, fighting each other for control. They liked our admiration, but when we did something they did not like, they demanded payback.

The sacrificial system is a natural outgrowth of these perceptions. We eat, so the gods eat also. Our civilizations compete; so should the gods. Some of us are stronger than others, so must the gods be like this as well. It makes sense that a tribe, or nation, would like to have the most powerful god on their side. The ancients would proclaim: "My god is stronger than your god, and we'll prove it. We'll attack you, defeat you, enslave/kill your men, capture your women, and take your lands and possessions. Winning proves that we are right."

The issue then becomes: how do we get the *big* god to be on our side? We give him something. What does he want? Worship? Probably. Food? Maybe. Something that we consider valuable? Yes, that will do it. How about the death of our firstborn? That would be the most we could possibly give and it certainly would demonstrate our loyalty. Then the big god will lead us into battle and help us wipe out our enemies.

There is still a problem to consider. What if things don't go our way? There is a famine. The enemy comes in and destroys a city. Some disease plagues us. Two possibilities could explain it: Maybe we have the wrong god, or maybe we displeased our big god in some way. If we have the wrong god, the answer is simple. Switch gods; find one that is bigger. If we got the big god angry, we devise rituals to atone. These inevitably must involve sacrifice on our part, the costlier the better.

Ancient cultures universally utilized sacrificial systems. This makes sense. If the gods want something of value, let's kill it ritualistically. The ancient norm was that there could be no atonement without blood. The descendants of Abraham were no exception.

Sacrificial rituals serve another important purpose; they satisfy humanity's proclivity to scapegoat.[84] From a modern perspective, this is a difficult concept to grasp. Those who consider themselves enlightened and modern generally believe that people are basically good. I've heard Oprah Winfrey say, "If a person knows to do better, they will do better." In other words, it's a matter of education.

Religious systems portray something different. They teach that human beings are flawed. So, which view is correct? According to the psychologist Carl Jung, people think themselves to be better than they actually are. He also says, "People will do anything, no matter how absurd, to avoid facing their own souls." So, let's delve a bit into human proclivities. Conflicts typically emerge when different individuals or groups want the same thing. This might be position, reputation, wealth, land, power, sex, and many other things. Anger and jealousy first rise to the surface among those without. Then, there is the urge to take, either by force or deception, feeling justified in the process. Of course, the ones possessing the thing will retaliate. A conflict follows and if the defeat is complete, the victor records their side of the story. More likely though, the revenge motive kicks in, and this leads to an escalating back-and-forth feedback loop.

Without an escape valve, total destruction is inevitable. Fortunately for us, ancient people found an ingenious solution to maintain order, at least within the group. They devised rituals, which involved blood, a public killing for all to see. These observances accomplished several things. First, the liturgies brought a sense of togetherness to the community. Everyone was "in the same boat." Second, the unity reduced the immediate thirst for violence and conflict. Finally, by directing the simmering conflict onto a scapegoat, the people would temporarily feel cleansed. Kill an animal and atone for the people. The gods are satisfied and the people absolved.

So, ancient peoples formalized various kinds of ritual sacrifices. These served to hold societies together and avoided them from coming apart at the seams. Unfortunately, a sacrificial system is only a partial solution; to be effective, the ceremonies had to be repeated over and over. Since anger gradually builds again, more scapegoats are needed.

---

[84] Refer to René Girard's writings on mimetic theory.

Perhaps this is why the regulations described in the book of Leviticus were necessary for the times.

We no longer practice scapegoat ceremonies in the West. The Christian influence is part of the reason for the shift. It is true that the Eucharist symbolically involves Christ's body and blood. Yet, this is very different. We remember that Jesus was the scapegoat who was violently murdered. We also remember that he was innocent. Most importantly, by partaking in the Eucharist, we identify with him. This means that if we take this sacrament seriously, we will turn away from revenge and replace it by praying for and loving those who seek us harm.

Nevertheless, even without ritual killings, humanity still looks for scapegoats. Human history is laden with wars. The sides of every conflict have reasons and justifications. We lie to ourselves and to each other and ignore the facts that go against our predispositions. The enemy needs to be defeated, sometimes eliminated. Sometimes it is a person. Sometimes it is a group. Sometimes it is another nation.

For much of my life, the political scapegoat was communism. It had to be contained; we had to prevent the Soviet Union from forcing their system throughout the whole world. We were the good guys. Our system emphasizes freedom and democracy, a government by, for, and of the people. Surely God must be on our side. Fortunately, because both sides were afraid to use nuclear weapons, the third world war didn't happen. Then, suddenly and unexpectedly, in 1989, the Soviet Union fell apart. The Berlin wall fell, signifying the end of the communist threat. Humanity breathed a collective sigh of relief. Optimism reigned. It is true that Red China was still a communist nation, but in time, they didn't seem so bad. Today, they are competitors, but not mortal enemies.

The media anticipated and touted *the peace dividend*. Without the communist threat, peace could finally reign and resources could be directed to important causes. Unfortunately, peace never happened. Instead we continue on a cycle: Whenever we get rid of the bad guy, another bad guy comes to the fore. When there is no threat, we turn on each other. More victims need to be sacrificed; we just need to find out who. It could be a political leader, like Obama or Bush. It could be a group like *Black Lives Matter* or the *Tea Party*. It could be a political party, Democrat or Republican. By popular narrative, republicans favor big business, destruction of the environment, and unlimited gun rights. They pursue a war on women and on minorities. Meanwhile the other narrative goes: the democrats push for more government, meaning less freedom. They support unrestricted abortion rights. They are anti-God and pro-regulation.

Following the communist threat, the infighting was on for a while, but then a group of Islamists flew into the World Trade Center on September 11. We united briefly because this outside threat brought us together. We were all Americans again. Signs went up. *We stand together.* Unfortunately, the unity was short-lived. The two-party split became wider and wider, till compromise was impossible. The political primaries didn't help. More extreme voices began to dominate the system. The Republicans became a racist basket of deplorables. The Democrats became anti-patriotic socialists.

Donald Trump gets elected, a perfect scapegoat. If he dies or gets impeached, much of the country will breathe a collective sigh of relief. They'll feel better, but for how long? Only till another scapegoat is needed. The cycle will repeat, and repeat, and repeat. This is the way our systems work, whether they be religious, political, or economic.

We may not engage in ritual killing of animals, but the sacrificial system of scapegoating is alive and well. Violence, revenge, and anger flow freely through all our systems. Tensions rise, war ensues. It starts with words, and then violence follows. Out of violence comes order, at least for a time. Then the cycle repeats. The human species is violent at its core. The religious, economic, political systems contribute their parts to the puzzle.

Scapegoating always requires a victim. There is the one that goes willingly. There is the one who goes with a fight and calls for revenge. In both cases, once dead, the victim does not come back. The one offering the sacrifice has inflicted the most powerful weapon, death. The victim dies and the offeror feels vindicated. The atonement is complete.

In the Old Testament, we read in Kings and Chronicles about the good kings. Three of them were Solomon, Hezekiah, and Josiah. After dedicating the temple, Solomon offered 22,000 oxen and a 120,000 sheep (2 Chron. 7:5). Hezekiah offered a thousand bulls and seven thousand sheep. According to 2 Chronicles 30:24-26, there was no Passover celebration like that since the days of Solomon. Finally, Josiah contributed 33,000 oxen to his passover celebration. The priests offered many more thousands of animals for the event. 2 Chronicles

35:18-19 states that no passover matched this one from the days of Samuel the prophet.

Apparently, the chronicler was quite proud of these things. The more animals they could burn up, the better. These accounts are from Chronicles, the books of the Bible that were written after the first temple was destroyed. These books extol the priestly class, who sought to restore the sacrificial system, and who would preside over it and the nation. The age of kings was over, signifying a great transfer of authority and power. The rule by the priests would continue till AD 70, when the Romans would demolish the second temple.

Did God approve of these massive passover celebrations? I think not. Do we have some evidence? I think we do. Consider the three great sacrificial heroes. Ten tribes were ripped from Solomon's son (1 Kings 11:13). Hezekiah was told that Babylon would plunder the temple and make eunuchs out of his offspring (2 Kings 20:18). The author of Kings reports that Judah would be destroyed, despite Josiah's faithfulness (2 Kings 23:26). Apparently, the sacrifices didn't do much good. All they accomplished was the killing of many innocent animals.

The Old Testament presents a mixed message when it comes to animal sacrifice. Leviticus establishes the system with very detailed instructions concerning the ritual procedures and how they could lead to the forgiveness of sins. The prophets present a different picture, sometimes declaring that God never approved of blood sacrifices in the first place.

When we read the sections of the Bible (i.e. Leviticus) that pertain to the sacrificial system, it is important to understand the context. It is interesting to note that the book of Leviticus does not contain the words for repentance, grace, mercy, or kindness. The people of the time had no concept that they could obtain forgiveness by repenting and appealing to God's mercy for forgiveness. God was perceived as pure, distant, and harsh. So how were they to obtain release from the feelings of guilt that we all have when we do wrong? The answer: A visible, tangible mechanism was necessary. Priests were needed as mediators because the guilty were in an unclean state. As such, they were in a condition of fear and therefore could not directly approach God.

The sacrificial system was imperfect, but it worked well for the people of the time. It did have some positive aspects. For example, it demonstrated the need of reverence towards God. It also distinguished the sacred from the profane. Some things are special and when they are misused, it is to our detriment. These concepts have been largely lost in our generation. This being said, the sacrificial system was never meant to be permanent. Jesus and the prophets reveal a better way to approach God.

Through the years, many times, I picked up the Bible, opened to Genesis and began to read. I fully intended to continue reading every book ending with Revelation. I did succeed a few times, but not many. Genesis and Exodus went quickly, although they have their share of troubling verses. Then comes Leviticus. Immediately, the first chapter describes a burnt offering, where some poor animal is burnt to a crisp, and I start slowing down.

For one thing, the process is quite gruesome. The person bringing the offering puts his hand on the young animal and kills it. Then the priests cut it up and sprinkles the blood in a specifically prescribed manner. Finally, the animal gets burned. There are two things that specifically make me recoil. First, the process is to provide atonement. For what? This chapter doesn't say. Second, God enjoys the smell of the burned-up animal; it is a sweet savor. Ugh. Well, at least this offering is voluntary. I think: "If I were a Jew, I'd skip this one. I would never do it." I keep reading.

The second chapter is the food offering. This is better, and the priests get to eat a meal. I don't mind this one. While it cooks, God also likes this smell. The peace offering comes in chapter three. I think: "Okay an animal dies, but the priests get another meal." The only strange thing here is that God owns the fat. Well, okay, I'm not much for fat anyway. I wonder why God wants the fat.

Then comes chapter four; the burnt offerings return. This time it's a sin offering. The ritual is done to somehow forgive sin. About this time, I've had enough. I'm glad none of this applies anymore. For years, I let it go and continued reading somewhere else, perhaps Psalms, Luke, or even Galatians; someplace in the Bible where God seems to fit the image presented by Jesus.

I don't think I'm alone. I've never heard a pastor do expository teachings through each chapter of Leviticus, verse by verse. Come to think of it, pastors generally skip the Old Testament entirely. I wonder why. I think I know. From our modern cultural context, there is a lot of stuff there that just doesn't sit right.

Unfortunately, I can't let this stand. We must do better than ignoring those portions of our scriptures that make us shiver. What explanations are out there? A common Christian response is to say that the sacrificial system ended with Jesus. Okay, but why was it there in the first place? It points to Christ, the sacrificial lamb. So you mean that God needed to command, for a thousand years, ritual slaughter and burning of animals to successfully point to Jesus? Sorry, I don't buy it. There must be a better answer.

Since animal sacrifice is prescribed by Jewish law, what do the rabbis say? Those from the orthodox sect are anxious to build the third temple and resume the practice. Their attitude is, "The law of Moses commands it; that settles it." The temple institute in Jerusalem is actively preparing the utensils and priestly garments; they are getting ready.

The rabbinic sites comment that ritual killing of animals is more merciful than what we do in the slaughter houses. That answer reminds me of my son coming home with a failing grade and saying, "Todd did even worse." He thought he was okay because his grade was the second worst in the class. I agree that slaughter house procedures which are not humane should be changed. That, however, doesn't justify the ritual slaughter or the waste of meat that goes with it.

It bothers me when Christians join in the effort to rebuild the temple so that the animal sacrifice rituals can restart. The idea is to speed up the fulfillment of end-time prophecies. This way we can get on the rapture highway to heaven before the antichrist arrives. But, how do we know that our end time interpretations are correct? The Jews in the first century were expecting the imminent arrival of a Davidic warrior; instead they got Jesus. More importantly, our job as Christians is to advance God's kingdom on earth, not to get a quick exit to the clouds. Third, and most serious, Christians then become no different than the Iranian mullahs. Those fundamentalist Muslims actively cause strife throughout the Middle East and the world because, they believe, this will usher in their Mahdi. In either case, Christian and Muslim end-time fanatics think they'll be safe while the Jews experience another slaughter, even worse than the Holocaust. Jesus tells us that we can be recognized by our love. How does this fit?

Jews, in each generation, reflect, argue, and reinterpret the law. This practice began with the prophets early on. Consider Jeremiah. He lived in a time when immorality and oppression were rampant. He witnessed huge sacrificial celebrations. Jeremiah, as did all prophets past and present, represented the conscience of the nation. He openly challenged the sacrificial system. The following verses summarize his views, speaking for God:

> Will you steal, murder, commit adultery, swear falsely, make offerings to Baal, and go after other gods that you have not known, and then come and stand before me in this house, which is called by my name, and say, "We are safe!"—only to go on doing all these abominations? Has this house, which is called by my name, become a den of robbers in your sight? You know, I too am watching, says the LORD.
>
> Thus says the LORD of hosts, the God of Israel: Add your burnt offerings to your sacrifices and eat the flesh. For in the day that I brought your ancestors out of the land of Egypt, I did not speak to them or command them concerning burnt offerings and sacrifices. But this command I gave them, "Obey my voice, and I will be your God, and you shall be my people; and walk only in the way that I command you, so that it may be well with you." (Jer. 7:9-11, 21-23)

Jeremiah was indignant over the people's hypocrisy, especially that of the priests who oversaw the practice. Jeremiah then states, surprisingly, that God never commanded sacrifice on the day when the Israelites were delivered from Egypt. These are amazing verses. They apparently disavow much of the Book of Leviticus.

Jewish rabbis debated Jeremiah's verses over the centuries. Maimonides, a twelfth century Jewish sage who is widely admired to this day, discusses the sacrificial system in his book, *Guide to the Perplexed* (3.32). He provides an interesting hypothetical scenario. Suppose a prophet came along and declared that we should not pray, not fast, and not seek help from God in distress. We should only meditate on God's goodness. For the religious, this teaching would be rejected because those things are deeply embedded in their way of being. Similarly, animal sacrifice was embedded into the ancient mind. Maimonides suggested that God's plan from the beginning was to wean his people away from this practice. His goal was always to work within our systems, and eventually show us a better way. Forgiveness requires confession and repentance, which embodies a change in attitude. Unlike the other false gods, the true God does not require blood for atonement. He tolerated the practice for a time.

Maimonides' interpretation fits with the various Old Testament prophets and the Psalms. They don't always seek to abolish the practice outright but emphasize that the attitude of the heart is what counts, not sacrifice. Repentance leads to forgiveness, not the blood of an animal. The fiftieth Psalm is especially strong:

> Hear, O my people, and I will speak, O Israel, I will testify against you. I am God, your God. Not for your sacrifices do I rebuke you; your burnt offerings are continually before me. I will not accept a bull from your house, or goats from your folds. For every wild animal of the forest is mine, the cattle on a thousand hills. I know all the birds of the air, and all that moves in the field is mine. If I were hungry, I would not tell you, for the world and all that is in it is mine. Do I eat the flesh of bulls, or drink the blood of goats? Offer to God a sacrifice of thanksgiving, and pay your vows to the Most High. Call on me in the day of trouble; I will deliver you, and you shall glorify me.
>
> But to the wicked God says: What right have you to recite my statutes, or take my covenant on your lips? For you hate discipline, and you cast my words behind you. You make friends with a thief when you see one, and you keep company with adulterers. You give your mouth free rein for evil, and your tongue frames deceit. You sit and speak against your kin; you slander your own mother's child. These things you have done and I have been silent; you thought that I was one just like yourself. But now I rebuke you, and lay the charge before you. (Ps. 50:7-21)

Until recently, the general opinion of biblical scholars was that the Levitical system was unique, very different, from other surrounding cultures. Recent archaeology reveals something different. In his book, Moshe Weinfeld, demonstrated many similarities, including requiring a priestly class with similar special garments, slaughter procedures, and distinctions between clean and unclean animals.[85] There were a few unique differences. A major one was the prohibition of man-made graven images; in the Levitical system, no one would see who God is until many centuries later, when Jesus revealed what he is like. A second difference was the idea that all the gods of the ancient world were fake; there is only one true God.

In other respects, the sacrificial system was simply status quo, and the prophets and psalmists challenge it in many places. Micah asks: "Will Jehovah be pleased with thousands of rams, with ten thousand rivers of oil? Shall I give my firstborn for my transgression, the fruit of my body for the sin of my soul?" He then answers his own questions, "God requires us to do justice, love mercy, and walk humbly before God."

David comments in Psalm 40, "Sacrifice and offering You did not desire; My ears You have opened; burnt offering and sin offering You have not asked." Hosea in chapter six states, "For I desired mercy and not sacrifice, and the knowledge of God is more than burnt offerings." Jeremiah in chapter 6 tells us, "I desired mercy and not sacrifice, and the knowledge of God more than burnt offerings."

Isaiah is particularly blunt. In chapter 66, he states, "He who kills an ox is as if he killed a man; he who sacrifices a lamb is as if he broke a dog's neck; he who offers an offering is as if he offered swine's blood; he who burns incense is as if he blessed an idol."

Isaiah is at it again in the following dramatic passage.

> Hear the word of the LORD, you rulers of Sodom! Listen to the teaching of our God, you people of Gomorrah! What to me is the multitude of your sacrifices? says the LORD; I have had enough of burnt offerings of rams and the fat of fed beasts; I do not delight in the blood of bulls, or of lambs, or of goats.
>
> When you come to appear before me, who asked this from your hand? Trample my courts no more; bringing offerings is futile; incense is an abomination to me. New moon and sabbath and calling of convocation—I cannot endure solemn assemblies with

---

[85] Moshe Weinfeld, *The Place of Law in the Religion of Ancient Israel.*

iniquity. Your new moons and your appointed festivals my soul hates; they have become a burden to me, I am weary of bearing them. When you stretch out your hands, I will hide my eyes from you; even though you make many prayers, I will not listen; your hands are full of blood. Wash yourselves; make yourselves clean; remove the evil of your doings from before my eyes; cease to do evil, learn to do good; seek justice, rescue the oppressed, defend the orphan, plead for the widow.

Come now, let us argue it out, says the LORD: though your sins are like scarlet, they shall be like snow; though they are red like crimson, they shall become like wool. (Isa. 1:10-18)

The new Testament writer of Hebrews adds his voice to the challenge. He insists that the blood of bulls and goats cannot take away sin. God has no desire for them and takes no pleasure in them. Instead, God seeks the sacrifice of praise and is well-pleased when we do not forget to do good and share (Heb. 10).

The religious leaders in the bible did not like the message of the prophets. Those leaders often were the worst. Isaiah, for example, lived just before the fall of the northern kingdom. He was despised, and when he was found hiding within the hollow of a tree, he was cut in half.[86] This was not at the hand of the Assyrian conquerors; it was by his own people.

Often, the most ardent supporters of the sacrificial system are Christians who see it as part of God's perfect plan, who set it in place in his divine wisdom. They then point to New Testament verses of support. The Book of Hebrews, for example, tells us that almost all things under the law are purified by blood. To this I ask, which law? Ours or God's? The temporary Levitical system required blood, but as I've shown above, God doesn't.

One might ask, doesn't the sacrificial system point to Jesus? Yes, it does. We, and our systems, require blood. When Jesus enters the scene, God says: "You need a sacrifice? Okay, I'll provide the sacrifice. This time, though, it won't be a ram. It will be me."

---

[86] Jerusalem Talmud, Sanhedrin x, Babylonian Talmud, Yevamot 49b, compared to Hebrews 11:37.

There are verses often cited by defenders of the Levitical system. For example, Matthew chapter 3 documents Jesus telling a person cured of leprosy to go to the priest and make an offering. In this case though, its purpose was to be a testimony to the priest. Jesus did not say whether he thought the ritual was good or bad.

A second example appears in Luke chapter two. It describes Mary going to the temple to satisfy the law of purification, which requires a blood sacrifice. A third example describes Paul taking a Nazarite vow, which is completed with a blood sacrifice. Neither of these two accounts say anything about supporting the practice. Mary's purification was simply an event in her life. We have no idea why Paul took the vow. Perhaps it was to avoid trouble when he went to Jerusalem.

Let's now consider a couple of the sacrifices recorded in the Bible before Moses. The first sacrifice in the Bible is early on, the fourth chapter of Genesis. Cain and Abel both presented an offering to God. Abel's was respected, but not Cain's.

Why was Abel's sacrifice accepted and not Cain's? Hebrews 11:4 implies that Abel gave in faith, but Cain's out of obligation. It is interesting that both Abel and Cain assumed that a sacrifice was required to obtain God's favor. Abel gave something more valuable, the death of an animal. Cain only had grain to give. How did they know what God thought? Perhaps Cain inferred God's displeasure because something bad happened to him. Maybe there was a famine. Cain's crops failed, but Abel's flocks prevailed. He became jealous and angry, first cursing his situation, and then blaming God. Finally, he took matters into his own hands and committed murder. In my opinion, this is not the story of an insufficient sacrifice; it is all about the evil that rises up because of envy.

The next account is a familiar one: Abraham's attempt to sacrifice Isaac. Like many people, I have issues with this passage.

The Book of Jasher states that Isaac was boasting to Ishmael. He said, "Even if God needed me to be a sacrifice, I would be willing." If true, Isaac thought that human sacrifice was a valid option. He should have been careful about what he said when boasting. Perhaps Abraham was listening.

In any case, we're told that God tested Abraham by telling him to kill his son. He had no intention of letting Abraham do this. As in many places in the Bible, God makes a statement that invites a response. In my opinion, God was opening the door for Abraham to object. He didn't. My problem is not the request, it is with Abraham. Why didn't Abraham protest? He objected to the destruction of Sodom because his nephew Lot was there. Why not appeal for his son? Would any reasonable father simply get up in the morning and go on his way to provide his son as a burnt offering? Was Abraham so entrenched in a culture of sacrificing firstborns that it seemed normal?

Today, many Christians honor Abraham for this incident. I don't. Some Christians internalize the message that it sends. If Abraham was willing to sacrifice his son and God the Father sacrificed his son, then it is okay for missionaries to abandon their children as part of their calling. If you are a parent, consider when your child was five-years old. Would you send them a thousand miles away to be raised by strangers in another country? This is what happened to my wife and she suffered for it. Child sacrifice is wrong, whether it involves a burnt offering or not.

People say that Abraham had such faith that he knew God would raise Isaac from the dead. The proof text is the verse, "I and the boy will go on to this way and worship, and come again to you." Is that evidence of faith or did Abraham simply avoid revealing to Isaac what he had in mind?

The account continues with Isaac carrying the wood for the sacrifice up the mountain. How bizarre; Isaac was to carry the wood to be used for his own sacrifice. I suppose Abraham, now an old man, was too weak. Why didn't he at least use a donkey?

In Sunday School classes, we see Isaac as a small child. This was not the case. Jewish tradition indicates that Isaac was 37 at the time, and Sarah immediately died of grief when she heard what her husband was doing. Genesis chapter 23 states that Sarah died at age 127 (37 years after Isaac's birth). We know that Isaac was old enough to carry all the wood up the mountain, so the Jewish tradition is plausible. Finally, Abraham returned down the mountain; no Isaac. What happened? Allow me to offer my scenario. It speculates, but it is completely consistent with the text.

Approaching the top of the mountain, Isaac asked, "Hey dad, where is the sacrifice?" He had no idea at this point what his father had in mind. Abraham replied, "Don't worry, God will provide a lamb." Isaac helped to set up the alter, and then Abraham began to tie him up. At first, because he had faith, he fully expected the lamb to show up out of nowhere. He didn't expect that his father would actually try to kill him. But then the knife appeared. Isaac thought: "No way; how can this be happening? Does my father plan to give the inheritance back to Ishmael?" It was time to escape. Isaac struggled. Abraham then heard a voice in his spirit, telling him to stop. During the delay, Isaac managed to get free and depart down the other side of the mountain. Abraham looked over and seeing a ram caught in a thicket, completed the sacrifice. In the end, Abraham returned to his servants alone.

What happened after this? Abraham's life fell apart. God said: "I see that you were willing to sacrifice your only son. You think that I'm like all the other deities; I am not. It is time to eliminate human sacrifice. Nevertheless, I'll still honor my promise to bless you and multiply your offspring."

Abraham went home and found that his wife Sarah died of heartbreak. He already sent Ishmael away and now Isaac was gone too. The next we hear of Isaac is that he is living in the south country. Abraham, a stranger in this land, was alone with all his possessions.

What was he to do? First, he took care of Sarah's burial. Next, he took steps to reconcile with his son. He sent his servant to find Isaac a wife. Apparently, it worked. In Chapter 25 we learn that Isaac returned, loved his new wife, and was comforted after his mom's death.

What is the moral of this story? Abraham was willing to make a burnt offering of his son. God said no, human sacrifice is not allowed. Why did he wait to the last minute to put a stop to it? That was the most effective way to make a point. This incident was the first step in weaning these people away from burnt offering sacrifices. First, don't sacrifice people, then later, stop sacrificing animals. Our God is not bloodthirsty like other deities. Approval and forgiveness require repentance, not the blood of an innocent victim.

The teachings of Jesus conclude this discussion. If Jesus reveals God the Father, then the Father is like Jesus. So, what does Jesus say on the subject? On one occasion, the Pharisees mocked him for associating with sinners. Jesus responded by quoting the prophets, "But go and learn what this is, I will have mercy and not sacrifice. For I have not come to call the righteous, but sinners to repentance." Another time, the Pharisees accused the disciples for picking grain on the Sabbath. Jesus replied, "If you had known what this is, 'I desire mercy and not sacrifice,' you would not have condemned those who are not guilty." In Mark chapter 12, Jesus stated that the great commandment is "more than all offerings and sacrifices." The clincher comes when Jesus overturned the tables of the money changers.

> Then they came to Jerusalem. And he entered the temple and began to drive out those who were selling and those who were buying in the temple, and he overturned the tables of the money changers and the seats of those who sold doves; and he would not allow anyone to carry anything through the temple. He was teaching and saying, "Is it not written, 'My house shall be called a house of prayer for all the nations'? But you have made it a den of robbers." And when the chief priests and the scribes heard it, they kept looking for a way to kill him; for they were afraid of him, because the whole crowd was spellbound by his teaching. And when evening came, Jesus and his disciples went out of the city. (Mark 11:15-19)

Jesus quoted from the same chapter where Jeremiah states that God never commanded animal sacrifice. There are parallels. The time of Jeremiah was just before the destruction of the first temple. The time of Jesus was shortly before the destruction of the second temple. In both cases, the priests were running a big business. They were the one-percent of the day. They abused their power and oppressed the poor. The sacrificial system was a bloody, corrupt mess. More notably, he stated that the temple was meant to be a house of prayer, not as a house of sacrifice as stated in 2 Chronicles 7:12. Jesus was not to be the Davidic warrior, and he was overturning the elitist sacrificial system. This event was crucial; it directly led to his crucifixion.

We can say that Jesus did act and teach against blood sacrifice. We can also say that he never said anything in its support. The sacrificial system was humanity's attempt to limit the violence inherent in its nature. Jesus, I believe, came to show us a different and better way.

According to Hebrews, Jesus' blood speaks better than that of Abel. Abel cried for revenge; Jesus said, "Forgive them, because they don't know what they are doing." He was the ultimate sacrifice, the scapegoat.

Unexpectedly and to the horror of his crucifiers, Jesus did not stay dead. Instead, he was vindicated and rose again. The scapegoat must always remain dead for the principalities and powers of our world to persist. Jesus conquered death, but instead of inflicting pay back, his message is "Peace be with you." This ushers in an entirely new system, the Kingdom of God. As Jesus conquered death, so will all who become citizens of his kingdom. Jesus Messiah is Lord. This is the Christian gospel.

Chapter 9

Biblical Violence

> The god of the Old Testament has got to be the most unpleasant character in all fiction —Richard Dawkins.[87]

Most atheists, in my observation, do not object to the concept of a deist god. This is a god, or intelligence, that orchestrated the creation of the natural order but now is not involved. I've heard Richard Dawkins concede that though he disagrees, a strong argument could be made for such a god. The issue, if I am correct, is whether this intelligence is personal. Does he care about each of us individually? If he is personal, I think most atheists have real problems giving allegiance to the God as presented in the Old Testament. We Christians tend to avoid the difficult passages; atheists do not.

The three major religions that hold to a personal god are Christianity, Judaism, and Islam. The first two consider the Old Testament to be sacred scripture. Muslims respect parts of the Old Testament but believe that it has been corrupted. The Quran is their sacred scripture. Both of these holy books feature much brutality. One could reasonably ask: "Why should I believe in a faith based on a holy book which contains and condones violence and genocide?" This question cuts to the heart of each of these three major faiths. In the face of weak answers, atheism is waiting at the door.

Although I've read the Quran and many of the Hadiths, I don't intend to attack or justify any of the violence described there. I'll keep my comments directed at the Bible. When we objectively read this book, we quickly encounter examples that are offensive from a modern viewpoint. There does seem to be a pattern, though. The difficulties seem to lessen as we move through history. The early books have many examples of divine violence. Through the old prophets, Joshua, Judges, and Samuel, we see wars, genocide, and more wars. The latter prophets are less violent as they reflect on the condition of their culture. You don't see them complaining about failure to obey

---

[87] Richard Dawkins, The God Delusion, 51.

problematic Torah laws such as hand amputation. They tend to speak out for the orphan, the widow, the foreigner. They often predict destruction but don't eagerly await it. They do use very violent imagery in their poetry, and some of the imprecatory prayers in the Psalms are quite violent. All of this reflects the people of the times. But when we get to the New Testament, the violence stops.

Yes, a few of Jesus' statements do seem to promote violence when critics take them out of context. For example: "Do not think that I have come to bring peace on earth. I did not come to send peace, but a sword." But Jesus is not encouraging his followers to fight. *Bring a sword* is an idiom meaning *bring division.* Jesus is predicting that this division would lead to the intense persecution that believers would experience at the hands of the Romans and other empires to follow. It was a prediction that proved to be entirely correct. Eusebius, in *the History of the Christian Church*, graphically describes the horrors of these persecutions.

As a Christian, how should I deal with biblical violence, especially Old Testament violence? It is certainly not a newly discovered problem. Marcion, an early second-century Christian, wanted to throw out the entire Old Testament. He considered God, as presented there, to be a Demiurge. He believed there were two gods. The Demiurge and the one presented by Jesus. Orthodox Christianity eventually excommunicated Marcion, albeit for other reasons. Regardless, orthodoxy does not agree that the God of the Old Testament is different from the God of the New. Why?

Throughout time, people unexpectedly received revelations pertaining to the nature of God and of the Universe. These sometimes were directed to giants of the faith, people like Abraham, Moses, and David. Other times, they come to those whom one wouldn't expect, such as Balaam, Saul, or even various Greek philosophers and modern scientists.

What does one do after receiving a new revelation? Of course, they will recognize that they have received something special. Sometimes they'll take credit, as if it came from their own superior intellect. Other times, they'll be a bit less arrogant. In any case, they'll tell others. Eventually, they or someone else will write it down for posterity. Unfortunately, the written word will undoubtedly be clouded by cultural assumptions and personal biases.

By inspiration, our Bible is a record of God's revelations to us written by many authors over thousands of years. So, how do we understand and apply the truth of these insights to our lives?

According to Mathew, Mark, Luke, and John, we learn that Jesus represents the perfect image of the Father. This is a clue. If we filter the writings through the lens of what we know about Jesus, it is possible to lift the truth of the ancient revelations from the text. The ancient church fathers did this, so it is helpful to highly value their insights and traditions. The Bible is a collection of God's revelations, but only Jesus is the living Word.

Returning to Old Testament violence, the problem is not with God; it is with the ancient people that wrote about that God. They recorded their perceptions as they struggled to understand the revelations they were receiving. Ancient law codes were harsh and quick to prescribe capital punishment. It is understandable that Mosaic law does the same. Note though, that even in the Bible itself, harsh penalties were rarely carried out. Torah scholars indicate that the death penalty is an indication of the seriousness of an offense, but as a rule mercy should prevail.[88]

Warfare was violent in the ancient world. When attacked, people either would run or die. Married women were killed; single women were conscripted as wives. It is important to read the Old Testament in its historical context.

That said, historical context is not a free pass. If these are our sacred scriptures, we need to deal honestly with the violence they contain. I'll first consider the Old Testament violence committed by the Israelites, and not by God. There are many accounts of these in the Old Testament. Instead of going through them one by one, I'll focus on the one that I consider to be the worst. This one appears at the end of the Book of Judges. It provides a glimpse of the state of humanity thousands of years ago. I'll summarize and then give my thoughts.

The Levites were the wealthy and religious priestly class. They were the ones that you would think would have the highest ethical standards. In the time of the Judges, you would be wrong. One of these Levites owned a concubine. In those days, a concubine had the status of a second-class wife. She was often not much more than a sex-slave.

---

[88] Dennis Prager, *The Rational Bible – Exodus,* 290-292, 320, 429, Rabbi Moshe Feinstein, *Igros Moshe, Chosen Mishpat,* (vol. 2), 68.n

The account tells us that this particular concubine was unfaithful, but it doesn't say how. I think the Levite was an abusive jerk, because she escaped and ran back to her father's house. In Old Testament times, running from your husband would be considered unfaithfulness. The Levite followed her, spoke nicely, and persuaded her to return with him. Even today, this is what abusers do. In any case, she didn't have much choice. The father doted all over the Levite. I don't think he wanted the responsibility of caring for his daughter. So they left and began their journey back to Jerusalem. On the way back, they stayed a night in Gibeah, a town controlled by the tribe of Benjamin. The Levite thought Gibeah would be safer than staying in an area controlled by foreigners. When an old man saw that they were travelers, he volunteered to let them stay at his home. This is common courtesy in the Middle East, even to this day. So far, so good.

Then the violence starts. The town's men, being drunk, began beating at the door. The Levite, being afraid, cast his concubine to them. After all, she was just property, a concubine. The town's men raped her repeatedly all night. It was so violent that she died in the morning. As bad as this part of the story is, it doesn't end here. It gets worse.

The Levite cut her body into sections and sent a piece to each Israelite tribe. This led to a genocidal war, almost wiping out the Benjaminite tribe. But the account still doesn't end. More atrocities follow. The Israelites feeling guilty wanted to appease the remaining men from Benjamin by giving them wives. They couldn't provide wives from their own tribes because of a vow they made. The law of Moses commands that you must honor your vows. What were they to do? Ah, an obvious solution emerges. They attacked Jabesh-gilead, a city that didn't participate in the slaughter. They killed the men, their wives, and their children leaving only 400 virgins alive. These were kidnapped and given to the remaining Benjamin men. Problem solved.

This account is most certainly not something that parents would read in the evening to their children. It is simply awful. Why is it in the Bible? I think it is there to illustrate the power of the darkness that overwhelmed the ancient Middle East. This account is bookmarked in Judges with the quote, "In those days there was no king in Israel. Everyone did what was right in his own eyes." It was a time of lawlessness. Apparently, the surrounding peoples were not much different.

There are other accounts of atrocities in the Old Testament. At least none of them are as gruesome as this one. For example, there are times when God "delivers an enemy into their hands." Then, instead of showing compassion, the people perform what today would be considered war crimes. God is not to blame for the wickedness of people who claim to act in his name. God is not to blame when a group yells *God is Great* and runs to battle. This is true even if they win.

There have been innumerable atrocities committed in the name of God over the course of human existence. Just in the last few years we've publicly seen Christians lined up and beheaded. We've seen genocide against the Yazidis, Mandaeans, and Christians in Northern Iraq. All this evil was done in the name of God. Not too many years ago, we saw Rwandan Hutus mass-murder a million Rwandan Tutsis. Most, on both sides, were Christian, some even going to the same churches before the massacre. The tensions between these two people groups were exasperated by Europeans who played one group against the other to gain access to their natural resources. We can't blame this on God. We can't even blame this on religion. We are an extremely violent species.

Suppose we were born in the times of the Israelite judges. Would we have been different? Can we guarantee it? Take anyone today, whether intellectual, sophisticated, atheist, religious, conservative, or progressive, and put them back at that time. This means all of us. Would we be different? We'd like to say yes. But is that true? We'd be wise not to moralize over these ancient texts.

A central human trait is imitation. In a broad sense, we imitate the god we believe in; that god can be religious, secular, or political. When I read war accounts in the Old Testament, I filter it through this lens. Is it God commanding these things, or is it people sick with violence? God, in my opinion, slowly works through the ages to transform our species away from these things. Not by force, but by grace and patience. I hope we are listening. Otherwise, the potential horrors of using our weapons of mass destruction bode far worse than anything these primitive people did.

So much for ancient Israelite violence. In the bible, there is much more to consider. I can classify these into three categories. These are New Testament violence, places where God commands people to kill, and places where God kills.

New Testament violence is the easiest of the three. The last book of the Bible comes to mind first. Note that nothing in the Book of Revelation has literally occurred, though it features lots of violent imagery. It is a cosmic play, a book of symbols that reflects the first-century drama between the Roman Empire, their religious system, and the early Christians. It applies to us, in that empire and secular religion still exist, having the potential and power to oppress should we get too comfortable. In Revelation, Christians do not inflict the violence, and neither does God. Jesus on the white horse is drenched in blood; it is his own blood. He defeats the enemies by the Sword of his Mouth, not by weapons of war.

Admittedly, Revelation is confusing. It is difficult for us thousands of years later to understand the symbolism. Many capitalize on this by writing end time books and composing dramatic movies. What do we make of the dragon, harlot, beasts, seals, trumpets, and vials? It is not possible to come to a reasonable understanding of this book without a detailed first-century background. Fortunately, there are scholars who carefully work through the book in a responsible way. I'll come back to this in a latter chapter.

For now, let's return to instances of violence in the New Testament. Ananias and Sapphira lied about the proceeds of a property they sold. Peter was livid. He angrily confronted Ananias, who immediately fell dead. A short time later, Sapphira met the same fate. The account does not say that God killed them, but those present undoubtedly thought so. I'm sure they were gripped with fear. This event was so noteworthy that it found its way into the book of Acts (Acts 5). We don't know what prompted Peter to confront the couple. Evidently, he found out something about what they were doing and was angry enough to address the situation sternly, loudly, and publicly. We don't know their ages. We don't know their health. All we know, according to the account, is that they dropped dead on the spot.

Sudden death is not an unusual medical event, though two in a row certainly is. Psychological stress tests often involve rapid-fire grillings with harsh reprimands when answers are incorrect. This stress accentuates abnormal heart rhythm, which becomes difficult to control afterwards, sometimes for hours. Stress can easily trigger a sudden death incident. In an article in the Annals of Internal Medicine, G L

Engel discusses examples of sudden death following stressful events such as a major life changes, periods of grief, "voodoo curses," etc.[89]

My wife Viv, recalls a situation when she was very angry at one of our children. She thought of hurting them, but when she realized what she thought, she immediately repented and sought forgiveness. That evening she attended a prayer meeting. One of the men looked at her and said loudly, "You said some evil things to your child this morning."

How did he know? She told no one. She repented. Doesn't that count?

Viv froze. For the entire prayer meeting, she couldn't say anything. She tells me, "It was like being made of ice inside." Later, the man apologized. Viv was still frozen. All she wanted to do was leave, to get out of there as fast as possible. What if she had had a heart condition? I'm glad she didn't.

This is my conclusion: God did not kill Ananias and Sapphira; Peter did.[90] He was like the man in the prayer meeting. He was loud. He was harsh. He assumed that the Holy Spirit was with him. I'm sure the couple already felt guilty. This incident occurred shortly after the first Pentecost. I bet that Peter thought he was hot stuff at this point. If he had been gentle and discussed the situation in private, perhaps the incident wouldn't have occurred. The lesson to us is: don't act in this way. Christians should never publicly ridicule and charge others like Peter did. Harsh words can and do kill people. This comes from a satanic accusatory spirit, not from God.

Another possible New Testament criticism concerns the angel of the Lord spilling Herod's guts after he was hailed as a god (Acts 12). The critic could say: "See, God is still violent in the New Testament." The secular historian, Josephus, presents a detailed version of this same event.

> Now when Agrippa had reigned three years over all Judea, he came to the city Caesarea …There he

---

[89] G.L. Engel, "Psychologic stress, vasodepressor (vasovagal) syncope, and sudden death." *Ann. Intern. Med.* 89 (1978) 403–12.

[90] It is interesting that the 2nd century church father Clement of Alexandria came to the same conclusion (*Stromata,* I:XXIII). He writes: "Peter in the acts is related to have slain by speech only those who appropriated part of the price of a field and lied." (translated in *Anti-Nicene Fathers* Volume 2).

exhibited shows in honor of the emperor…On the second day of the festival, Herod put on a garment made wholly of silver, and of a truly wonderful contexture, and came into the theater early in the morning; at which time the silver of his garment was illuminated by the fresh reflection of the sun's rays upon it. It shone out after a surprising manner, and was so resplendent as to spread a horror over those that looked intently upon him. At that moment, his flatterers cried out…that he was a god; and they added, 'Be thou merciful to us; for although we have hitherto reverenced thee only as a man, yet shall we henceforth own thee as superior to mortal nature.'

Upon this the king did neither rebuke them, nor reject their impious flattery. But as he presently afterward looked up, he saw an owl sitting on a certain rope over his head, and immediately understood that this bird was the messenger of ill tidings, as it had once been the messenger of good tidings to him; and he fell into the deepest sorrow. A severe pain also arose in his belly, and began in a most violent manner. He therefore looked upon his friends, and said, 'I, whom you call a god, am commanded presently to depart this life; while Providence thus reproves the lying words you just now said to me; and I, who was by you called immortal, am immediately to be hurried away by death. But I am bound to accept of what Providence allots, as it pleases God; for we have by no means lived ill, but in a splendid and happy manner.'

After he said this, his pain was become violent. Accordingly he was carried into the palace, and the rumor went abroad that he would certainly die in a little time. But the multitude presently sat in sackcloth, with their wives and children, after the law of their country, and besought God for the king's recovery. All places were also full of mourning and lamentation. Now the king rested in a high chamber, and as he saw them below lying prostrate on the ground, he could not himself forbear weeping. And when he had been quite worn out by the pain in his belly for five days, he departed this life, being in the fifty-fourth year of his age, and in the seventh year of his reign.[91]

This event happened in history. The angel of the Lord, in this case, was an owl, which signifies a bad omen in many cultures. If one is to criticize the New Testament for recording Herod's death, then also criticize Josephus' secular version. Was he already sick? Would he have died anyway? Did God do it? Was God justified? Was some spiritual agent involved? You decide.

Turning to the Old Testament, it is important to understand that this 39-volume library that comes to us contains different and conflicting voices. This includes the voices of the people and the voices of the prophets that reflect on those voices. It is the drama documenting how an extremely violent, primitive people were coming to know their God. Sometimes, many times, they didn't get it right. In this chapter, I intend to interpret the accounts using Jesus' teachings as a guide. If Jesus reveals the Father, then the Father is like Jesus. Therefore, I find it necessary to use Jesus as a filter in order to responsibly address the very reasonable and difficult charges about Old Testament violence.

There are many Old Testament verses of violence that we can consider. It is not my intent here to go through them all. That would be a long book and I've not worked through every instance. Some of them might be the result of evil spiritual forces doing things that are wrongfully attributed to God. We'd have to consider each account individually to arrive at reasonable hypotheses that fit the data. I can say that I didn't cherry-pick the ones that I will address here; I worked through the ones that bothered me the most. In light of this, I am confident that there are rational explanations for the rest.

A man was gathering sticks on the Sabbath, probably because his family was cold. He was caught by some of the people, who took him to Moses to stand trial. Moses didn't immediately react, but he locked the man up. After a time, the Lord told Moses to stone the man to death. So the people brought him outside the camp and did the deed (Num. 15). What happened to the man's family? We don't know.

There is a parallel incident in the New Testament. This account is not in the earliest New Testament manuscripts; some source

---

[91] Flavius Josephus, *Jewish Antiquities*, 19.343-350.

documents place it in different spots within the gospels of John and Luke. Finally, later documents settled on John 8. I believe that the account was legitimate, but not part of the original publication. It took a while for scribes to decide where in the gospels it should go.

In this incident, the Scribes and Pharisees brought Jesus a woman caught in adultery. Apparently, the accusers let the man who participated go free without punishment. They charged, "The law of Moses commands stoning, what do you say?" It was a set up; they were trying to corner Jesus into saying something they could use against him. Jesus responded, "The one who hasn't sinned should cast the first stone." They all walked away, one by one. Finally, Jesus told the woman, "Neither do I condemn you, go and sin no more."

The woman in adultery account is eerily similar to the incident faced by Moses. Let's contrast the two. Suppose he responded like Jesus. Would that have ended the matter? But he didn't. At first, he delayed by locking the man up. When forced to decide. He said, "The Lord said to stone the man."

This tells me a few things. Moses, at first, was reluctant to carry out the stoning. Otherwise, he wouldn't have locked the man up while he pondered what to do. Maybe he hoped that the whole thing would blow over. When it didn't, Moses made a political decision. He didn't want to be charged with hypocrisy should he let the man go. This would violate the law that he recently established.

This account teaches me that verses which declare, "The Lord says" should be carefully examined through the lens of the life of Jesus. When his disciples were working on the Sabbath to pick grain, violating the same law that got the stick gatherer stoned, Jesus said, "The Sabbath was made for man, not man for the Sabbath. So, the Son of Man is lord even of the Sabbath (Mark 2:27-28)."

I do not believe that God favored the stoning. It is true that, according to the Bible, Moses prayed. Perhaps God replied with a question. "What do you think should be done"? Then, because Moses already had formulated a plan, he was not really listening. He believed that God agreed with his predetermined decision. Don't we do this today? People often see God in their own image and not the other way around. When this happens, it is easy to pray for confirmation, not direction. Based on the New Testament clarification provided by Jesus, the man gathering sticks should have been released.

Similar logic can apply to another account initiated by the prophet Samuel:

> Samuel said to Saul: "The LORD sent me to anoint you king over his people Israel; now therefore listen to the words of the LORD. Thus says the LORD of hosts, 'I will punish the Amalekites for what they did in opposing the Israelites when they came up out of Egypt. Now go and attack Amalek, and utterly destroy all that they have; do not spare them, but kill both man and woman, child and infant, ox and sheep, camel and donkey.'" (1 Sam. 15:1-3)

The Amalekites must have been up to something to get under Samuel's skin. He was a prophet, so he had the authority to say, "Thus says the Lord." This being said, as we look at this passage, it doesn't make sense. Did God suddenly remember something that happened four hundred years in the past? Why should the descendants pay for the sins of their ancestors? If the Amalekites were irredeemably evil, why didn't Samuel say that? Why the animals? Why the children?

There are discrepancies in this chapter. Verses 8-9 state that Saul killed all the people, but spared only King Agag and some livestock. Yet, verse 33 implies something different.

> Then Samuel said, "Bring Agag king of the Amalekites here to me." And Agag came to him haltingly. Agag said, "Surely this is the bitterness of death." But Samuel said,
>
> "As your sword has made women childless, so your mother shall be childless among women."
>
> And Samuel hewed Agag in pieces before the LORD in Gilgal. (1 Sam 15:32-33)

Samuel was killing Agag because he left mothers childless in previous battles. But that is exactly what Samuel wanted Saul to do, making Samuel guilty of the same thing. Furthermore, if Agag's mother was to be left childless, doesn't this imply that she was still alive? How could that be possible if Saul already killed all the women?

A short time later, in chapter 27, David is still fighting the Amalekites, so how could Saul have killed them all? There has to be more going on in this chapter than what is apparent from a modern perspective. There are many places in the bible where the word 'all' does not mean 'all' as we understand this word today. Sometimes hyperbole is used that is misinterpreted by a literal reading of a text. Samuel could not have meant the command as we often understand it.

A clue could relate to Samuel's anger. Saul spared the king, perhaps so he could later form an alliance. Saul also allowed his troops to take the loot; that wasn't the point of the battle.

There are other issues with this passage. Saul didn't seem to object to the original command. He could have said, "No, I won't." Many Old Testament commands invite an objection. All too often the objection never comes. Later, after the slaughter, Saul was confronted for sparing the king and some plunder. He didn't say, "It was wrong, and I couldn't do it." Instead, he tried to wiggle out of his problem by offering the remaining animals as blood sacrifices. Saul had no problem mass-killing the Amalekites. He just wanted some goodies for himself and his troops. I consider Saul to be worse than Samuel because he is the one that inflicted the atrocity.

I have another problem with this passage. If God really commanded the murder of people, then there is the potential for him to command it again. One could say, "He doesn't do that anymore." But what if he does? Would we obey? ISIS and radical Islamists kill in this way. They are sure that they are killing in the name of God. It was not very long ago when Christians proclaimed Manifest Destiny while they cleared North America of most of the indigenous population. America was the new Israel, the *City on the Hill*.[92] Jesus addresses this bluntly, "Indeed, the hour is coming when whoever kills you will think he is offering service to God." His statement applies today and in Old Testament times. It applies even when the victims are not believers.

I have one more example to share. The Israelites prayed before exterminating the tribe of Benjamin. Should we attack the tribe of Benjamin (Judg. 20:18). The people wanted God's approval. They wanted God to be on their side. They got their answer. God said, "Sure, go ahead." But then they lost twenty-two thousand men. Did God really say to go ahead? Was it God's perfect will that twenty-two

---

[92] John Winthrop, *City upon the Hill* (1630).

thousand troops should fall in battle? More likely, God was saying: "Your decision is already made up; so do what you are determined to do. I'll not be a part of it."

We should be careful when we interpret verses like "the Lord said," or when "Go and I'll give them into your hands," or "go avenge yourselves." These are the kind of things leaders always say to justify a war. We still do it today. Before invading Iraq, leaders said, "This is a just war; God is with us." Apparently, God was not. We are dealing with its aftermath many years later.

Is there such a thing as a just war? Perhaps. One example might be to restrain a genocide. Is there ever a justification for violence? I think yes, but rarely. There are times evil must be stopped. It is not loving to let a person to continue committing a rape. It is not loving to let a person with an automatic weapon continue to wreak havoc on innocent victims. This being said, many of the wars in the Old Testament did not need to happen. They were a product of the people and the times. They were doing the best they could with the revelation that they were willing to hear.

There are places in the Old Testament where God kills. This raises the question: does he have the right? Suppose that this Universe is nothing but a huge computer animation. Does the system's engineer have the right to shut off the power? I suppose he does. We wouldn't like it, but we'd have nothing to say. Would it be immoral? Considering all the things that humanity has done over its existence, who are we to judge?

God's right to kill is not the best question to ask, however. A more relevant question would be: is pulling the plug consistent with his nature? According to the disciple John, God is love. According to John's gospel, God so loved the world that Jesus entered into our darkness to redeem us individually, our species collectively, and the entire world itself. He demonstrated his love by willingly going to the cross and declaring, "Forgive them for they know not what they do." During an incredibly violent act on the part of empire and religion, Jesus reacted without violence. Perhaps, with this in mind, we have a chance to unravel the areas where God killed people in the Old Testament.

Before considering specific examples of God's violence, it is important to keep in mind that in ancient times, bad things were almost always attributed to God, the gods, the destroyer, or the angel of the

Lord. In my opinion, when God is involved, he tends to act in the most unexpected way. For example, in a battle against the Midianites, God first picked Gideon to lead. He was a man with lots of doubts, the least in his family and from the least of the clans of the tribe of Manasseh. Gideon certainly was a most unlikely choice. Then his army was reduced from many thousands to 300. Finally, the victory was won because the Midianites got confused and began killing each other. As I read the Old Testament, I see a pattern. God either gives fair warning, or he accomplishes his purposes in a very unusual way.

Let's now return to specific examples of violence attributed to God. The first of these occurs when David was transporting the ark of the covenant back to Jerusalem (1 Sam 6). One of the oxen stumbled and Uzziah instinctively grabbed hold of the ark to prevent it from crashing to the ground. He died instantly. The account tells us that God, who was angry, killed him. David naturally became angry and left, leaving the ark with one of the local inhabitants.

As we consider this passage, it is important to first determine what the author was trying to convey. David recently was crowned king. He prevailed in a string of military campaigns. God was with him and he wanted to rejoice and give praise. Everything was going as planned. Suddenly, everything changed. Reality has a way of interfering with our assumptions. The God who David thought he knew did not behave in the way he expected. Rejoicing and praise were replaced with fear and anger. Certainty was gone.

Is this not the way we respond today? TV evangelists promise wealth and prosperity if we have enough faith and obediently send them money. What happens when things don't work out? Chaos arises in our spirit along with fear and anger. We don't control reality. We don't control God.

The author of Second Samuel of course, sought an answer. David put the ark on a cart, which violated one of the Mosaic laws. It specified that the ark must be carried by priests. The author thinks: "Yes, that must be the reason." We today do the same thing. We say things like: "I didn't pray enough," or "I wasn't faithful enough." Once we have a plausible answer, control is reestablished and the crisis is resolved. God again becomes predictable.

Did God strike Uzziah? Of course, like most ancient people, that is what David would think. Apparently, the author of second Samuel thought the same. Even today, many of us blame God when things don't go as we expect. We shout to the heavens with raised fists. But are our presuppositions correct? Suppose Uzziah had a heart attack? Wouldn't David still think that God was to blame? Wouldn't Samuel write the account as it comes to us?

The lesson for us in this chapter is to understand the words of Jesus: "In the world you face persecution. But take courage; I have conquered the world!" Are we willing to maintain our faith even when confronted with the inevitable realization that we are not in control? There are no rituals or magic spells that we can use to guarantee success. All we have is our relationship with God and the promise that he will walk with us through the trials. Yes, we can pray and sometimes amazing answers come. Unfortunately, other times God's will does not match ours. Often, the unexpected occurs.

In ancient times, everything was blamed on the gods. Why would we expect different? In our times, we have more information and more scientific knowledge. Because of this we should be better able to discern the natural from the supernatural. Similarly, many of the plagues in the Bible could have been natural events. Of course, we would expect the people of the time to attribute them to the gods. The same is true for earthquakes, fires, and many other events.

This doesn't explain away all of the places where God killed people. Let's look at a few more examples. One of these is recorded in the first chapter of the second Book of Kings. The King of Israel sent fifty men to arrest the prophet Elijah. Fire came down from heaven and consumed them. This happened a second time. Then the third time, the captain of the guard begged for mercy. Elijah relented and went with him.

The New Testament sheds light on this event in Luke.

> And they went and entered into a village of the Samaritans to make ready for Him. And they did not receive Him, because His face was going toward Jerusalem. And seeing, His disciples James and John said, Lord, do You desire that we command fire to come down from heaven and consume them, even as Elijah did? But he turned and rebuked them and said, you do not know of what spirit you are. For the Son of Man has not come to destroy men's lives, but to save.

> And they went to another village. (Luke 9:54-57 MKJV)
>
> The earliest manuscripts and most translations, including the NRSV, present Jesus rebuking the disciples, but they skip the explanation.

Jesus was not happy with his disciples. They were resorting quickly to violence. In my mind, this passage in Luke causes me to look deeper into the Old Testament account. Is there an alternative explanation? When I read the Elijah verses, I notice that it follows the rule of three, as do lots of jokes. The first time X happens. The second time X happens again. The third time, punch line and we laugh. I see the author using a similar literary device to emphasize the authority that Elijah had as a prophet. As Jesus could have called legions of angels to prevent his crucifixion, Elijah could have called down fire from heaven and prevent his arrest. Based on Jesus' reaction to his disciples' request, I do not believe that fire came down literally from heaven.

Let's now consider the ten plagues of Egypt. Why exactly ten? This is a symbolic number used many times in the Bible, the number of completeness. Why those plagues? It is long known that each plague applies to one of the Egyptian gods. The account, as written, demonstrates that the God of Abraham, Isaac, and Jacob is superior to those other gods. Note the items in the following list:

1. **Water to blood**: Hapi, the god of the Nile
2. **Frogs**: Heket, the frog god of childbirth
3. **Gnats (after striking the dust of the earth)**: Geb, the god of the earth
4. **Flies**: Khepri, the Egyptian god had the head of an insect.
5. **Cattle**: Hathor, with the head of a cow.
6. **Boils and sores**: Isis, Goddess of medicine and wisdom
7. **Hail**: Nut, the goddess of the sky
8. **Locusts**: Seth, the God of storms, disorder, and warfare
9. **Darkness**: Ra, the sun god
10. **Firstborn**: Pharaoh who was worshiped as a god

Let me summarize. Do I believe that Moses existed? Yes. Do I believe that there was significant supernatural activity during the time of the delivery from Egypt? Yes. After a couple centuries of no activity, these sudden and unexpected interventions explain why the Exodus story became central to Judaism for millennia. Do I believe that there was a series of events that increased in intensity that finally persuaded Pharaoh to let the people go? Yes. Do I believe that these events targeted the Egyptian Gods? Yes, the Bible confirms this in Numbers 33:4. Do I believe that God delivered the Israelites from slavery in Egypt? Yes. It is unlikely that a nation would make up a story starting with their being slaves, and then call attention to that lowly beginning throughout their written records. Do I believe they crossed the red sea on dry land? Yes. Exodus 24:16 tells us that a strong east wind blew all night to dry out a temporary land bridge. Did the entire Egyptian army drown? Some did, I wouldn't hazard a guess of how many. Do I believe that God killed "all" of the firstborn of Egypt? No, I believe the word "all" is used as a point of emphasis. During the fifth plague (Exod. 9:6) "all" the cattle died. If this were literally true, then why were livestock present during the following plague of hail (Exod. 9:19), and how could there be firstborn cattle to die in the final plague (Exod. 12:29). They were already dead. How could the Israelites of the time know this even if it were true? I believe God intervened using the minimal amount of force to accomplish his purpose. At each step, a fair warning was given. One might ask: Why use force at all? Perhaps a demonstration of power was required to get the attention of the people of the time.

Another Old Testament account comes from the Book of Second Kings. Jerusalem was surrounded, and The Assyrians were poised to attack. Sennacherib, king of Assyria, mocked the king of Judah, trying to get him to surrender. He boasted that the God of Israel will be as useless as all the other gods that his army previously defeated. But overnight, the angel of the lord struck down one 185,000 Assyrian soldiers.

I have a number of things to say about this passage.

The sudden turn of events in this account reminds me of a more recent encounter. On October 6, 1973, the Syrian, Egyptian, and Jordanian armies unexpectedly attacked Israel on the Yom Kippur holiday. The Israelis were outnumbered by a factor of ten to one, and they were unprepared for battle. During the course of the following few days, they first held off, and then they successfully defeated the invading forces. Many military analysts have studied this unlikely victory in the years that followed; no reasonable explanation has emerged.

There were a number of miraculous events recorded during this war that I could recount, but I'll summarize the one that is similar to the ancient Assyrian attack described above. On the first day of the Yom Kippur war, the Syrian army quickly advanced into the Golan Heights with 1,400 tanks. They were near a mountain ridge by the Valley of Tears overlooking the largest Israeli cities. The opposing force, commanded by Avigdor Kahalani, only had about a dozen tanks available. The Syrians were poised to eliminate the state of Israel. Suddenly, they stopped. After the war, Israeli security officers questioned a Syrian commanding officer. They asked, "Why did you stop?" He replied that he saw a long row of white angels on the mountain line and a white hand motioning for him to stop. So he did.[93] What would have happened if he had not?

In the Old Testament account, apparently, Sennacherib did not stop. Assyrian records give their account of trapping Hezekiah, the Israeli king, like a bird in a cage, yet Sennacherib returned to Assyria in defeat and died not long after.

Next, let's look at the 185,000 who, according to the text, were struck down. How many Assyrians were there? Old Testament writers played around with numbers in ways that we no longer fully understand. For example, the first census after the Exodus records over 600,000 men of fighting age. Is this literal? I doubt it. The book of Numbers tells us that there were 22,273 firstborn males in Israel one month old and older. With more than 600,000 fighting age men, each family would have to average more than thirty male children, which is unrealistic. Scholars propose various solutions to the dilemma,[94] but their hypotheses cannot be proven. Perhaps the author did something simple, like multiplying all the census numbers by 10, the biblical number for completeness and perfection. In any case, it is odd that the count of Assyrians is an even number of thousands. Would the Israelis really count of all the dead bodies?

---

[93] "Yom Kippur War Miracle," https://www.nehemiaswall.com/yom-kippur-war-miracle Accessed March 28, 2018.

[94] Colin J. Humphries, "The Number of People in the Exodus from Egypt: Decoding Mathematically the Very Large Numbers in Numbers I and XXVI", Cambridge University.

God strikes violently several times in the book of Numbers. The rebellion of Korah is one of these. The people were frustrated with Moses because he did not fulfill his promise to lead the people to a better future. They wanted power to be shared. Because of this, Korah and two other leaders confronted Moses. They plotted an insurrection, recruiting 250 other tribal leaders to join the rebellion. The account tells us that the earth opened and swallowed the three men along with their wives and children into Sheol alive. Fire devoured the 250 involved in the insurrection. A plague finished off those who were still complaining that Moses killed their countrymen.

A traditional explanation for Korah's rebellion is that God's entire plan of redemption was in jeopardy. If these men were allowed to continue, Israel would never have become a nation and the advent of Jesus would not have been possible. In this case, the violence was not out of anger or wrath, but necessary to move the plan forward.

Another possibility occurred to me as I considered Paul's reference to the event in First Corinthians 10:10. He says that the destroyer killed the murmurers, not God. Who was the destroyer? When we read biblical passages containing the word, *destroyer*, or the phrase, *angel of the Lord*, we generally assume that the author is referring to a supernatural agent. This is not always true. The destroyer sometimes refers to a nation (Babylon[95]) or even a person (Samson[96]).

Could Moses and his supporters possibly have been the destroyer? Consider the following scenario. There was an insurrection and it was bloody. It started when Moses and Aaron killed the leaders of the rebellion. This triggered a fight, which resulted in the death of 250 men. The congregation became angry, charging Moses with the killings,[97] and this caused the insurrection to expand. Those supporting Moses and Aaron proceeded to squash the rebellion with more killing. Out of violence came order. The earthquake, fire, and plague, in this case, are metaphors. There are many places in the Bible where these words are used as such. This scenario is possible, is it not?

In the poetry written by the prophets, God directly takes credit for many disasters, though he always gives fair warning. As I think about these examples, it makes sense. I believe that God restrains human evil

---

[95] Jer. 25:9, Jer. 6:26.
[96] Judg. 16:24.
[97] Num. 16:41.

in more cases than we know, yet in some cases he lifts his restraint by choosing not to intervene. At these times, God is responsible because he could have prevented the thing from occurring. For example, in Isaiah 5, he signals to the Babylonians to come and destroy Israel. What kind of signal? He just lifts his restraint and lets them do what they want to do anyway. There is no guarantee that God will always act to restrain humanity from doing its worst. I believe the *Day of the Lord* is when this happens. He lets us directly face the consequences that have been building up, sometimes for centuries.

The Old Testament books, are largely unchanged since the time of the Dead Sea scrolls. I would propose that the current form of most biblical texts date to the Babylonian captivity, some six centuries earlier. Before that, I believe that the texts fluctuated. For example, Exodus 22:29-30 calls for human sacrifice. There are other verses instructing the Israelites to redeem their sons to avoid the practice. Were those verses added later? Maybe. Hilkiah, during the reign of Josiah, discovered a scroll apparently gathering dust (2 Kings 22:8). That discovery led to a revival. Many scholars believe that the scroll they found was the Book of Deuteronomy. The vocabulary and style of the writing differ significantly from the other four books of Torah and is similar to the books ascribed to Jeremiah. I don't take a position on this, but it is something worth considering. This has no impact on whether the Old Testament is inspired. If true, however, it does require us to carefully study the texts to discern the accurate contexts.

As a Christian, I am free to apply what I know of Jesus to evaluate Old Testament texts. This enables me to discover scenarios to potentially explain what took place. The Old Testament is important because it points to Jesus, and gives context to the New Testament, not because it is word-for-word accurate.

Chapter 10

The Angry God

> If you believe that God is good and that he loves you without regard to whom you are or what you do, you will worship Him wholeheartedly. You will praise him with thanksgiving. If you believe he is angry against you, you will come to him with fear and trying to appease his anger. And you don't know when His anger will be over. Such a god keeps you in a perpetual psychological anguish. That is the typical kind of god we usually worship. That is the typical god approved by authority.[98] —Bangambiki Habyarimana

How do we perceive the God of the Bible? Is he easily angered? Does this anger keep us in perpetual psychological anguish? Or does God truly love us unconditionally? The Old Testament is not always clear. This is understandable. The authors were trying to understand the true nature of the God of Abraham, Isaac, and Jacob. Early writers perceived him to be like the other deities, but much more powerful. As such, he required sacrifices from the people to atone for their shortcomings. They thought he would lead them into battle and fight with them to bring victories. If they fell short of his expectations, they expected wrath and anger. This perception describes a god who ordered genocide, inflicted plagues for minor offences, and brought destruction when the people grumbled.

Over time, the Israelites more and more perceived God to be longsuffering, merciful, slow to anger, one who did not take pleasure over the death of the wicked. God was willing to work with the people as they developed, weaning them, little by little, away from their misconceptions.

In New Testament times, people wrestle with these conflicting presentations. Jonathan Edwards and preachers in the early days of America perceived an angry god who was ready to judge.

---

[98] Bangambiki Habyarimana, *Pearls of Eternity*

> The bow of God's wrath is bent, and the arrow made ready on the string, and justice bends the arrow at your heart, and strains the bow, and it is nothing but the mere pleasure of God, and that of an angry God, without any promise or obligation at all, that keeps the arrow one moment from being made drunk with your blood.[99] — Jonathan Edwards

Sometimes New Testament believers imitated this angry god, and this led to atrocities including conquests, inquisitions, and the like. Other times, believers imitate the merciful God and successfully reflect his image to the world.

Most careful readers of the Old Testament understand the tensions that are present. It is interesting how the ancient texts invite us into these tensions as we attempt to understand the context. This is the genius of the Old Testament. Throughout history, readers debated, as the prophets received further revelations. However, it took Jesus to settle the issue. It is he who reveals what God, the Father is really like. John 5:17, for example, states "I tell you, the Son can do nothing on his own, but only what he sees the Father doing; for whatever the Father does, the Son does likewise." This verse and others like it teach us to filter the ancient texts through the life, death, and resurrection of Jesus. Any Old Testament account that conflicts with these revelations reflect an incomplete image of the Father held by ancient authors. A full revelation required God's direct incarnation into the world. In this way the Old Testament points to Jesus. We don't discard the ancient texts. Instead, we filter them to experience the entire drama of redemption.

Wrath

> It is hardly to be believed how spiritual reflections when mixed with a little physics can hold people's attention and give them a livelier idea of God than do the often-ill-applied examples of his wrath. —Georg Christoph Lichtenberg

---

[99] Jonathan Edwards, "Sinners in the Hands of an Angry God"

In the Bible, God's wrath and anger show up over a hundred times. What are we to make of this? Let's consider a couple of examples.

> On the way, at a place where they spent the night, the LORD met him and tried to kill him. But Zipporah took a flint and cut off her son's foreskin, and touched Moses' feet with it, and said, "Truly you are a bridegroom of blood to me!" (Exod. 4:24-25)

The sin? Moses' son was not circumcised. But then forty years went by in the wilderness and no one was circumcised. God didn't seem to be disturbed by that. The next mass circumcision is described in Joshua 5:3 as the Israelites were entering the promised land.

Like many biblical narratives, we lack details. In this case, an incident that transpired over days or weeks is reduced to a couple sentences. Here we are more than 3000 years later living in a very different culture trying to hermeneutically fill in the blanks. How do we do this? Consider the following possibility.

Moses and Zipporah were arguing. One of them thought that circumcision was unnecessary. The fight escalated. Finally, Zipporah and the children left, returning to her father's home. The family would not reunite until much later in the wilderness (Ex 18:1-5).

During the fight, God intervened saying: "Circumcision is the sign of my covenant with the children of Israel. It certainly is important." He didn't answer with words though. Instead, he dramatically got their attention by allowing Moses to become seriously ill, even to the point of death. What did Zipporah think? "God is actually going to kill him. He really is going to do it!" So, it all comes down to perception. God never had the intention of killing Moses. His anger was not the issue; the importance of preserving the Abrahamic covenant was.

A second example occurs shortly after God delivers his people from Egypt when they worship a golden calf. The dialog between God and Moses that follows is very Jewish-like and contains a tinge of humor. God first disavows everything that came before: "Go down at once! **YOUR** people, whom **YOU** brought up out of the land of Egypt, have acted perversely (Exod. 32:7)." Apparently, Moses, not God, is now the one who delivered them. They are Moses' people, not God's. Next God threatens to entirely wipe out the people and start over with Moses.

> The LORD said to Moses, "I have seen this people, how stiff-necked they are. Now let me alone, so that my wrath may burn hot against them and I may consume them; and of you I will make a great nation." (Exod. 32:9-10)

This statement invites, expects, and even seeks, an objection. Moses does indeed do just this. Note his response:

> O LORD, why does your wrath burn hot against your people, whom you brought out of the land of Egypt with great power and with a mighty hand? Why should the Egyptians say, 'It was with evil intent that he brought them out to kill them in the mountains, and to consume them from the face of the earth' (Exod. 32:11-12)?

So, God relents, but he had no intention of carrying out the threat. This conversational dialogue illustrates how he sometimes communicates with us at our level, in a very humanlike manner. I find it amazing that the creator of the Universe would do this.

There is a deeper question here, though. How do we describe the emotions of the eternal God? Would he even have emotions? A rough example would be to try to project a three-dimensional view of the ocean onto a photograph. I remember doing this once. I was by the ocean in Northern California and snapped lots of pictures. The scenery was amazing. This was before the days of cell phones. I was very disappointed when I saw the developed prints. They did not come close to capturing the experience. It didn't capture the wind, the warmth of the Sun, the motion of the waves, and the feeling of the day. Essential information was lost. What if we further projected that scene onto a line? Then all we would have are shades of colors. We couldn't even discern what the original picture was about. Every reduction of dimension loses information.

Psychologists uses the term, "projection," to describe ink-blot tests. People look at random blots and then describe their perceptions. If a person sees bombs, bullets, and explosions, a therapist might conclude that something is amiss. There are times when we are experiencing a certain emotion, so we assume others are feeling the same way. If we lie, then we think others do also. We might project our negative emotions onto someone else. We feel isolated, then we think that others don't like us. Our perspectives can easily cloud our outlook.

The biblical authors had a typical Middle Eastern frame of reference. Their perception of nature and the gods that controlled it was scary. They observed famines, earthquakes, floods, lightning strikes, and fires. Of course, they attributed these things to the wrath of the gods. The ancient Israelites would think that their new God Jehovah would act in similar ways. Why would they think otherwise? It is the way that ancient deities behaved. But were they correct?

Sometimes things attributed to God could be entirely incorrect. Consider the well-known story of Sodom and Gomorrah.

> All its soil burned out by sulfur and salt, nothing planted, nothing sprouting, unable to support any vegetation, like the destruction of Sodom and Gomorrah, Admah and Zeboiim, which the LORD destroyed in his fierce anger. (Deut. 29:23)

Could this destruction have been a natural event? Josephus tells us that smoking tar pits surrounded the Dead Sea even in Roman times.[100] He describes the destruction as a divine fire caused by lightning. So, perhaps a lightning strike caused the oil and tar near the surface to catch fire. A meteor strike could also have ignited the pitch. In this case, God's visit with Abraham was out of mercy, not anger. Yahweh certainly didn't appear angry while he spoke with Abraham. In fact, he was inviting Abraham to appeal for the city, to intercede. Still, God was indirectly responsible for the following destruction. He let the thing happen and was not shy about taking credit. There are times when he intervenes to prevent a disaster; there are times when he does not. Should we, thousands of years later, assume that ancient perceptions were accurate? Our frame of reference is not the same. We should take this into account when we interpret the emotional words ascribed to God.

Anger is a secondary emotional response to a real, felt, or imagined grievance. In psychological terms, what causes anger and wrath? There are many reasons, but several quickly come to mind. People get

---

[100] Josephus, *Wars of the Jews* 4.8.4.

angry when they feel inferior or diminished in the presence of others. Their self-image is threatened. I doubt that God ever feels that his honor is in question. It seems to me that God was willing to work with the Israelites even though they presented him in an extremely unflattering way. Yet he didn't give up on them. We could say that he became sin for them.

We can get angry when we feel guilt. A man gets fired for coming to work late. By the time he gets home, he is seething. He is angry at himself. The anger is at the boiling point; it has to be released. But at who? At whoever confronts him. When his wife finds out, he explodes. I'm sure that God doesn't experience this kind of anger. If his ways are perfect, there is nothing to be guilty about.

People get angry when things don't go as planned. The water heater breaks and there is no money to fix it. A person comes home tired and discovers that a neighbor is complaining about some garbage that blew on their lawn. The list goes on. Do these kinds of things apply to God? Isn't God sovereign? Didn't he know that humanity would turn away from the beginning? Didn't he have a plan all along? Is his plan a backup, because the first one failed? Or was the current plan in place from the beginning? It seems to me that the above causes of anger and wrath don't fit when applied to God.

A final example occurs when we witness a situation that offends our sense of morality. For example, suppose we see a person abusing a child. Of course, most of us would react in anger, even wrath. The question to ask is: To where is the anger directed? Is it to the perpetrator, to the action, or to the condition that enabled the offender to behave in such a way? As humans, it is difficult to separate these things. Likely, we would direct our anger to the perpetrator. He or she is the one who is guilty. But what if the abuser is our child? Then the situation becomes more complicated. We are still angry, but now our attention shifts to the action and the reason for it. We might ask: "Why would you do this?" Our heart's desire is restoration, to set things right. Our response would focus on getting our child to come to grips with what they did, make amends, and repent. So when we sin, where is God's anger or wrath directed? What is his heart's desire, and what is the focus of his response? These are questions worth considering.

For Christians, Jesus is the full revelation of the Father. He tells us that he and the Father are one. He told Phillip that when this disciple saw him, he saw the Father. This gives us a frame of reference. It helps us reinterpret the words used that portray God as wrathful and angry.

I believe that God does have emotions, but the only way I have a chance to understand them is by observing Jesus. Jesus uses the word, wrath, once in the gospels. In Luke 21:23, he describes a time coming when believers should flee to the mountains. He describes that day as one of wrath inflicted on the people. It is interesting that this wrath does not originate with God. It comes from the Romans. It comes from empire. It is what empires do when they are threatened. They rule by force. One could say that God lifted his hand of protection and allowed it. Still, God was not the source. This prophecy was fulfilled in AD 70 when the temple was destroyed, and Jerusalem was sacked. Jesus is telling his followers, don't fight. Don't participate. Get out of there as fast as you can.

What example did Jesus present during his life? He always identified with the weak, the sinners, the downtrodden without any trace of wrath. He was angry at times, but this was directed towards those who oppress. Even here, his intent was to get them to repent. The Sermon on the Mount blesses the poor in spirit, those that mourn, the meek, the poor, the peacemakers, and those that show mercy. He gives voice to the downtrodden. On the cross, he willingly becomes the victim. Instead of conquering evil by force, he forgives and turns evil back on itself. His kingdom and his victory come through his death, confirmed by his resurrection.

This leaves us with the question, how do we interpret the *wrath* verses? Many recent scholars perceive God's wrath and love to be the same thing. Wrath is not opposite to love, indifference is, and God is not indifferent. When we are running and turning away, it is the fire of his love. This fire aims at the sin and its power over us. God will not allow anything that is harmful to our spirit to remain. It will burn those things away, and this burning can be a painful, but necessary process. For example, a hidden evil could be exposed in a most unusual way for all to see. An unexplainable set of coincidences might prevent a success that would lead a person in a bad direction. This kind of intervention could apply to individuals, nations, or to the entire species. The purpose is to provoke repentance, but not force it. God's heart's desire is to witness a turning back towards goodness. His actions are restorative, not punitive. God's wrath is for us; it is not against us. It is up to us to willingly walk towards the light and not scurry away. The intensity of God's light can easily harden the heart of a person determined to rebel, and this causes unnecessary pain. In this case judgement is necessary. It is the only way to set things right.

Hell

I don't think any discussion of hell is appropriate without first considering the Holocaust of World War II. Otherwise, it is easy to ignore the impact to those that we think are destined for that place. This is a real stumbling block to those outside the faith.

The Frank family were German citizens, and the father Otto served honorably in World War I. He was well-aware of the rising anti-Semitism, and so fled Germany in 1933 as the Nazis were rising to power. He applied for visas to emigrate to the United States in 1938 and again in 1941, but both times he was refused. As a result, with the help of Miep Gies, his family went into hiding, hoping to wait out the war. During the next few years his teen-age daughter Anne kept a diary. The following is a quote:

> Who has inflicted this upon us? Who has made us Jews different from all other people? Who has allowed us to suffer so terribly up till now? It is God who has made us as we are, but it will be God, too, who will raise us up again. If we bear all this suffering and if there are still Jews left, when it is over, then Jews, instead of being doomed, will be held up as an example. Who knows, it might even be our religion from which the world and all peoples learn good, and for that reason and that reason alone do we have to suffer now. We can never become just Netherlanders, or just English, or representatives of any country for that matter; we will always remain Jews, but we want to, too.[101] — Anne Frank

The Frank family almost survived. But late in 1944, likely through an informant, they were found and transferred to German prison camps.

---

[101] Ann Frank, *Diary of Ann Frank*, (4/11/1944).

Within a few months, Otto's wife died of starvation. Anne's former friends Hanneli Goslar and Nanette Blitz, had a brief conversation with her through a prison camp fence. Anne was bald and sickly, losing hope and wanting to die. She and her sister expired from typhus within the next month.

From ancient times, people speculated about what happens after death. Atheists claim that when the body dies, the lights go out and consciousness ceases. Christians reject this view. Many Christians are convinced that those who don't accept the risen Christ as savior are destined to eternal torment.

The Frank family living in Christian Europe, undoubtedly heard about Jesus. In light of their experience, are they without hope? Is this just? How can a Christian not wrestle with this issue?

The Bible is clear about some things and vague about others. Most Christians believe the following. Heaven, God's realm, is a real but temporary resting place for believers while they await the final restoration of all things. Eventually, they will resurrect with new incorruptible, physical bodies to live and prosper on the new earth. Heaven and earth will merge in this new reality and God's kingdom will reign. Everything will be made new. What is the nature of heaven? Other than knowing that it is a place of peace and rest, we don't know.

What about the others, those that don't go to heaven? For this there are many speculations. Universalists believe that the afterlife will be a period of refinement. Eventually, everyone will yield to God's irresistible love. Some envision a purgatory, a temporary period of suffering where people will have to face the wrong things they did in life. Others believe in hell, the place where souls suffer forever in torment. Christians understand that Jesus is Judge. He will be fair. He will not force anyone to join his new creation if they refuse.

As I stated above, the concept of hell, the place of eternal torture, is one of the biggest stumbling blocks to faith. It depicts an angry, wrathful god. We very likely would fear that god, but would we love him? That is another question. We might try to be good, generous, and fair, but would this be good enough? If proclaiming our belief in Jesus would save us, sure, we'd do it. We would proclaim the magic words and convince ourselves and the world that we believe. We might even stand firm in the face of mockery. But would our belief be one of the heart or would it be only in our head? If only in our head, we'd be destined for the fiery furnace anyway. Scary thought, isn't it?

The Angry God

How can a God of love sentence people to an eternal oven? If the penalty for sin is death, how does that translate to eternal torture? Yes, there are those who oppress, seek power, and treat others as objects to satisfy their own desires. Judgment for these is understandable. What kind of judgment should they face? Who decides? Fortunately, I'm not God, so I don't need to wrestle with these questions. Yet most of us judge others every day. A central message of the New Testament is: Judge not so you won't be judged by the same standards. It is hard to live by that rule, isn't it?

In the American colonial period, there were the great revivalists. They preached fire and brimstone messages. Turn to God or a horrible eternity awaits you. Let's imagine that we are back at that time. Consider living in the late-nineteenth century, somewhere in the western United States. Life is hard and there is not much recreation for a single young person. Perhaps they could shoot the tops off bottles or visit the local saloon on payday.

In comes a traveling preacher who sets up his tent. The tabernacle is put in place and gospel literature is readied for distribution. Out of curiosity, most of the town comes to listen. It is a real event. The sermon is a Charles Spurgeon message titled "Heaven and Hell." The preacher first tells the good news, and while doing so makes a serious attempt to connect with the hard-working audience:

> Many shall come from the east and west, and shall sit down with Abraham, and Isaac, and Jacob, in the kingdom of heaven. I like that text, because it tells me what heaven is, and gives me a beautiful picture of it. It says it is a place where I shall sit down with Abraham, and Isaac, and Jacob. O what a sweet thought that is for the working man! He often wipes the hot sweat from his face, and he wonders whether there is a land where he shall have to toil no longer. He scarcely ever eats a mouthful of bread that is not moistened with the sweat of his brow. Often, he comes home weary, and flings himself upon his couch, perhaps too tired to sleep. He says, "Oh! Is there no land where I can rest? Is there no place where I can sit, and for once let these weary limbs be still? Is there no land where I can be quiet?" Yes, thou son of toil and

> labor, "There is a happy land far, far away" where toil and labor are unknown.
>
> Beyond yon blue welkin there is a city fair and bright, its walls are jasper, and its light is brighter than the Sun. There "the weary are at rest, and the wicked cease from troubling." Immortal spirits are yonder, who never wipe sweat from their brow, for "they sow not, neither do they reap;" they have not to toil and labor.
>
> There, on a green and flowery mount, their weary souls shall sit; and with transporting joys recount the labors of their feet. To my mind, one of the best views of heaven is that *it is a land of rest*—especially to the working man.[102]

The audience listens intently. The vision of a land of rest sounds appealing, but many are confused about the jasper city, and why such a place is a good thing. The preacher desperately wants to win converts; the eternal fate of those listeners depends on him. He transitions to the second part of the sermon. As he continues, the goal is not to appeal to reason and logic; that would take too long and likely be ineffective. The appeal must be to the emotions. It is time to scare the hell out of those present.

> The second part of my text is heart-breaking. I could preach with great delight to myself from the first part; but here is a dreary task to my soul, because there are gloomy words here. But, as I have told you, what is written in the Bible must be preached, whether it be gloomy or cheerful. There are some ministers who never mention anything about hell. I heard of a minister who once said to his congregation, "If you do not love the Lord Jesus Christ, you will be sent to that place which it is not polite to mention."—But, in hell, there is no hope. They have not even the hope of

---

[102] C. H. Spurgeon, Sermon (No. 39-40), Tuesday Evening, September 4, 1855, In a field, King Edward's Road, Hackney,
http://www.spurgeon.org/index/cindex.htm Accessed 9/25/09.

> dying—the hope of being annihilated. They are forever—forever—forever—lost! On every chain in hell, there is written "forever." In the fires, there blaze out the words, "forever." Up above their heads, they read "forever." Their eyes are galled, and their hearts are pained with the thought that it is "forever." Oh! if I could tell you to—night that hell would one day be burned out, and that those who were lost might be saved, there would be a jubilee in hell at the very thought of it. But it cannot be—it is *"forever"* they are "cast into utter darkness."

As the sermon ends, many quickly hustle forward to make their commitment. The tent meetings continue for a week or two and there are many baptisms, but interest inevitably begins to wane. The preacher counts his donations and moves onto another town. Some time passes, and the zeal fades. Life goes back to normal and the people live as if the preacher never came. It becomes a distant memory.

But fear not, another preacher comes to town with another of Spurgeon's sermons. This one is titled, "The Resurrection of the Dead." This preacher appears disappointed and somewhat angry because the town folk do not show proper Christian behavior, so he gets right to the point.

> Did our Savior mean fictions when he said he would cast body and soul into hell? What should there be a pit for if there were no bodies? Why fire, why chains, if there were to be no bodies? Can fire touch the soul? Can pits shut in spirits? Can chains fetter souls? No; pits and fire and chains are for bodies, and bodies shall be there.
>
> You will sleep in the dust a little while. When you die, your soul will be tormented alone—that will be a hell for it—but at the day of judgment your body will join thy soul, and then you will have twin hells, body and soul shall be together, each brim full of pain, thy soul sweating in its inmost pore drops of blood, and thy body from head to foot suffused with agony;

conscience, judgment, memory, all tortured, but more—your head tormented with racking pains, your eyes starting from their sockets with sights of blood and woe; your ears tormented with sullen moans and hollow groans. And shrieks of tortured ghosts.

Your heart beating high with fever; your pulse rattling at an enormous rate in agony; your limbs crackling like the martyrs in the fire, and yet unburnt; yourself, put in a vessel of hot oil, pained, yet coming out undestroyed; all your veins becoming a road for the hot feet of pain to travel on; every nerve a string on which the devil shall ever play his diabolical tune of hell's Unutterable Lament; your soul for ever and ever aching, and your body palpitating in unison with your soul. Fictions, sir! Again, I say, they are no fictions, and as God lives, but solid, stern truth. If God be true, and this Bible be true, what I have said is the truth, and you will find it one day to be so.[103]

The pattern repeats. Another preacher comes to town and delivers Jonathan Edward's sermon called "In the hands of an Angry God," where he pictures a god who sees all non-believers as spiders hanging on by a thread above the flames of hell. This god despises them and his wrath burns hot, yet it pleases him to hold off for the moment from cutting the strand. The preacher points out that God's patience may run out at any time, at which time the non-believer will get what they fully deserve, quick descent into the flames. Hell's mouth is open wide, and the Satan eagerly waits for permission to pounce on his prey.

The above accounts are representative of many religious tent meetings during the American period of Great Awakenings. Many went forward and were baptized, but what message did they receive and apply to their lives? There was a lot of fear taught, but I doubt anyone came away thinking that God is love (1 John 4:16). If they did repent and start to act differently, was it a heart-felt transformation? In some cases, maybe. Likely, it was because they wanted to escape a

---

[103] C. H. Spurgeon, Sermon (No. 66), Sabbath Morning, February 17, 1856, At New Park Street Chapel, Southwark, http://www.spurgeon.org/index/cindex.htm Accessed 9/25/09.

terrible destiny. The fact that most converts after a time returned to their normal behaviors testifies; fear-based decisions don't tend to stick after the fear subsides.

Another troubling aspect of this approach concerns the preachers themselves. Did they really love those to whom they preached? They would say they did, I'm sure. But their behavior indicates something different. The preacher comes, preaches, receives donations, and then moves on. The words sound angry, which makes sense because they are imitating the god who they serve. This is not a pattern of loving one's neighbor. It is hit-and-run religion, with collection-box payback. Long term relationships are traded for the next town's visit. In my opinion, this kind of evangelism exemplifies the worst of Christianity.

As I considered the hell question, I've come to recognize several elements that lead a person to believe in a place of eternal torment.

The first is genuine; people interpret verses differently. Other elements are more disturbing. Our founding fathers were largely members of the Enlightenment, and many of them did not believe in hell. Yet many of these same leaders supported evangelical preachers that did. Benjamin Franklin, for example, was a good friend to George Whitfield, and he published every one of the evangelist's sermons. One might ask why? The reason is simple. Franklin and many like him were convinced that hell was necessary to restrain the behavior of the general population. Even if it was a false teaching, the threat of eternal punishment was beneficial for society.

It appears the passion for hell comes from those who support its existence. When the concept is challenged, the common reaction is defensiveness and anger. It seems that, in many cases, proponents want hell to exist and would be disappointed if it did not. This reminds me of Jonah, who preached that Nineveh would be destroyed, and later, when it didn't happen, he became angry at God. Why? He was angry because God showed mercy. Shouldn't we all hope for God's mercy, even if we think it might not happen? To pray and hope for mercy is always a good thing; it demonstrates good fruit. Don't you think?

One might argue, but what if there is no mercy. We will be responsible for all of those we didn't warn; their blood will be on our hands. Ezekiel implies this in chapter 33 of his book; a watchman who doesn't sound the alarm is responsible for the blood of those he didn't warn. My mother-in-law once suffered extreme sorrow when an acquaintance committed suicide. She exclaimed, "I'm responsible. I'm responsible. She's in hell now because of me." Should we be happy to share our faith? Sure. Are we modern-day Ezekiels? No. We need to read the Book of Ezekiel in context.

I do not agree that the blood of the unsaved is on the hands of a believer; we each make our life choices and walk our own journeys. Good news that carries an ultimatum of torture is not good news. We can share without threats, which are generally ineffective and cause division. Among believers, many denominations are convinced that hell exists and are sure that most of humanity will end up there. Unfortunately, they all too often point the rod of judgment at each other. I've heard people say, "Those Catholics, they're going to hell," or "Those Lutherans, they're going to hell." Belief in hell inevitably leads to inter-denominational conflicts like these.

Let's now consider the verses and arguments for hell. The word *hell* appears fifty-four times in the King James Version; thirty-one times in the Old Testament. One possible reaction is, "There you have it; the Bible says it, so it is true whether we like it or not." It is not so black and white, however. I did concordance searches for the word in seventeen translations. There are significant differences of opinion among translators, whom I assume are all proficient in Hebrew and Greek. Douay-Rheims had the most: ninety-four. Weymouth and Young both had zero occurrences. The other translations had various counts in between.

How can this be? As I pondered a solution, I've found two plausible explanations. The first relates to when the translation was made. Hell does not mean the same thing today as it did originally. It has a Germanic etymology referring to the netherworld of the dead. Norse pagans believed that a god named Hel ruled over an underworld having the same name. This is very different than the meaning conveyed by the word today.

There is a second reason for translation differences, worldview bias. If one is convinced that hell exists, this belief likely will cloud how a translator renders certain words; of course, the reverse is also true. If one does not believe in hell, it will similarly affect the translation.

In scripture, in the clear majority of cases, hell translates from the Greek word *hades* or the Hebrew word *sheol*. These two words have similar connotations. Sometimes they convey *the grave;* other times they refer to the place where the dead go while awaiting judgment (the netherworld). In a few cases, the word *pit* is used instead. I can see how early translators into English would use *hell* to convey a similar meaning. Today, however, this meaning is not accurate. There is no implication that either *hades* or *sheol* represents a place of eternal punishment. In fact, the Jewish Publication Society consistently translates *sheol* to the word netherworld, which seems to me to be the most accurate.

This does not settle the issue however. There are other words translated *hell*, and *tartarus* is one of these. This word has an interesting etymology; it comes from Greek mythology. It originally was a prison for defeated gods. For example, when Zeus defeated the Titans, a race of powerful deities, they were imprisoned there. As time went on, Tartarus became a place of suffering. Tantalus, after cutting up his son and feeding him to the gods, had to forever stand neck-deep in water but never could get a drink. Tartarus appears once in scripture (2 Pet. 2:4); the author declares that God did not spare the angels but confined them in Tartarus to await judgment. The context here is similar to Revelation 20:2, where the Devil is bound for a thousand years. Apparently, Peter is using the original meaning (a prison) of the word. I seriously doubt that he is giving credence to Greek mythology.

Another word translated to hell is *Gehenna*. In the Old Testament, *Gehenna* is the place where some Jews sacrificed their firstborn to the god Molech. Jeremiah testifies to God's displeasure at the practice. The valley of Hinnom is mentioned a number of times in the Old Testament in connection with this practice. After the Babylonian exile, the Jews returned and made the valley into a huge garbage dump. It was a place where the fires burned continuously. Sometimes criminals were thrown into the fire after they were executed. If garbage or the dead didn't make it into the valley, maggot worms would be there to consume the remains. In this sense, the fire is never quenched and the worms never die. Think about it. What goes to a garbage dump? Those things that have no use. What does a garbage dump do to those things? It destroys them. Jesus seems to use the word Gehenna as a synonym for fire. He uses the fire metaphor to reveal God's eternal passion to burn away anything that is evil and refine anything that is good. In this sense, we all need to pass through the fire.[104]

---

[104] 1 Cor. 3:15, Mk. 9:47-49

Gehenna appears twelve times in the New Testament source documents. Eleven of these occurrences are in the three synoptic gospels where Jesus is speaking. Three are duplicates. Seven of them are in the gospel of Matthew. Some are warnings to the religious, especially those who are quick to judge and slow to forgive. Some are encouraging us not to be afraid of short-term consequences. The eternal view is more important. And others have nothing to do with eternal punishment. For these, as I mentioned above, *Gehenna* is the necessary fire to burn away the evil present. To summarize, the word *Gehenna* does not mean hell in the way that our Western minds think. *Gehenna* indicates judgment, but is it hell? I don't think so.

I'm sure that the people in the first century understood the phrases *worm that does not die* and *unquenchable fire*. Maggots were constantly present around the literal garbage dump and fires were always kept burning. I'm also sure that the Pharisees understood what Jesus meant. He was calling them criminals, and as criminals wind up in the literal *Gehenna*, so they would wind up experiencing judgment. But is there anything here that is eternal? No.

Some use the parable of Lazarus and the rich man to prove the existence of hell. Lazarus is in the bosom of Abraham, and the rich man experiences severe heat. First of all, this is a parable, so I would argue that its symbols are not literal. Second, it happens before the final judgment, since the rich man's relatives are still alive. So it cannot be hell. Finally, the bosom of Abraham is a metaphor meaning a place of comfort while awaiting judgment day. Here again, the rich man is not in hell.

There are verses in the New Testament that speak of everlasting fire, punishment, or destruction. There are others that speak of forever and ever. How do we interpret these?

We first need to carefully define words like forever, everlasting, and eternal. These words have very different connotations. Forever is the weakest of the three. The Western interpretation is time that goes on, and on, and on, without end. A verse from song, *Amazing Grace*, presents the European concept.

> When we've been there ten thousand years
> Bright shining as the Sun.
>
> We've no less days to sing God's praise
> Than when we've first begun.

But is this what forever means? There are many forevers in the Bible that had ends. Israel was to return from Babylon and live in peace forever. There were memorials that were to be a sign so people would forever remember. We can easily find similar examples. Apparently forever was not forever, and it soon becomes apparent that the word does not necessarily mean what we think it does. Possibly it means that the endpoint is not yet determined. Things will continue until the situation changes or until the endpoint is established.

We use this meaning today. A teenager might say to their girlfriend or boyfriend, "I will love you forever," and then a month later, the love is gone. How many times have we stared forever at a computer screen? In the Old Testament, people often say, "Oh King, may you live forever." They, of course, knew the king would eventually die, though his length of days was not yet determined. There are many Old Testament promises declaring things to last forever that did indeed end.

Let's consider the words, everlasting and eternal, using the following verse:

> He stopped and shook the earth; he looked and made the nations tremble. The eternal mountains were shattered; along his ancient pathways the everlasting hills sank low. (Hab. 3:6)

Here these words do not have the same meanings that modern readers assign to them. Mountains and hills may seem to be permanent, but obviously they are not. It is true that they last as far as one can envision, to a vanishing point beyond the horizon. It is like forever, but the end is a long way off, much longer than the lifespan of a king. It could mean till the end of the age or till the new creation. It could mean till judgment day.

Are the words everlasting and eternal synonyms? Consider the differences in the various translations of Matthew 25:46:

1. go away into **eternal** punishment, but the righteous into **eternal** life (ESV).
2. go away into **everlasting** punishment, but the righteous into **everlasting** life (LITV).
3. will be punished **forever**. But the ones who pleased God will have **eternal** life (CEV).
4. go away into **everlasting** punishment: but the righteous into life **eternal** (KJV).
5. go away to punishment **age-during**, but the righteous to life **age-during** (YLT).

Notice the translator disagreements. The bolded words above are translations of the same Greek word, but with different connotations. There is a sense of finality in this verse. Once judgment occurs, the sentence is final. The punishment, whatever that might be, cannot be revoked.

Nevertheless, in our time, we distinguish between the meanings of everlasting and eternal. Scientists tell us that without space there is no time, the fourth dimension that began with the Big Bang. With this understanding, Jesus' statement "Before Abraham was, I am," is profound. What he was saying was, "I am from eternity, the existence beyond time." Eternity wraps around this temporal existence where we live. It is like a great sphere that surrounds a speck of dust called time. Eternity is entirely different from hours, days, years, and millennia continuing on and on. A problem with many translations of the Bible is they do not distinguish between the words, everlasting and eternal. This is understandable. There was no concept of existence without time. So, the translators interchange the words. In ancient times, there simply was no way to clearly convey the differences.

Another phrase in the New Testament that people attribute to hell is *outer darkness*. Matthew indicates that some will be cast to outer darkness where there is weeping and gnashing of teeth.

The twelfth century Jewish sage Maimonides, in his book, *the Guide to the Perplexed*, portrays the next world as a kind of large expanse. Some individuals will be far from the king, even as far as another country. Others will be closer, perhaps near the palace or even inside. A few will be in the presence of the king.

This illustration could be a picture of what is to come. Those who are righteous will be close by and in service to the king. Others, in outer darkness, could be far away, experiencing great anger and remorse. Nevertheless, their nature will not allow them to move closer where they can experience God's blessings. Their distance depends on how much they can still reflect God's image. Those whose identity is so entwined with money, sex, power, or other idolatries are very far distant, in outer darkness. So, maybe multitudes will be in the new creation, but to some it will be paradise, and to others a great disappointment. CS Lewis, in his novels *The Great Divorce* and *The Last Battle*, presents a view of the afterlife in these terms. Is it possible that those in outer darkness could eventually move closer to the light? Maybe. We can hope.

Let's now consider the lake of fire. In Egyptian mythology, this is where the devourer of souls Ammut, threw the unworthy rather than eating them. Their fate was everlasting restlessness, which was called the second death. In Jewish tradition, the lake of fire meant something quite different. It referred to the Dead Sea. According to the first century Greek geographer, Strabo: "It abounds with asphalt, which rises, not however at any regular seasons, in bubbles, like boiling water, from the middle of the deepest part."[105] Nothing lives there. From the Jewish point of view, things that are thrown into it are those that are spiritually dead. It could be another way to say *outer darkness*.

No Christians would think of Ammut when they ponder the phrase "Lake of Fire." They often do associate the place as one of eternal restlessness, though. When they do this their views are more Egyptian than Jewish.

Matthew 7:13 teaches: "Enter through the narrow gate; for the gate is wide and the road is easy that leads to destruction, and there are many who take it. For the gate is narrow and the road is hard that leads to life, and there are few who find it". If this verse refers to the final judgment, almost all of the people alive in the world will wind up in hell. At the same time, most adherents to the doctrine of an eternal hell support the concept of the age of accountability. A child who dies before the age of eight will go to heaven. Every year, millions of children die and we grieve when we experience such a tragedy. But why? By reason, the odds of these children going to heaven should they grow up is very low. I doubt that very many Christians have considered the gravity of this dilemma. It seems that we are okay

---

[105] Strabo, "Geographica", book 16 chapter 2, section 42.

saying that adults who never hear the gospel are dammed. It is far more difficult to assign children to this same fate.

The dilemma is lessened when we attribute verses like that one just cited to the present. Then, when we encounter words like condemned, salvation, and contempt, we would understand them to relate this life. Most are condemned to live a life that is far less fruitful than that which is possible. This is our default state without Christ.

Admittedly, the above reasoning is not conclusive. There are many ways to interpret the same words of scripture. There are other verses to consider, and each can lead to long debates. I believe that God has a way of surprising us and breaking apart our rigid doctrines. Nevertheless, I do not think that a biblical case can be made for a place where people will be eternally tortured. I don't deny that there will be judgment, but I believe it will be fair and proportional. I hold this view because I trust John when he says: "God is love." An eternal furnace for the lost, if it exists, would be a contradiction.

I also hold my view because Jesus tells us that a good tree does not produce rotten fruit. In my opinion, the fruit of the doctrine of hell is rotten throughout. It causes its adherents to be judgmental, which conflicts with those teachings commanding us not to judge. If we perceive a god of retribution, we tend to be that way ourselves. The eternal fate of an individual is between them and God; I have no part in the equation.

In fact, the doctrine of hell leads to wars. How can the more than two-billion Christians ever live in harmony with the one and a half billion Muslims when each condemns the other to hell? How can Christian denominations get along among themselves? On the surface they try, but in their hearts, they think the other is going to the awful place. The bigotry may be hidden, but eventually it reveals itself.

The hell doctrine leads many to believe that those that go there deserve it. The colonial period saw mainstream Christians encounter people whom they considered depraved, and therefore, they had no problem committing genocide on a large scale. Those outside the faith, the pagans, were separated from their families, made into slaves, and even had their humanity questioned.

Nobody fully understands what awaits us after death. Our spiritual traditions give us a glimpse, but still, we only have vague impressions. Jesus indicates that some who have no clue will be accepted, and others who think they are safe will experience rejection. My dad was an atheist. Many of us have family and friends whom we love but who do not believe as we do. I would rather keep a positive hope for their fate and look forward to seeing them in the next life. Thinking they are all in hell is not productive; it is depressing.

Jesus tells us "no one comes to the Father but by me (John 14:6)." I agree. This means that Jesus is the gatekeeper, not I. He decides.

Ann Frank and her family died a horrible death in the Holocaust. Many of the German guards were Christian. The Lutheran and Catholic establishment in Germany were largely sympathetic to the Nazis as they rose to power. I fully understand why many Jews could no longer accept any god, let alone the Christian God. Does a God of love understand?

Christopher Columbus' crew practiced cutting peaceful indigenous people in half with single blows of their swords.[106] They were Christian. Do you think those indigenous people could be receptive to the Christian message? Are the German guards going to heaven along with Columbus' crew? Are the victims destined for hell? I believe God always identifies with the victim. Jesus proved that on the cross. I trust that Jesus, as gatekeeper, will undertake the responsibility to judge perfectly.

I suppose that it is possible for one's humanity to deconstruct after death if they persist in rebelling from the Creator's love. In my opinion, however, Christians need to move beyond the belief in hell. It is impossible for us to love our neighbor if we do not. In many cases it creates devils that become instruments of judgment, hurling scriptural fire at those who could otherwise be friends. This is destructive and unnecessary. It is wrong.

---

[106] Refer to the writings of Bartelome de Las Casas and David Stannard, *American Holocaust*, Oxford University Press (1992).

Chapter 11

Peace with God

> Calvinism is known by an acronym: T.U.L.I.P.: **T**otal Depravity, **U**nconditional Election, **L**imited Atonement, **I**rresistible Grace, **P**erseverance of the Saints
>
> Someone has said that no theology is worth believing that cannot be preached standing in front of the gates of Auschwitz. I, for one, could not stand at those gates and preach a version of God's sovereignty that makes the extermination of six million Jews, including many children, a part of the will and plan of God such that God foreordained and rendered it certain. I want young Calvinists (and others) to know and at least come to terms with the inevitable and unavoidable consequences of what this radical form of Reformed theology teaches. And I want to give their friends and relatives and spiritual mentors ammunition to use in undermining their sometimes overconfidence in the solidity of their belief system.[107] —Roger E. Olson

Since the earliest centuries of Christianity, Western believers have attempted to understand God and his plan of salvation. Mainstream Christianity agrees that Jesus will return to judge the living and the dead. Postmodern culture rejects this truth claim because of its apparent exclusionary nature. Whether this charge is valid depends on the nature of the judgment. Reformed theology, which is commonly known as Calvinism, believes that God pre-elected a small number who are destined for eternal life; these will be saved whether they like it or not. The rest are destined for eternal torment. This view certainly is exclusive. The overwhelming majority are rejected, even if they

---

[107] Roger E. Olson, *Against Calvinism: Rescuing God's Reputation from Radical Reformed Theology,* 25.

never heard the salvation message or if they were victims of Christian atrocities.

Cognitive Dissonance

Cognitive dissonance is the psychological conflict experienced when an individual simultaneously holds two or more contradictory beliefs, ideas, or values. Most of the time, people are unaware of the antithetical aspects of their convictions. A crisis occurs when they are confronted with information that conflicts with existing assumptions.

Christians, like all people, are very prone to cognitive dissonance. Let's take a step back to the 18th century for an illustration. In 1772, John Newton wrote the lyrics to the beloved hymn, Amazing Grace. The folklore surrounding the composition goes as follows. John's father commissioned a sailor to find his son who was missing in Africa. He was found and was rescued from slavery. On the way home a strong storm ensued causing the ship on which he was traveling to be in severe danger. John repented, converted to Christianity, and wrote Amazing Grace. The tune was a Western African song of mourning that he heard sung by slaves from the belly of slave ships.

It's a great story, isn't it? Unfortunately, it is incomplete and largely false. John did convert to Christianity during a storm. He was rescued from slavery. Everything else is imaginative storytelling. The famous melody did not merge with the lyrics until many decades later; the actual composer is unknown. Before his conversion, John was a very profane sort of person. The crew of the slave ship Pegasus, on which he served were fed up, so they left him with the slave traders on the coast of Africa. He was a slave for eighteen months, but never experienced the harsh treatment to which the Africans were subjected. After his conversion, John did not immediately transform. He was less profane but continued working on slave ships for nine more years, ultimately achieving the rank of captain. Then, while preparing to embark on another mission, John suddenly took ill. If it were not for this illness, the song Amazing Grace likely would not exist. In his own words:

> I never had a scruple upon this head at the time; nor was such a thought once suggested to me, by any

friend. What I did, I did ignorantly; considering it as the line of life which Divine Providence had allotted me, and having no concern, in point of conscience, but to treat the Slaves, while under my care, with as much humanity as a regard to my own safety would admit.[108]

It was not till many years later that John, then a minister of the Gospel, publicly apologized:

> If I attempt, after what has been done, to throw my mite into the public stock of information, it is less from an apprehension that my interference is necessary, than from a conviction, that silence, at such a time, and on such an occasion, would, in me, be criminal. If my testimony would not be necessary, or serviceable, yet, perhaps, I am bound, in conscience, to take shame to myself by a public confession, which, however sincere, comes too late to prevent, or repair, the misery and mischief to which I have, formerly, been accessory. I hope it will always be a subject of humiliating reflection to me, that I was, once, an active instrument, in a business at which my heart now shudders.[109]

It took this Christian minister, 33 years to come to grips with his actions. This is cognitive dissonance of the highest order. To his credit, John did acknowledge the unconscionable treatment of slaves on their journey from their homes to America. I won't describe those here; you can read the full 1788 article, which is posted online. Two items, though, I find particularly chilling. The English made the economic calculation that it maximizes profit to load a boat with over two hundred slaves, knowing full-well that a quarter to a half of them would die on the voyage. The profit-to-cost ratio decreased when boats were loaded with less. Economic expediency prevailed over loss of human life. The American landowners made a similar calculation. It is cheaper to work a slave to death in nine years and then replace them, than to treat them humanely, and have to provide for their old age.

---

[108] John Newton, "Thoughts on the African Slave Trade," (1788).
[109] Ibid.

These people called themselves Christians. It never occurred to them that their actions were among the worst evils imaginable.

Amazing Grace is one of the most beloved songs ever written. It has impacted millions and been translated into many languages. Most of the words are fine, but I dislike the phrase, "That saved a wretch like me." When I think of the word wretch, it conveys the following meanings: scoundrel, villain, reprobate, good-for-nothing, creep, swine, lowlife, scumbag, scuzz-ball, and sleaze-ball. As bad as John Newton was, was he those things? If we say yes, then the large number of Christians in the 1700s who supported slavery would qualify. Who among us could guarantee that we would have been different if we lived in those times?

Words like wretch come from Calvinistic thinking. The unsaved are totally depraved, while those who are saved, the good-guys, are redeemed. This kind of thinking degrades those that we consider to be *other*. Every human being has the stamp of God's image. That image might be dimmed and distorted, but it is still there. Many of those outside the Christian faith live lives that are good and honorable; sometimes they put Christians to shame. To claim that they are wretched and totally depraved is simply wrong.

There are other implications. If we say someone is wretched, it is not much of a leap to believe that they deserve whatever misfortune they experience, especially if they are unwilling to convert. This is what leads to things like the slave trade and modern sex trafficking.

If one asks a Jewish person, "What is the worst sin?", the answer likely will be, "*Doing evil in the name of God.*" This is the third commandment, "You shall not carry the Lord's name in vain." It is the only one of the ten where God says, "I will not hold them guiltless." This command does not mean saying in an animated voice, "Jesus Christ," or "Oh my God." Rather, it is a believer carrying the royal signet ring of the King and using it to justify and do evil. There is nothing that will faster push people away from the God of the Bible than when his followers misrepresent him by doing evil in his name. Our prayer should be: "God, show me what I don't see and those things that I would rather cover over. Please, provide for my basic needs, but keep me from any evil that hides behind the culture of the day."

The Atonement

> Beside our picture of the unjust man let us set one of the just man, the man of true simplicity of character who, as Aeschylus says, wants "to be, and not to seem, good." We must, indeed, not allow him to seem good, for if he does, he will have all the rewards and honors paid to the man who has a reputation for justice, and we shall not be able to tell whether his motive is love of justice or love of the rewards and honors. No, we must strip him of everything except his justice, and our picture of him must be drawn in the opposite way to our picture of the unjust man; for our just man must have the worst of reputations even though he has done no wrong. So, we shall be able to test his justice and see if it can stand up to unpopularity and all that goes with it; we shall give him an undeserved and lifelong reputation for wickedness, and make him stick to his chosen course until death…The just man, then, as we have pictured him, will be scourged, tortured, and imprisoned, his eyes will be put out, and after enduring every humiliation he will be crucified, and learn at last that in the world as it is we should want not to be, but to seem, just.[110] —Plato

Plato surely had no idea that he was being prophetic. Yet, his account eerily predicts what happened to Jesus, centuries later.

Who killed Jesus? The organized mob did. It was an orchestrated effort by the rulers of the time. Pilate represented Rome. Herod represented the Jews. The Pharisees and Priests represented the Jewish religious system. They all united to make Jesus the scapegoat.

Why? Jesus represented a threat. Rome would not accept the message. Persecutions of the first several centuries of Christianity prove that. The religious leaders would not accept the message either. He threatened to upend their entire sacrificial system. Eliminating him

---

[110] **Plato**, Plato's Republic, "The Perfect Man," (360BC) Socrates speaking to the philosopher, Glaucon.

meant things could go back to normal. Everything would function as always, as though he never existed.

The harshest weapon at their disposal was to inflict a humiliating, torturous death. As Isaiah 53 predicted many centuries before, he went willingly to the slaughter. In this way, he took the wrath and darkness of humanity onto himself. Pilate asked him, "Don't you know that I have the power to condemn you to death?" Jesus replied, "No one takes my life, I lay it down freely." He had the power to call thousands of legions of angels to his defense, but he did not.

So he was crucified. But unexpectedly, he did not stay dead. He rose. When he did, he didn't call for payback, but declared: "Peace be with you."

One could ask: "What does all of this have to do with us?" Paul provides a partial answer in the following quote:

> For I delivered to you as of first importance what I also received: that Christ died for our sins in accordance with the scriptures, that he was buried, that he was raised on the third day in accordance with the scriptures. (1 Cor. 15:1, 3-4)

He provides a more detailed answer in Philippians Chapter 2, where he quotes a very early Christian hymn, which many scholars date to within months of the crucifixion.[111]

For about a hundred years, verses like those cited above sufficed to tell us what Christ's death means for us. But then, Church structure began to take shape and longer doctrinal statements, or creeds, began to appear. Jesus saved us from our sins. How? He died on the cross. Why?

The why, in light of the above discussion, is simple. He had to die because the world systems would not tolerate anything else. God did not require the sacrifice; we did. He entered the world knowing the darkness that he would bear.

But how did he save us from sin? Dozens of atonement theories attempt to rationally answer this question. These include substitution, recapitulation, penal substitution, Christus victor, ransom, government, moral, guaranty, vicarious repentance, accident, martyr,

---

[111] Refer to the section on the resurrection in chapter 3 of this book.

and declaration. I'm sure if we think about it, others can arise as well. Many of these overlap; others clearly contradict each other. It would be really boring to describe each of these in detail, then to list who believes them, and finally critique each of their implications. I won't do this. Rather, I will explain issues that I have with a few of the most popular of these and then conclude this section.

Atonement theories rest on one's view of God the Father, humanity, and the power of the Satan. Often, their formulation relates to the background and culture of those creating them. A few are weird and simply don't need a response.

A first question is: how do we view the condition of humanity? Are we evil to the core or are we lost? Are we wretches or are we sick? Does God the Father act as a courtroom judge, or does he act as a physician to heal?

Penal substitutionary atonement sees God as a judge, actually an angry judge. This is understandable because John Calvin and other reformers who formalized the theory were trained as lawyers. The theory goes like this. God is perfectly just, and when we sin, we offend him and each other. Justice must be satisfied. He wants to forgive, but perfect mercy is in conflict with perfect justice. He must find a way to do both. Jesus, innocent because he is perfect, can take our place. God pours infinite wrath upon him which satisfies the dilemma. Jesus physically bears the sin of us all, making mercy available for those who accept him.

The penal substitution model has many problems for me. Let's bring it into human terms. There were many times where someone did or said something hurtful to me. It never occurred to me to require equal compensation for the wrong. When I could, I simply forgave. Likewise, Steven in the Book of Acts, while he was being stoned, asked God not to hold the wrong against them. I suppose there were times when I considered the thought of payback, but afterwards, this would make me feel petty and small. If I, as an imperfect person, can forgive wrongs without a required price, how much more so would God?

Penal Substitutionary atonement theory assumes that every sin must be punished by God. Is this true? For those of you who are parents, is this the way you act with your children? Suppose your child does something wrong, and they come to you truly sorry. Is punishment unconditionally required in every circumstance? Yes, consequences follow wrongdoing, but punishment? According to many scriptures, God calls us to repent, and if we do, our sins are forgiven. A heart of repentance is the key. The foundation of Penal Substitution shakes apart if we remove the assumption that every single sin must be punished.

Even worse than this is the idea that I would heap punishment for someone's wrong toward me onto someone else. If my child offends me, should I attack my wife, even if she were willing? My wife Viv recalls an early memory. She, as a child, did something wrong. Maybe it was a lie or a task that was left undone. To demonstrate grace, her mom, with her dad's approval, handed Viv a stick. Instead of having her father inflict punishment on her directly, she was to inflict it on her mom, a willing substitute, who said: "Strike me." The incident caused Viv to cry and cry. It remains a painful memory to this day.

I don't deny that there are instances where someone can intervene on behalf of someone else. If a person steals, someone could come forth and pay the bill. If someone breaks a window, someone else can repair it. This is hugely different. These examples are restorative, not retributive. The thought of Jesus being pounded with the Father's wrath makes me cringe. Furthermore, If Jesus' death satisfied the required payment for our sins, the Father shows mercy, not forgiveness. The debt was paid, so there was nothing left to forgive. So, with penal substitution theory, there is no forgiveness of sin.

In Luke's gospel, Jesus is talking with the father while he is on the cross. For example, he says "Father, forgive them; for they do not know what they are doing"[112] and "Father, into your hands I commend my spirit."[113] Was the Father listening? How could he be if he was pouring his wrath on Jesus? Those verses seem to imply that God, the Father, was present, but not in a wrathful way.

Another question: How does the Father think? Is it true that the Father cannot look at sin? The Old Testament prophet Habakkuk thought so: "You who are of purer eyes than to see evil and cannot look at wrong."[114] Yet Jesus hung out with sinners, not the righteous. When accused by his critics, he responded, "Those who are well have no need of a physician, but those who are sick. I came not to call the

---

[112] Luke 23:34
[113] Luke 23:46
[114] Hab. 1:13

righteous, but sinners." Jesus acted as a physician, not a courtroom judge. For me, this eliminates the penal substitution theory. It cannot be true. There has to be a better explanation.

Let's consider another approach to atonement, substitution theory. This one also involves paying a price. Anselm, an eleventh century priest devised this explanation. He lived in a feudal era. Divine right meant that honor was due the lords. If their honor was challenged, there was a price to pay. Similarly, the theory goes, our sins are an affront to God's honor, which must be restored. Jesus offered himself as an innocent sacrifice, and because he is perfect with infinite worth, his sacrifice was sufficient to restore the Father's honor.

This theory is better than penal substitution, but still falls short in my opinion. It is weak people who worry about their honor. Jesus was not born among the wealthy; he was born in a stable. He came from Nazareth, and "Nothing good comes from there." I doubt that God, the creator of the Universe, is worried about his honor. It would be like my being offended because a chipmunk screams at me. I think we can do better than this atonement theory, too.

Ransom theory was the predominant view from the time of Constantine till about AD 1000. A price is still required, but this time, the payment goes to the Satan. The Satan legally owns humanity because of Adam's sin. To free us, a ransom must be paid to him. The Satan makes an agreement with God. He is allowed to kill Jesus, who is God incarnate, and this releases us from his bondage. CS Lewis' *Lion Witch and Wardrobe* illustrates this approach. I don't like this theory either. I don't think the Satan has this power. Jesus metaphorically sees him falling from heaven (Luke 10:18). He was cast down, not paid. The Satan, along with his systems of scapegoating, accusing, and violence, is a defeated foe.

Western culture tends to have a legal focus, and the above atonement theories fit that mindset. It is *not* a Jewish concept, however. The Jewish concept of atonement is that of a kinsman redeemer. According to this idea, Christ is one who was willing to come to this earth knowing the violence it contains. In this way, he identifies with our imperfections, our sins, shares in our darkness, and even in death.

We, as individualists, think of the atonement as a way for *me* to escape. I submit that this is not the primary issue. The real issue was whether the whole of humanity should have a future. There is a significant difference thinking this way. It joins me with my neighbor because we are in the same boat. Perhaps, like animal sacrifice, penal and substitutionary atonement were temporary understandings that were necessary until humanity was better able to understand the reasons for Jesus' coming.

The recapitulation theory, held by the Orthodox Church, provides another alternative to the atonement question; it is one that goes back very early. Irenaeus elaborates this in his book *Against Heresies* (AD 185).[115] Recapitulation sees humanity as separating itself from God, not the other way around. It sees God as a consuming fire of love working to repair the breach. We, in this fallen state, are incapable of finding our way back. We are lost and sick, needing help. Jesus, in God's perfect love, entered this world to become the *True Adam*. His life reveals the heart of the Father. Where Adam failed, Jesus succeeded and was able to reunite humanity with divinity. All who willingly say Yes to God will also be united through Christ. As he lives, so will those who live their life in him guided by the Holy Spirit. Basically, Jesus recapitulates (restores) the fallen human nature. You can see this theory illustrated through YouTube videos showing the gospel in chairs.

The last theory that I'll briefly mention is Christus Victor. The penalty for sin is death, so humanity needed a redeemer. Jesus, God himself, entered the world for this purpose. When he did, all of the evil forces gathered together for battle. They inflicted a humiliating, painful death. It was their hour (Luke 22:53), but Jesus bore all that these dark forces of the world could inflict.

When he rose from the dead, everything changed. He was vindicated. He defeated evil, conquered death, and achieved a complete victory over the principalities and powers. God the Father restored to him full dominion over the cosmos, and all things were put under his feet. Jesus became the true Davidic king of Israel and Lord of the world. The Kingdom of God was established.

Because of Jesus' faithfulness, humanity can be reunited with divinity. As we all were formally subject to death, now anyone who repents and submits to his lordship can be made spiritually alive, new creations and citizens of the Kingdom. Through the workings of the

---

[115] Irenaeus, Against Heresies 3.18.7; 3.21; 3.22; 5.20.

Holy Spirit, the fire of the Father's love then can be applied to our hearts, gradually burning away anything that is harmful to our souls.

Christians have debated the *How Jesus saves me* question for thousands of years. At times, I've leaned towards various atonement theories. I favor the Orthodox recapitulation view. I'm also attracted to Christus Victor, even though this one is relatively recent. I see the Father and Son as united always. I see them both demonstrating love and compassion. We serve a good Father who loves us and seeks restoration. His love is a consuming fire that will burn away all of the evil that is harmful to our soul; it is up to us to be willing to trust him in this.

Let me summarize with a few of my thoughts. Many thousands of Jews were crucified in the first century. The Romans used crucifixion as a public demonstration to anyone who might be considering rebellion. It was the most horrific form of execution that they could devise, meant to dissuade anyone from even thinking of challenging the system.

The crucifixion of Jesus was unique in several ways. First, both Pontius Pilate and the religious leaders knew that he was innocent. The passion accounts make this clear. Second, although Jesus knew that he was innocent too, he did not resist. He was the victim who responded in forgiveness, confident that he would die and then be vindicated through the resurrection.

Who killed Jesus? The religious and political systems did. We did. In this way, he bore our sins. The price was huge; the creator of the Universe suffered a humiliating death hanging between two criminals, killed by the wrath of his creations. It was the necessary ransom to free us from the power of death.

The purpose of Jesus' life, death, and resurrection form a web of meaning and mystery. By his life, he reveals the true nature of God. He is not distant, but eager to walk with us through life's trials, even to the point of death. His resurrection demonstrates that the journey does not end with death. By trusting in this hope, we become new creatures transformed by the Holy Spirit for life in a new creation where justice reigns and everything is made right.

Metaphors can be a helpful mechanism to explain the atonement. All metaphors are incomplete, but these work for me.

Consider a baseball game where team *humanity* is in an intense competition with team *Death and Sin*. It is two outs and we're in the bottom of the ninth inning. Bases are loaded, but we are down three to zero. I'm coming to the plate with eternity on the line. Unfortunately, in my whole life I never hit the ball or even ever fouled one off. What is the manager, God the Father to do? He sends up his Son as a substitute hitter. Born as a human, Jesus steps up to the plate. Here comes the pitch! It is a crucifixion right down the middle. Jesus slams it out of the park. Team *humanity* wins a great victory. *Death and sin* suffer a resounding loss. Praise God that Jesus is on our team.

My second metaphor follows. The Bible tells us that the wages of sin is death. Before Jesus, millions died and stayed dead. In biblical terms, they descended to Sheol (Hades). There was a gate there, but no one could open it. Jesus, as God, took on the human condition in its corruptible state, even to the point of sharing in death. When descending into Hades, because he was innocent, he was vindicated; death could not hold him. With the keys to the kingdom he opened the gate and as the gatekeeper, he enabled an uncountable number who were imprisoned to go through to eternal life. This metaphor presents a God of love, a unified Trinity, with Jesus as the gatekeeper.

When I think of God the Father, I'm drawn to the famous parable of the *Prodigal Son*. I prefer to call this parable *the Loving Father*. The son returned afraid of what his father would do. He fully expected judgment. The father instead, when seeing his son from a distance, runs to meet him. He has compassion, embraces him, gives him the best robe, and prepares a celebration. He does not worry about his honor. He does not require payback. He does not demand that his other son restore the squandered funds. This parable describes the Father, our God. He is one that we can love with our whole heart.

Jesus demonstrates *the Loving Father* parable with his life. He did not even wait for the rebellious human race to seek forgiveness. He ran into our dark world knowing that he would be rejected and killed. He also was aware that many millions would continue to mock and belittle his sacrifice in the centuries that followed. Imagine: The Creator of the universe coming into our world to reconcile us to himself. It is amazing to consider.

Salvation

The often-quoted verse states: "I am the way, and the truth, and the life. No one comes to the Father except through me (John 14:6)." These famous words are beloved to many, yet if misunderstood, provide a mandate that separates peoples into groups and, more times than we would like to admit, can lead to violence. For example, Thomas Aquinas, a renowned early church philosopher, justified the inquisition and believed that if a person refuses to assimilate into Catholic Christianity, that person should be considered a heretic and killed.[116]

In the run up to WW 2 many, possibly the majority, of German Christians supported Hitler's rise to power. During the Holocaust they were often the ones who herded Jewish prisoners to the gas chambers. On Sundays, these same people visited their churches and peaceably sang Christian hymns together. While all of this was happening, many Jews, resigned to their fate, sang an ancient hymn called *Ani Ma Amin*.

I Believe
I believe with complete faith
In the coming of the Messiah, I believe.
I believe in the coming of the Messiah
In the coming of the Messiah, I believe
I Believe in the coming of the Messiah

And even though he may tarry
Nonetheless I will wait for him
And even though he may tarry
Nonetheless I will wait for him

Nonetheless, I will wait for him
I will wait every day for him to come
Nonetheless, I will wait for him
I will wait every day for him to come
(Ending)

---

[116] Thomas Aquinas, *Summa Theologica*.

Pious Jews commonly sing this hymn as part of their daily morning prayers. How can it be that these who suffered genocide on earth, in the heart of Christian Europe, now are destined for an even greater judgment? The picture makes no sense. How can Christians expect Jews to recognize the historical Jesus after experiencing thousands of years of anti-Semitism and persecution?

Suppose that we were taught from a young age that martyrdom was a virtue which we could achieve by strapping on a suicide belt. Can any of us guarantee that we wouldn't do it? Suppose we were a Native American who saw the Methodist Missionary Colonel Chivington, wipe out our family at the Sand Creek Massacre. Would we be open to hear about the love of Jesus? Assume we were born in Haiti and saw the Jesuit Columbus and his crews test their mettle by cutting our friends in half with single swipes of the sword. Could we guarantee that we would be open to the Christian message? Is there no hope for those whose life experiences make it impossible to accept the historical figure of Jesus?

The parable of the soils often is used as an object lesson to distinguish those that are saved from those that are not. The hard soil represents unrepentant sinners and the soft soil stands for those who are open to the evangelical message. Yet, though all of us have some soil in our hearts that is soft and receptive, we also have other soil that is rocky, and even more that is hard and stubborn. Who among us can say otherwise? Interpreting the parable of soils in this way—in which all the soils are to be found in each of us—keeps us from dividing the world into saved and unsaved. It is a picture that represents us all. It forces us to recognize there is a flood of potential chaos as well as potential good that runs through the center of each person's heart.

It is important to understand what we are saying when we announce to an indigenous person that unless they call on the name of Jesus, they are destined for judgment. It comes across as saying, "You can be okay, but too bad for all those from your culture that came before." This is a hard teaching. Indigenous peoples traditionally feel strong connections to their ancestors. If the doctrine is true, its net effect is that God favors Europeans over all other peoples. For a good part of the last two millennia, Christianity was largely centered in the West.

There are verses in the Bible that imply something entirely different. Three that come to mind are Matthew 25, Romans 2:4, and Matthew 7. In the first of these, Jesus declares that there will be judgment, but the outcome of that judgment is not so obvious. Some, not knowing who he was, would be accepted. Why? Because their compassion for the thirsty, hungry, unclothed, sick, imprisoned is equated with compassion for Jesus, who identifies with the suffering. Others who thought they were doing great things in Jesus' name would be rejected because they lacked such compassion. This includes many who are pastors, missionaries, and spiritual leaders. The second verse Romans 2:4, indicates that nations, though they didn't have access to God's law, may indeed by nature have a thirst to do what it says. These are a law unto themselves. Finally, Matthew 7 stipulates that not everyone who calls Jesus Lord will be part of his kingdom. Verses like these, and others with similar messages, inform me to obey Jesus' admonition to avoid judging others. These verses tell me that I don't have the right to presume to know another's eternal destiny.

One might ask then, what do we do with the verse, "I am the way, the truth, and the life, no one comes to the Father but by me"? Do we just throw that verse away? The answer is *no*: this verse shows Jesus to be the gatekeeper. It is he who will decide the part that each of us will have in the world to come.

Jesus is the truth; this is true. He tells us to spread the Good News throughout the world and make disciples; this is true. Many in the world are lost; this is also true. But the eternal fate of those outside of Christianity is God's business, not ours.

One might ask, "Why then did Jesus tell us to spread the Gospel?" The answer: Because people need to know the incredible price that God paid to reconcile the world to himself. Because the Christian message is good news, which enables us to be secure in our relationship with the Almighty. Life in Jesus guided by the Holy Spirit is a transforming experience. It furthers the project of bringing the Kingdom of God to earth. Living God's way brings joy and fulfillment that cannot be achieved otherwise. It doesn't require a stifled, inhibited life; it rather leads to a life of courage, joy, and meaning. It frees us from those things that enslave and kill our souls. The message is not just a utilitarian effort to reserve people's spots in the afterlife; it is valuable in its own right.

PART 4

End Time Frenzy

> I think this is irresponsible preaching and very dangerous, and especially when it is slanted toward children, I think it's totally irresponsible, because I see nothing biblical that points up to our being in the last days, and I just think it's an outrageous thing to do, and a lot of people are making a living—they've been making a living for 2,000 years—preaching that we're in the last days."[117] —Charles M. Schulz

Over the last 2,000 years, a significant percentage of Christians of every generation believed that theirs was the last. In my opinion, the focus on the End Times is a major source of division in the Church, and it discourages our children. It is also a vehicle that charlatans use to get rich. Most importantly, it presents a major barrier for people who would otherwise be open to accept the Good News. False prophecies cause many to discount the Christian gospel altogether.

Our job, according to Jesus, is to be found faithful and caring; we should not be "packing our bags" anticipating the ultimate trip to Heaven. In this last part of the book, I'll work through verses, which people use to convince us that these are the last days. Are there ways to interpret these verses so that we don't become consumed with the hype?

---

[117] Charles M. Schulz–Creator of the Charlie Brown cartoon series, "Charles M. Schulz: Conversations".

Chapter 12

Signs of the Times

> Our earth is degenerate in these latter days. There are signs that the world is speedily coming to an end. Bribery and corruption are common.[118] — Assyrian tablet 2800BC

> What has been is what will be, and what has been done is what will be done; there is nothing new under the Sun. (Eccles. 1:9)

Occasionally, I like to perform a google search for the word, *prophecy*. About ten years ago I remember getting five million hits. I did this again recently. This time, I got 57,300,000 hits. Many have opinions, and they are quite ready to express them.

As I told earlier, my 17-year-old son died unexpectedly in a tragic accident. At that time, Family Radio was a popular Christian radio station. My family and I enjoyed the music, audio book readings, and the Bible reading time. The founder, Harold Camping, hosted a nightly Bible question and answer program. He was a sincere enough person, living off the proceeds from having sold his civil engineering business. As far as I know, he never took a salary from Family Radio. Right around the time of my son's death, Camping wrote a book called *1994*. He believed that the Lord would return during the Feast of Tabernacles of that year. He left a bit of wiggle room, saying that there was a 1% chance that the Lord would not return. I'm not sure of what methodology he used to calculate the probabilities. Likely none.

Viv and I respected Camping and the station that he founded. We were also vulnerable with our sadness. Could he be correct? If so, we would be reunited with our son in short order. Grief impacts people in strange ways, doesn't it? But the feast of Tabernacles came and went and nothing happened.

---

[118] *Isaac Asimov's Book of Facts* (1979) Assyrian clay tablet approximately 2800 BC.

Seventeen years passed, and Camping was at it again. This time we didn't take his prediction seriously. Nevertheless, we were curious to observe how people would react. His new date pointed to May 21, 2011. Billboard signs sprang up with the slogan, *Not 2012*. They were competing with the reset of the Mayan calendar. Camping wanted to emphasize that his prediction was correct and the Mayan one false. Some people used all their savings to purchase End Time advertisements and rent billboard space. May came and went. Nothing happened.

Camping, as he put it, "faced the music" with a press conference shortly after. He claimed that he miscalculated and as such revised his date to October 21. No wiggle room this time; October was going to be the end, no doubt about it. The press could have scalded him with embarrassing questions, but they were rather benevolent. After all, Camping was about ninety years old. I suppose if someone makes it that far, there are allowances. Well, October came and went and as expected nothing happened. Camping had a stroke shortly after. He did, to his credit, say that he was wrong and would never set dates anymore. A while later he died. Still, the damage to many vulnerable people was done.

Anticipation of cataclysmic events is nothing new. At the time of Jesus there was great excitement, not for the end of the world, but for the arrival of the messiah. The first century was a very troubling time, likely worse than today. The people cried out for deliverance. The writers of the Dead Sea Scrolls bandied about code words like *lion of wrath, flattery seekers, children of darkness, teacher of righteousness, wicked priest, man of the lie,* and the *Kittim*. Today we do the same. Popular terms include *antichrist, 666, New World Order, rapture, tribulation, Armageddon,* and *second coming.*

In the first century, many believed there would be more than one Messiah. The military leader from the lineage of David was to annihilate all the enemies of God. The war scroll describes forty years of setbacks leading to the ultimate victory. *True Israelites* would then rule the entire world from Jerusalem. The second messiah from the priestly line was to fulfill the prophecies of Isaiah. His birth would be of a miraculous nature. He would suffer persecutions and a violent death. He would be called *the Son of God*. After the war, all evil would be destroyed and true temple worship set up. The Dead Sea Temple Scroll describes this worship in the finest detail. The utopia it describes seems to me to be rather harsh and uncompromising. In any case, the expectations led to many supposed messiahs. Eventually, the temple was destroyed and after the AD 135 Bar Kokhba rebellion, the name of the Jewish homeland was changed to Palestine. Jews subsequently were not allowed back. Much blood was shed. Wars were fought for nothing. Even the famous Jewish sage Rabbi Akiba fell for the hype.

First century believers expected the Messiah to return in their lifetime; this likely included Peter, Paul, and John. Their expectation and hope came directly from New Testament scripture. The key is Mark 13:30, "This generation shall not pass away until all these things have taken place." Jesus apparently used the term *this generation* in other quotes to refer to that particular generation. Why would Mark 13 be different? In any case, nothing happened. As a result, those early believers were forced to revise their theology. Church fathers, like Clement, Justyn Martyr, Tertullian, and others began interpreting the verses of Matthew, Mark, and Luke as having been fulfilled when the temple was destroyed in AD 70. Today, this interpretation is labeled the preterist view.

There were many end time prophecies through the ages. Around Y1K, there was a flurry of them. Interpreters considered the thousand years in the Book of Revelation to be a literal number. There were more predictions around the year 1030, approximately a thousand years after the crucifixion. Another bunch appeared a thousand years after Constantine's conversion to Christianity.

The predictions did not end as the centuries went on. Martin Luther taught that the world would end in 1600 at the latest. Charles Wesley predicted 1794. Jonathan Edwards prophesized 2000. Joseph Smith, founder of Mormonism, thought he would see Christ come in the clouds when he was 85 years old; he died at 35. The Great Disappointment happened on October 22, 1844 when William Miller's followers sold their belongings and waited patiently at the top of a mountain. Nothing happened. One can only imagine the embarrassment they endured as they trekked back down. Then Ellen White, the founder of the Adventists, set several dates around 1850.

Herbert Armstrong, founder of the Church of God, predicted 1936, and again 1975. Chuck Smith of Calvary Chapel looked to 1981. Gordon Lindsay, founder of *Christ for the Nations,* anticipated the tribulation before 2000. Pat Robertson predicted 1982, and in his book *The New Millennium* suggested a new date: April 29, 2007. Hal

Lindsey looked to 1988, and then proposed 2000. Brother Kenneth Hagin predicted 1997. Jerry Falwell of the moral majority expected Jan 1, 2000 to be the fateful day. Kenneth Copeland thought that February 11, 2000 would be the end of the 6000th year since Adam. Grant Jeffrey suggested Oct 9, 2000. Tim LaHaye of the Left Behind series expected global economic crisis in 2000. Of course, we can't forget the book, *Eighty-Eight Reasons for 1988*.

There are repeat offenders too. The Jehovah's Witnesses predicted 1914, 1915, 1918, 1920, 1925, 1941, 1975, and 1994. Michael Rood proposed 1999 and several dates afterwards. Monte Judah made similar predictions around the same time. Author Marilyn Agee has the record as far as I can tell. She predicted the end at least fourteen times.

More recently, we've heard about blood moons, the shemitah, signs in the heavens, deadly comets, planet X, and Nibiru. With YouTube and social media, end time predictions are accelerating. We might say the prediction of the month makes its splash and then quietly melts away. One popular way to avoid the embarrassment of being wrong is to simply change the prediction before the time arrives. A second is to leave some uncertainty in the prediction. Another technique is to just lay low for a while and then return with another prediction a few months later.

There are many downsides to end-time predictions. Not the least of these is their effect on those outside the faith. Christians become a laughing stock, and rightly so. They are perceived to be irrational believers of nonsense. Followers of a prophet might overlook false prophecies because they have a lot invested emotionally. To those outside the faith, it gives Christianity a bad name.

A second downside is especially true of American evangelicals. The rapture is primarily popular in the United States. We are so blessed in this country; do we really think we are favored over believers in other countries? Why should we be raptured to avoid tribulation when there are great tribulations happening now in many parts of the world? Christians are being wiped out throughout the middle east. North Korea police puts parents, children, and grandchildren of a Christian family into horrible work camps. I wonder what they would think if we told them Christ might come and rapture Americans before the coming of the Great Tribulation. I wonder.

End time prophecies are divisive to those within the Church. I once read an Internet article by pastor Bill Barnwell of Royal Oak Church, who doesn't buy in to the end time hype. He documents the following email sent to him that is representative of the fundamentalist mindset.

> When the RAPTURE of the CHURCH takes place, and mark my words it will, then maybe then you will see the light! After you have been left behind you are going to look back on all the people that you deceived, who will probably be in your face at that time, and hopefully repent of the false gospel that you are teaching! It's not too late to be saved during the 7-year tribulation period but it will be harder when you hear the Christians, who became Christians after the Rapture of the Church, are being beheaded for the witness of Jesus! Hopefully you and those who partake of your beliefs will see the light before Christ comes for the Church![119]

Christians are to be recognized by their love. One Christian here considers another unsaved because he doesn't believe the same things about the rapture and the tribulation. It is an example of a doctrine that produces bad fruit.

There are other downsides. End time prophecies discourage the next generation. I remember how my kids reacted when they heard end time prophecy. They began to lose interest in life and assume a "what difference does it make attitude." This is unfortunate. What we do while we are alive is far more important than what we hope will happen in the future. Now matters.

Then, what is the impact on someone who believes a prophet, and their prophecies don't come to pass? What did the people do who sold their houses in the 1800s and waited for the Lord to return? What did those 50,000 in London do in the 1700s who ran from the great flood that never happened? What about those who spent life savings on

---

[119] Bill Barnwell, "The Troubling Worldview of the 'Rapture-Ready' Christian," (Feb 7, 2007), http://theapologeticsgroup.com/wp-content/uploads/2012/06/Troubling-Worldview-of-Rapture-Ready-Christians.pdf

billboards in 2011? It can cause a faith crisis. It is one thing if a person turns away because they have reasonable doubts over the truth of Christianity. It is another if they lose their faith because of the damage done by false prophets. As Christians, we should build each other up with sound doctrine and support each other in practical ways. We should not create unnecessary stumbling blocks.

Another problem with false predictions is the disappointment when the bad thing doesn't happen. Do we really want a Great Tribulation? Do we really want Jews to face a crisis far worse than the Holocaust? Are we disappointed when it doesn't happen? If so, we really need to ask ourselves, "What kind of people are we?" Shouldn't we rather pray for God's ongoing mercy for humanity and our world? The ancient prayer, "Lord have mercy on us and on the whole world," seems more appropriate.

One of the worst effects of end time prophecies involves people who want to help God along. People anticipate a coming war with Iran, the rebuilding of the third Jewish temple, the reestablishment of the sacrificial system, and the appearance of the antichrist. Some groups want the United States to attack Iran to trigger Armageddon. Others are raising money to rebuild the temple and favor blowing up the Muslim Dome of the Rock so this will be possible. There is apparently no thought concerning the ramifications of these things, because they think they are right. God help us if people like this get into power. They would impact our foreign policy, cause real and unnecessary problems for the world, and ignite extreme human suffering.

This reminds me again of the Dead Sea Scroll writers and Judea around the time of Christ. They were ready to follow any messianic leader, believing the Lord would support them in their efforts. The result was near destruction of the Jewish people and thousands of years of persecution thereafter.

Suppose we ask a typical American evangelical the question, "Is this the last generation?" I think most would expect the answer to be an emphatic, "Yes!" If we ask, "Will there be a rapture?" Again the answer is, "Yes!" What about the tribulation? Again, "Yes!" Will the Church go through that hard time? The answers get a bit nuanced here. People fall into the categories of, pre-tribulation, mid-tribulation, post-tribulation, and pre-wrath. Will we see the antichrist? It all depends on when we are caught away to meet Christ in the air.

Christians are vulnerable to false predictions. The reason is because the teachers they respect emphasize the verses that support their views of the end. They conveniently ignore or reinterpret those verses that warn not to do this. For example, after Jesus provides detailed descriptions pertaining to the destruction of the second Jewish temple, he rattles off a series of parables to serve as warnings. One describes virgins who run out of oil while waiting for the bridegroom to return. A second parable focuses on a servant who gets drunk and starts beating his fellow servants while the owner is away. Another discusses the consequences of when servants do not properly invest the talents entrusted to them. Jesus indicates that the end will come unexpectedly, like a thief in the night, and no one knows the day or the hour. The message is: don't worry about when. We should focus on the work to be done now.

The false prophets avoid these warnings in several ways. For example, they might manipulate the context of the following verse in Thessalonians.

> But you, beloved, are not in darkness, for that day to surprise you like a thief, for you are all children of light and children of the day; we are not of the night or of darkness. (1 Thess. 5:4-5)

It is true that this verse tells us that the end will not be a surprise to the faithful. But it is not because they have advance knowledge that the time of the end is near. Rather, it is because they are found faithful whenever that time comes. Whenever it happens, it is okay.

Another way to circumvent Jesus' warnings is to pick verses apart. We are told that no one knows the day or hour. Some will argue, "Yeah, but we can know the month, year, or season." This is parsing words and missing the point in my opinion.

In the first century, the religious leaders rejected Jesus. They were not anticipating a non-violent messiah. He was not what they expected and not what they wanted. How do we know that we are not guilty of the same thing as we wait for his second coming? I expect that there will be many surprises. In the meantime, there is good reason to rethink the passages that so often lead to the unhelpful conclusions that I've been describing.

End time prophecy comes primarily from the book of Revelation and scattered verses elsewhere. The preterist interpretation holds that all of these predictions were entirely fulfilled in the first century. Some of their arguments are persuasive in my view. Others seem forced. In any case, let's analyze those verses that many use to formulate their end time predictions.

The Temple Destruction

The three synoptic gospels feature a dialogue between Jesus and his disciples. The disciples were admiring the magnificence of the second Jewish temple. It was a sight to see, even from the Mount of Olives, two miles away. Herod was known for constructing amazing building projects. The temple complex was roughly the size of a football field with the main structure being approximately ten stories high. The disciples must have thought it to be indestructible.

Jesus responds to their admiration in an unexpected way. "The whole thing, in this generation, will be destroyed. Not a trace will remain." Can you imagine the impression this made on the disciples? The temple was the center of Jewish worship. To a Jew, it was more than that. It was the center of the world. It was the place where God and heaven met the earth. Using Druidic terminology, it was a thin place.

Jews in the first century had no expectation for the world to end. End of the age to them meant the end of the Romans. It meant the establishment of a new physical holy kingdom that would last forever. The city of Jerusalem was to be the center of this kingdom.

Put yourself back at that time. What would you say next? The answer is obvious. When? When will this take place? When will the current age of oppression end? It is an expected question. Jesus then, in rapid fire, rattles off a series of things to look for. These include false messiahs, earthquakes, famines, wars, and signs from heaven.

Many of the things that Jesus predicted did happen in the first century. There was a severe famine that swept the empire. Tacitus reports repeated earthquakes in AD 51; Josephus states that Judea experienced an earthquake that impacted the entire cosmos; he reports many strange signs that occurred in those years. Conflicts between the Romans and Jews were continuous. Several civil wars plagued the empire. We tend to downplay the things that happened in the distant past because we weren't there. To the people living through these events, these things were life-changing. Instead, those living in comfortable settings are using statistics to plot an increasing number of earthquakes in our century.

Matthew and Mark indicate that the physical signs were birth pangs. Intense persecution was to follow. Luke places persecution first. Maybe both were true. There surely were intense persecutions before and afterwards. Christians were burned alive under Nero for his entertainment and many were crucified; others were fed to lions in the Roman Coliseum while excited fans watched. Jesus indicated that the time would be cut short. If that level of persecution were continuous, persisting for years on end, maybe no one would have been able to endure; Christianity would be wiped out at its beginning. It was a truly a time of Great Tribulation.

Jesus warned his disciples. "When you see Jerusalem surrounded by armies, flee." History records that his followers took this warning literally and ran to the mountains. This was one of the reasons the Way separated from its beginnings as a Jewish sect. The *fleeing to the mountains* is connected to another coming event foretold by Jesus, the Abomination of Desolation (Matt. 24:15). This happened a first time in 167BC, when the Greek ruler Antiochus Epiphanes mockingly sacrificed a pig on the temple altar.[120] Jesus indicates that a similar defilement would happen again, and his prediction was literally fulfilled. Titus joined his father Vespasian at Ptolemais on the Phoenician coast in April of AD 67. From here, they launched the Roman invasion of Galilee. The campaign ended with the destruction if the second temple in August AD 70. Josephus describes dead bodies all over the temple as the Romans laid siege.

> And are not both the city and the entire temple now full of the dead bodies of your countrymen? It is God, therefore, it is God himself who is bringing on this fire, to purge that city and temple by means of the Romans, and is going to pluck up this city, which is full of your pollutions.[121]

---

[120] 1 Maccabees 1:54
[121] Josephus, *The Jewish War*, book 6, chapter 2 paragraph 1.

The Romans also defiled the temple by offering pagan sacrifices there before its final destruction.

> AND now the Romans, upon the flight of the seditious into the city, and upon the burning of the holy house itself, and of all the buildings round about it, brought their ensigns to the temple and set them over against its eastern gate; and there did they offer sacrifices to them, and there did they make Titus imperator with the greatest acclamations of joy.[122]

After Jesus provides details about the destruction of the temple, he dramatically switches his language. He begins using apocalyptic symbols. Neither the Sun nor the Moon will shine, stars will fall from the sky, the powers of the heavens will be shaken, a great trumpet will sound, all the tribes of the earth will mourn and faint in fear, the seas will roar, and the Son of Man will come in the clouds to gather the elect from the four winds of heaven. These are word pictures that can be interpreted in many ways.

This kind of dramatic visual imagery appears frequently in Old Testament poetry. They stir the emotions and the imagination. Artists and musicians can appreciate this far better than those focused on rational thought, and who demand certainty. Jesus wins, love triumphs, all will be set right. The symbols signify major, cataclysmic shifts in history. Coming in the clouds, for example, is a metaphor meaning vindication.[123] The four winds of heaven frequently means the known world and does not necessarily reach to the Americas or Australia.[124] These symbols may very well apply to the entire New Testament period, but they might also apply specifically to the age of the apostles. I'm sure that the first century believers thought they were for them. The verbiage gives us a sense of what is to come, but I think it is a mistake to use them for specific literal predictions.

Matthew's gospel provides a provocative statement that seemingly addresses those living in the first century. He writes: "This generation

---

[122] Ibid. book 6, chapter 6, paragraph 1).
[123] R.T. France, *The Gospel of Mark* and N.T. Wright *the New Testament and the People of God.*
[124] Dan. 8:8, 11:4, Zech. 2:6.

will not pass away until all these things have taken place (Matt 24:34)."

That generation did indeed see many, if not all of those things take place. Heaven and earth were coming together. Death was defeated at the cross. God's kingdom was coming to earth. Paul tells us in Colossians 1:23 that the gospel had already been preached to all creatures under heaven. The events leading up to the temple's destruction took place. Great persecutions occurred. The vindication of Jesus and his message came. The momentous shift in history happened.

But questions remain. What does the phase *all of those things take place* really mean? Does Matthew mean *have taken place* or does he mean *begun to take place*? Was he referring to that particular generation, the last generation, or both? What is meant by "pass away?" (Are not the first century generation believers alive with Jesus still)? Which of Jesus' prophecies have already been satisfied and which suggest multiple fulfillments? The answers to these questions are not clear. Perhaps we are simply not supposed to know more.

The Rapture

The rapture is a doctrine that implies that we will suddenly fly away to meet Jesus. This doctrine was popularized by Darby in nineteenth century England, though it never caught on there. It is primarily an American evangelical belief. But is it true? Its primary proof text is from a First Thessalonians letter.

> For the Lord himself, with a cry of command, with the archangel's call and with the sound of God's trumpet, will descend from heaven, and the dead in Christ will rise first. Then we who are alive, who are left, will be caught up in the clouds together with them to meet the Lord in the air; and so, we will be with the Lord forever. (1 Thess. 4:16-17)

Most American evangelicals read this verse literally. NT Wright, one of the foremost Biblical scholars of our time, interprets it differently. It contains apocalyptic symbols including a command crying from heaven, the voice of an archangel, and a trumpet. This is a clue. The event is engaging our imagination and our senses of sight and sound. Wright observes parallels to the arrival of the Roman emperor when returning from battle. The people leave their homes and line the roads. They meet the emperor and travel back to the town with him to celebrate the victory.

A foretaste of this happened when Jesus approached Jerusalem on a donkey on Palm Sunday. The streets were lined and the people yelled: "Hosanna to the Son of David! Blessed is he who comes in the name of the Lord! Hosanna in the highest!" Jesus was the true king, not Caesar. The Pharisees told him to rebuke the crowd. He refused. He wasn't coming to conquer by force as his arrival on a lowly donkey demonstrated. He was coming as king, nonetheless.

The Thessalonian letter paints a similar image, using apocalyptic language. In this case, all who are alive, together with all who arise, go out to meet the arriving king. As Moses came down from the mountain at Sinai, Jesus will come down from the clouds. All return with him to earth to fully establish his kingdom in victory on earth. The Caesars of the world are no more.

The Antichrist

Central to end time fervor is the quest to identify the antichrist. In the recent past, the antichrist was Kennedy, Clinton, Obama, Erdogan, Hitler, and many others. The Pope is always a leading candidate. Presently, if you perform an Internet search, you'll find that Trump and his son-in-law Kushner are near the top of the list. I believe that this focus is hurtful and not worthy of the Christian tradition.

Antichrist theology comes from the books of Daniel, Revelation, First John, and First Thessalonians. First John describes many antichrists already present. He doesn't clearly say that there will be a single very bad one who appears at the end of time, though he doesn't deny this either. John, in my opinion, was very likely addressing an early form of Gnosticism. This became a significant threat to orthodox Christianity in the second and third centuries. Gnostics considered all matter to be evil, and because of this, Jesus' life could not be physical; it was an illusion.

Second Thessalonians contains verses commonly believed to refer to the antichrist. They describe a man of lawlessness that will appear.

> As to the coming of our Lord Jesus Christ and our being gathered together to him, we beg you, brothers and sisters, not to be quickly shaken in mind or alarmed, either by spirit or by word or by letter, as though from us, to the effect that the day of the Lord is already here. Let no one deceive you in any way; for that day will not come unless the rebellion comes first and the lawless one is revealed, the one destined for destruction. He opposes and exalts himself above every so-called god or object of worship, so that he takes his seat in the temple of God, declaring himself to be God. Do you not remember that I told you these things when I was still with you? And you know what is now restraining him, so that he may be revealed when his time comes. For the mystery of lawlessness is already at work, but only until the one who now restrains it is removed. And then the lawless one will be revealed, whom the Lord Jesus will destroy with the breath of his mouth, annihilating him by the manifestation of his coming. The coming of the lawless one is apparent in the working of Satan, who uses all power, signs, lying wonders, and every kind of wicked deception for those who are perishing, because they refused to love the truth and so be saved. (2 Thess. 2:1-10)

Most first-century believers, Paul included, expected a quick return of Jesus. Why would they think anything different? The gospel going out to the whole world to them meant the Roman empire. It didn't include the aboriginal Australians or people living in New Guinea. Apparently, there was a rumor going around that the Lord had already returned. The congregation feared that they had missed it. One of the purposes of Paul's letter was to reassure them. I think it likely that Paul was aware of Jesus' Mount of Olive discourse that we discussed above. This is evidenced by parallels between the above Thessalonians passage and Matthew 24. Paul knew that the end could not come until the temple was destroyed. When he referred to the man of lawlessness, the son of destruction, he probably was using code for a coming Roman emperor.[125] Those emperors presided over the Imperial Cult, which demanded that the populace refer to them as divine, calling them Lord.

The above verses in Thessalonians foretell that the man of lawlessness will utilize "all power, signs, lying wonders, and every kind of wicked deception." The historian Tacitus, documents two such deceptions performed by the emperor Vespasian. One of them, cited below, even mimics a Jesus miracle. These were false signs in that they were stunts performed to bring glory to the emperor.

> Of the Alexandrian people, one man who learned that there was decay of his eyes fell at his [Vespasian's] knees, imploring him with a groan for a remedy of his blindness, since the god Serapis advised him...he begged the princeps that his cheeks and circles of the eyes were deemed worthy to be sprinkled with his spit. Another man who was sick in his hand spoke to this same god and father [Serapis] with the result that his hand might be walked on by the Caesar's foot and footprints. At first, Vespasian laughed and these requests were rejected. Through these instances, he feared that he would acquire a reputation for vanity, but he was finally led to hope by the entreaty of these very people and the cries of adulation.
>
> Finally, he ordered them to be checked out by some doctors or to learn if such kinds of blindness or debility might be surmounted with human aid. The doctors talked in various ways: for the one man, the power of light was not gone and it would return if obstacles were removed; for the other man, his muscles slipped into a crooked form, but if he was held with good power, it was possible that he could be made whole .... if the remedies were performed, there would be glory for Caesar. But if they were of no importance to the unfortunate men, there would be mockery. Therefore,

---

[125] Refer to various commentaries on the verse. For example, F.B. Meyer or Ellicott.

> Vespasian imagined that all fortune was available to him, and nothing could be more incredible.
>
> With a happy appearance, he stood among the multitude which had gathered, and he performed the prescriptions. Steadily, the hand turned to use and the day shown again for the blind man. (Tacitus, *Histories*, 4.81)

Parts of the above quote from Thessalonians do seem to point to Jesus' second coming. Consider the phrase: "[the lawless one] whom the Lord Jesus will kill with the breath of his mouth and bring to nothing by the appearance of his coming." One could say that this was not fulfilled by any Roman emperor. Furthermore, no Roman Emperor ever sat in the temple of God "declaring himself to be God."

In any case, why are we Christians so determined to identify the antichrist? Do we wish for his arrival? Let's instead pray that "the one who restrains," continue to restrain. Let's hope that the third temple does not get built. If the end is not yet; there is still time to establish God's kingdom on earth.

The Great Falling Away

There are a number of verses in the bible that predict a great falling away and an increase of evil immediately before Jesus' return.[126] As I ponder this, I recall reading about many falling away periods in history. During the second half of the third century AD, persecution was particularly intense. These caused many Christians to abandon the faith.[127] Some even turned over the sacred writings to the authorities to be burned.

The period leading up to the Reformation experienced another great falling away. The Sale of Indulgences were supposed to reduce the time dead relatives spent in purgatory. The poor gave what they couldn't afford, and expensive building projects were undertaken. Those at the top of church hierarchy were super-wealthy, and attempts

---

[126] Matt. 24:12, 2 Tim. 3, 2 Pet 3
[127] Emperors Decius (AD 249-251), Diocletian (AD 283-305), and Valerian (AD 253-260)

to challenge their position were met with violence. More than a hundred years of bloodshed followed.

The start of a great falling away in America could be dated to 1925 with the Scopes Monkey trial. Convinced that they lost the culture, evangelicals retreated to their silos of faith. Instead of engaging the wider society, they decided to sit back and wait for Christ to return. End time prophecies increased, rhetoric became strident, and religion became political. These things caused Christians to be largely viewed as judgmental, hypocritical, and anti-science. At the same time, pastors started to function as CEOs and celebrities instead of shepherds. Megachurches and TV evangelists became the new face of Christianity.

In my opinion, it is a mistake to blame the falling away on the darkness of the times. Rather it is because the institutional church is no longer faithful to its calling. Instead of equipping individuals to engage the world using their specific talents, the focus is to recruit helpers to implement the Pastor's vision. The unfortunate implication is that fulltime Christian service is considered more important than the specific callings of everyday congregants.

Is this generation experiencing the final falling away where the love of many grow cold? I hope not. Time will tell.

Why the Fuss?

Why is there such a fuss about end times? There are many reasons. I've thought of a few, but there are probably others.

First, I believe it is a human desire to want to know what is going to happen. Fortune telling is big business. Astrology charts are one of the most popular sections of newspapers and news sites on the Internet. The chaos of the future is scary because it is unknown. We want to be in control, and the unknown can make us feel overwhelmed and helpless. A second reason is that we get tired of the trouble we face from day to day. A rapture would solve all the problems. We wouldn't have to face difficulties. Instead, we would simply fly away to the good place. A third reason is the prideful desire to have inside knowledge, the inside secrets, if you will. People join groups like the Prophecy Club to feel special, to be on the cutting edge.

Then there are those who believe the scary predictions portrayed in books like *the Late Great Planet Earth* and movies like *the Left Behind* series. These include seven years of unimaginable holocaust and violence, computer chips being inserted into people's brains, and devastation when huge numbers of people suddenly disappear. They feature an evil antichrist who rules the world. Who wouldn't want to escape from these things? If they are truly on the horizon, the rapture would be a good alternative. The books and movies are designated as quasi-fiction, but with a subtle implication that they are based on accurate biblical teachings. Those who buy into this, change their day-to-day life patterns and sometimes make unfortunate choices. There are instances where families are split apart. These books and movies lure the vulnerable and turn off the rational.

A last reason to fall for the end time hype is that we fear death. The rapture means we don't have to die. One would think that believers, of all people, should have the least fear of death. Yet, Christians tend to fear death as much as anyone else.

Let's sum up these reasons: The unknown is scary, we don't like trouble, we want to feel special, we seek secret inside knowledge, life is difficult, and we are afraid of death. These are strong motivations to focus on prophecy. All of this can be quite compulsive.

For Christians, it should be easy to recognize false teachings, especially when they concern prophecies. Unfortunately, this is not the case. With that in mind, let's look at how to keep from getting drawn into the trap of end time predictions.

Never put too much faith in a respected religious leader. John Wesley, Jonathan Edwards, and Martin Luther are well-known giants of the faith. Pat Robertson, Jerry Falwell, Kenneth Copeland, and John Hagee have huge followings. But popularity and stature don't make a person correct. Christians should never check their critical thinking skills at the door when it comes to prophecy. This is true for any doctrine of faith for that matter. Use your mind. Respected leaders are just people with the same problems and flaws as anyone else. Putting faith in certain people without checking their views against other standards leads to disappointment.

Another thing to watch out for is a prophecy that conveniently leaves out or twist verses that don't fit. The one that quickly comes to mind is "no one knows the day or hour." I've heard some end-time proponents say, "Yes, but that phrase about knowing the day or hour is a first-century idiom meaning the Feast of Trumpets." Baloney! There is no historical evidence for such an expression.

Third, it is dangerous to interpret ancient books in terms of current events. The events of every age are unique and dramatic. In the previous generation, we experienced World War I, World War II, the Holocaust, Communism, the establishment of the state of Israel, the six-day war, and the Yom Kippur war. In the current generation there are temple sacrifice preparations, nuclear proliferation, threats of radical Islam, a push towards globalism, the Internet, mass school shootings, major redefinitions of morality, and dangerous advances of technology. It is easy to say, "This proves it, we are at the end." Keep in mind, this is what every generation says. The job of a Christian is to live as a citizen of the kingdom in whatever time we're in.

Next, watch out for strange numerologies. This is the practice of either interpreting numbers in the Bible literally, or using formulas to compute some end date. The books of Daniel and Revelation, for example, contain mysterious numeric values like 1000 years, 666, 2300 days, 1335 days, 1290 days, three and a half years, and five months. The ancient authors do not treat numbers in a literal manner as does the modern world. Often, they use numeric values as symbols to mean something else. Consider how the numbers three, four, six, seven, ten, and twelve appear throughout the Bible. Sometimes these values are squared. Sometimes they are multiplied together. In most cases, the authors are conveying a concept, not a literal number.

Matthew's genealogy is an example. He records fourteen generations from Abraham to David, from David to the Babylon exile, and from Babylon to Christ. Literally, he was wrong. Names were left out. But literalism was not his goal; Mathew was making a point. The fourteenth of the month of Nissan is when the Passover is celebrated each year. It commemorates the Exodus when the Israelites were freed from slavery. Fourteen signifies deliverance. I think Matthew is using the fourteens in the genealogies to signify the deliverance that Jesus provides. A new Exodus is in view. To force modern usage of numbers on an ancient text is a futile practice. We should consider this before trying to determine the timing of the second coming.

Now that we've looked at what not to do, let's consider the opposite: how should we approach prophetic proclamations? There are a few criteria that I use. If a prophecy concerns the future, I start with a high level of skepticism. I listen to prophecies sometimes, but mostly for fun. It is amusing to see what the supposed prophets are saying this month and then hear how they backtrack after their predictions prove false.

If you tend to wonder, "Could it be true?" consider the following:

1. Are the prophecies specific enough to put to the test? If not, pay no attention.
2. Is there wiggle room designed to avoid accountability? If so, ignore.
3. Was a prophet ever wrong, even once? If so, ignore all their future prophecies.
4. Are the prophecies compatible with Jesus' teachings? If not, ignore them.

Prophecies in the Bible rarely have the purpose of prediction. They rather are there to comfort when times are hard and to challenge when times are easy.

Conclusion

All our doctrines should contribute to strengthen our relationship with God and our relationships with each other. End time prophecies tend to do the opposite. They can damage us so we don't see God in a good way. We stop thinking about how we can better love our neighbor and make this a world a better place. One might ask: "Why worry about this fallen creation? It will be burned up and replaced anyway. Won't all the work we do now be a wasted effort? Shouldn't we focus our efforts on evangelism?" These are fair questions.

I'll answer with an analogy. There was a recent TV series called *Extreme Makeover*. The producers, each week, select a deserving family needing help. Their home is falling apart and the family doesn't have the resources to make the necessary repairs. In a week's time, with the help of neighbors and volunteers, the house is completely revamped and remade. During the renovation, the network provides a hotel as a temporary residence for the owners. One might say that this residence corresponds to heaven while we await all things to be made new.

Upon the project's completion, the owners return and are escorted through their newly created residence. Each room contains important memorabilia from the original. The good from the old was transferred to the new. This often is the most inspiring part of the show. In the same way, the good we do in this life is not wasted. Its impacts will be transferred to the new earth. What we do now is important; it all matters.

What are we to believe about the end times? My belief is that scripture is not clear enough to tell us when with any degree of certainty. It is not for us to set dates. Will there be a rapture? Not like that portrayed in the movies. Will there be an antichrist that appears at the end? Very likely; evil is powerful and real. We can only imagine what could happen when a charismatic leader embodies that force having the power of technology at their disposal. Will there be a seven-year tribulation? If so, its nature will likely be something unexpected. Will there be a thousand-year reign of Christ? Probably not that literal length. Time will tell. Will there be a great falling away of the Church? Throughout history there have been many falling away periods and many revivals. I'm praying for another revival. Are there lots of false prophets around? Absolutely. Will Jesus return unexpectedly? Yes.

What about the Book of Revelation? Its interpretation has led to much confusion and division. Some church leaders over the centuries went so far as to propose that it should be removed entirely from scripture. I'll address these things in the following chapters.

Chapter 13

The Book of Revelation — Introduction

> I can in no way detect that the Holy Spirit produced it …they are supposed to be blessed who keep what is written in this book; and yet no one knows what that is, to say nothing of keeping it … My Spirit cannot adapt itself to the book. For me this is reason enough not to think highly of it: Christ is neither taught nor known in it.[128] —Martin Luther

The Book of Revelation is an ancient letter complete with an initial salutation and final blessing. Yet it is much more than a letter. It is a prophecy, but not a detailed point-by-point list of predictions whose secrets will be decoded in due season. Its imagery is violent, but its message comes from the Prince of Peace. It is steeped in Old Testament references, but often redefines their implications.

It is an apocalyptic message whose purpose is to explain spiritual realities behind events of the day. It digs deep into the spirit with a confusing collection of interrelated symbols and visions. It is a Greco-Roman drama, flipping between scenes with musical interludes. It engages the imagination, not logic. It functions as an integrated whole that invokes the senses. John, the seer, eats a book, visits the throne room of God, hears trumpets and orchestras, feels the smoke of a furnace, and smells the sulfur coming from the mouth of horses. It is baffling to the rational mind, but clearly describes with metaphors and pictures things difficult to explain in any other way. Interpreted responsibly, Revelation is important to every generation including our own. Interpreted irresponsibly, it is pure speculation with no meaning at all.

While Revelation does not inform us of the exact details of what is coming, it promises that God's kingdom will prevail. Heaven and Earth will merge and God's will for the Universe most certainly will come to fruition. Revelation encourages followers of the Way to continue as faithful citizens of the heavenly kingdom, and to look

---

[128] Martin Luther, *Preface to the Revelation* (1522).

forward to the day when its dominion fully enters our physical realm. Genesis and Revelation are appropriate bookends to the 66-book library that we know as the Bible.

It is impossible to understand the Book of Revelation without first understanding the world of the late first century when it was written. Let's enter that world.

Rome is the dominant superpower. Its citizens confidently proclaim the doctrine, Pax Romana, peace of Rome. Its manifest destiny is to rule the Mediterranean and all surrounding lands, expanding ever outward till all peoples, tribes and nations come under its influence. The purpose is to bring peace, rule of law, order, security, and stability to the ends of the earth. All of this will be accomplished through military might, peace through strength. Barbarous tyrants in rogue nations must be pounded and subdued. As long as the gods smile on the mission and the military continues to do its important work, the dream will move forward. Rome's democratic system is the gift to the world, for which its subjects should be grateful. It will rule forever.

The Roman rulers are placed in power by divine right. They are the friends of the gods and our mediators who represent humanity. Ever since a comet was observed hovering in the sky for seven days after the death of Julius Caesar, the populace has recognized that emperors are more than mere men. They are not quite equal to the gods, but will live with them and achieve immortality. Everyone recognizes that each emperor, starting with Augustus, is the Lord, the son of god, the savior of the world. This is the good news for all peoples of the empire.

The Roman Imperial Cult is the fastest-growing world religion, and it is happy to recognize the local gods of the provinces. They simply add newly discovered gods to the blessed pantheon. Rome embraces diversity. It is important, however, that the center of all worship be directed towards the great city which is blessed by her god, Roma. Citizens demonstrate patriotism by attending regular empire-wide celebrations and processions. These are generally well-received. The populace enjoys receiving coins thrown to them by the super-wealthy. Sacrifices are part of the rituals; it is important to maintain favor with the gods so Rome's divine mission will continue unimpeded. These activities promote unity and patriotism. Long live Rome.

On the Lord's day, we venerate the emperor at imperial temples. This is to show appreciation for the genius bestowed upon him by the gods. There are statues everywhere, reminding citizens of their obligations. The impressive Roman temples portray the greatness of the empire. The structure at Pergamum, for example, is one of the seven wonders of the world; it is a magnificent sight to see. These temples serve a double function as well: They are centers of commerce. You cannot buy or sell apart from the workings of these institutions. The merchants and traders regularly conduct their affairs through temple facilities, which are situated prominently at many city centers.

We Romans are suspicious but respectful of the Jews. They serve one God and would rather fight to the death than be willing to submit to our modest Roman requirements. This makes no sense. Why not just obey? You don't actually have to believe anything. Worship in the Roman world does not involve faith. Rather, it is driven by obligation. One must correctly and precisely follow the rituals. Nevertheless, because the Jewish faith is ancient, even more so than that of Rome, Jews have special status. At least they did till the Jewish war broke out.

Followers of the Way are another story. Like the Jews, most of them will not submit to Roman requirements. They worship a man who they claim rose from the dead as if he is a god. They are weak. Way-followers won't even fight; they die willingly for their superstition. How preposterous is this? Their worship is emotional. This is very suspicious and weird. It is particularly worrisome that they meet privately in their homes. This presents a serious threat to Roman rule. Who knows what they are plotting? It can't be good. This superstition must be forcibly dealt with. When we interrogate with threat and torture, those who relent, we can release. Those who won't, we'll execute. This should be sufficient to wipe out this recent form of atheism.

Persecution of Jesus' followers tends to be fierce in some places and sporadic in others. Under Nero's reign, it was especially intense. That was a bit more than twenty years ago. At the present, the followers of the Way and the Romans are tenuously getting along.

The Roman Imperial Cult is not enforced directly from Rome. There is simply not enough available manpower. Local authorities are entrusted to do the hard work. There are benefits directed to effective proconsuls. The more loyal ones receive more benefits. All wealth and power originate from the central glorious city.

There is a dark side of Roman rule, including economic oppression, and a great divide exists between the rich and poor. The one percent upper class tightly control the economy. Tacitus, a Roman senator and historian, writes:

> They have plundered the world, stripping naked the land in their hunger... they are driven by greed, if their enemy be rich; by ambition, if poor... They ravage, they slaughter, they seize by false pretenses, and all of this they hail as the construction of empire. And when in their wake nothing remains but a desert, they call that peace.[129]

John the Seer

It is the fifteenth year of Domitian's reign. John, the Seer, is on Patmos, a small island off the coast, near Ephesus. He is a follower of the Nazarene Chrestus, and he frequently visits congregations in Asia Minor. He is concerned for those gatherings and shares in their persecution. His testimony as a traveling prophet is likely why he is isolated on this remote island. His clockwise circuit includes seven metropolitan areas including Ephesus, Smyrna, Pergamum, Thyatira, Sardis, Philadelphia, and Laodicea. There are likely other cities that he visits, like Troas to the north and Miletus to the south, but on this particular day, his focus is directly on these seven.

Ephesus is a western coastal city, an important commercial center. It is the capital of the province of Asia. Its temple of Artemis, which like the Imperial temple of Pergamum, is a wonder of the world. The city contains a variety of other temples as well. In 29BC, Ephesus appealed to Rome and was granted permission to build a special temple for venerating Julius Caesar and the goddess Roma. Later, additional space was allocated for emperor Augustus and the local goddess Artemis. The Way congregation in Ephesus is solid in their beliefs, but they stay by themselves and rarely proselytize.

Smyrna, about 35 miles north, is also on the coast. There is hostility there from the Jewish synagogues. Rumors are concocted claiming

---

[129] Tacitus, AD 55-125, *The Agricola and the Germania*, (1894).

that Way-followers participate in barbaric rituals. The Romans seem to believe these things, and this leads to periods of severe persecution.

Pergamum, 45 miles further north, competes with Smyrna for the title *First City of Asia*. The Imperial Cult is strictly enforced here because this city is a principle Greco-Roman worship center. Its many temples, made from locally quarried black stone, honor gods like Athena, Asclepius, Dionysus, and Zeus. Refusal to participate is traitorous and only the godless and subversive will refuse. Followers of the Way are always at risk here, and some have been martyred. To avoid a similar fate, many of those remaining are beginning to conform to Roman requirements. In some cases, they engage in popular sexual practices as well.

Going about 40 miles southeast, we come to Thyatira. It is smaller than the three coastal cities, but well known for its manufacture of purple dye. It has strong trade guilds featuring expert artisans who produce fine cloth, bronze-works, and pottery. Way-followers here are known for their growing generosity and kindness, yet they are embracing teachings that synchronize with those of pagan traditions leading people away from the central beliefs.

Next comes Sardis, south of Thyatira by about 32 miles. Twice, this city was thought to be impregnable, but was unexpectedly taken by sneak attack. It is a prosperous city known for the golden sands of the river Pactolus. Strong guilds drive its economy marketing fruits and wool. The Imperial Cult is not quite as strong in this city, but there are rituals at the temple to Cybele. Sardis boasts one of the oldest congregations, but it seems to have lost its way. It has a solid reputation, but appears to be just going through the motions.

Philadelphia is 25 miles slightly southeast. Sometimes, this city is called *Little Athens* because of its plethora of temples and public buildings. It is an agricultural area known for its fine wine, attested to by the writings of the poet, Virgil. A massive earthquake in AD 17 hit Philadelphia particularly hard. As a result, the city is not subject to Roman taxation and has received significant aid from several emperors. The Way is small in this area and faces significant opposition from local Jewish synagogues. Nevertheless, it remains faithful.

Laodicea sits 48 miles south east of Philadelphia and 96 miles west of Ephesus, completing John's seven-city circuit. Situated on an important trade route, it is a major financial center. It has a state-of-the-art medical center for treating eyes and ears. The city's reputation for black wool produced from sheep with a violet glossy coat is known throughout the Roman world. Laodicea's only apparent deficiency is the lack of a good local water supply. Water is piped from a hot spring a few miles away. It has a nauseating smell and the lukewarm mineral-laden taste is awful. Laodicea is the richest of the cities on John's circuit. It is a popular retirement destination for wealthy Roman citizens. After a huge earthquake during Nero's reign, Laodicea was the only city to refuse imperial help. This is a source of pride for the city folk. The wealthy people in the Way-gatherings apparently don't care much for social issues. They feel that they have *served their time* and are blessed to live out their remaining years in luxury.

The Lord's day[130] is a holiday when all Roman citizens are required to give homage to Caesar. Followers of the Way are at most danger at this time, when rituals and temple sacrifices must be observed. John refuses to address Caesar as Lord and Savior, which explains his exile.

There are rumors going around that the tyrant Nero is not really dead but will reappear at some point. The previous years have been tumultuous. A famine swept the empire, serious earthquakes rocked a number of the provinces, and several civil wars wreaked severe damage. Things seem somewhat better now, but memories remain. The empire is again at full dominance. Persecution is less savage, at least in most places.

Yet many are wavering. It is sixty-five years since the crucifixion; only a few eye witnesses remain, and Chrestus has not yet returned. Things are stagnant and God's kingdom seems a long way off. The demands from the Imperial Cult and pressures from local pagans are hard to resist. There are many who are asking, "Can't we assimilate and follow the Way in secret?"

Suddenly, John receives a series of visions. They are vivid. They are frightening. They illustrate a fierce battle between Good and Evil. John ponders them carefully, and after a time weaves them into the Book of Revelation. Blessed are the *readers* and the ones in the audience who *hear*. This book is meant to be acted out. It is a drama in pictures.

---

[130] Coffman's commentaries on the Bible; Robertson's Word Pictures of the New Testament; and the International Standard Bible Encyclopedia, "Lord's Day."

With this in mind, I'm going to present Revelation as a play. Let me first interject a few reasons for taking this unusual approach. With all of the end time hysteria, it is easy to conclude that the book of Revelation is primarily for us in this "last day generation," not for those of previous generations. This conclusion is simply not true. It is also common for Revelation to be read as a book of violence, both by skeptics and people of faith. In my opinion, this is also not true. First century Christians had many advantages over us in understanding this book. They were steeped in Old Testament knowledge, compared to many modern readers who rarely read through the Torah and Prophets and because of this, they often miss the point. People of John's time were fluent in Greek and could appreciate those places where John intentionally used odd grammatical structures to refer to Old Testament quotations. On this point, non-Greek readers have no clue. Early Christian believers understood their world in ways that we do not. In light of these things, presenting Revelation as a play gives us a chance to pretend that we are in the audience as first century listeners. My hope is that presenting Revelation as a play will at a minimum be interesting, and possibly provoke some new ways of understanding this difficult book.

In preparation for this effort, I've read roughly a dozen books on the topic, all by renowned scholars. These include R. Bauckham, M. Gorman, B. Metzger, E. Peterson, P. Williamson, NT Wright, and others. I've also watched presentations given by biblical scholars and studied various biblical commentaries. Throughout my presentation, unless otherwise noted, wherever a Revelation translation appears, it is from N.T. Wright's *Kingdom New Testament*.[131]

---

[131] Wright, N.T., translator, *The Kingdom New Testament: A Contemporary Translation*, 1st ed., (Harper One 2011).

Chapter 14

John's Revelation Visions

As I visualize that I'm alongside John on his amazing journey, this is what I see.

Act 1: Seven Letters, Throne Room, and Seals

Scene 1 (Letters to the Congregations)

We hear a loud, booming, trumpet-like voice. Turning, I see southwestern Asia Minor with fires emanating from the seven congregations. The intensities of the fires vary. Laodicea and Sardis display a faint flicker. Philadelphia's fire, though very small, is at the same time, very bright. The others have different appearances. In the middle of this region stands a huge fiery figure. He appears as the Son of Man, who sits at the right hand of the Father and is to be worshipped by all tribes and nations. In this vision, the Son holds in his hands, the presbyters who are responsible for the well-being of John's seven congregations.

The Son of Man, the Alpha and Omega, the First and the Last, stands huge, so bright that we cannot bear to look. His hair is white, like those of the ancient of days with infinite wisdom. His eyes are as a consuming fire. It is a burning love reaching out to his followers, but perceived as intense wrath by those in flight. His feet appear as indestructible, eternal, burnished steel, not a mixture of iron and clay that will break apart under pressure. His voice is like that of many waters, penetrating and unmistakable, speaking truth which pierces soul and spirit like a two-edged sword. He is dressed in a royal robe fit for the true King of Kings, and wrapped with a gold belt, pure and righteous. John falls down as if dead.

The Son of Man gently touches John, which removes all fear. He is the first and the last, who has conquered death. He possesses the keys which release humanity from the prison of death and hades. He is the one who will, in victory, judge the living and the dead. His kingdom is at hand. This Son of Man has a specific message for each of the seven congregations. It is also for all Way gatherings, any that are able to listen.

To Ephesus: "Your patience is commendable and your doctrines are sound, but make sure to show love to those outside, who are lost. Share the Good News. The tree of life is available to everyone."

To Smyrna: "You've remained strong in spite of intense suffering. It is not over; a series[132] of intense, short persecutions are coming. Religious hypocrites will continue to dream up slanderous charges against you. Remember, death has been defeated; it has no sting. Remain faithful; there is nothing to fear. You will receive your Crown of Life."

To Pergamum: "You are struggling to survive in the center of the evil world system. Stay strong; don't compromise under the pressure from the Imperial Cult operating in Satan's dark black rock temples. Eat the manna provided by God, not meat sacrificed to idols. Be encouraged. The word of truth will judge all evil. Receive the bread of life and your new name will be inscribed on special white marble."

To Thyatira: "Continue to reach out to the lost and needy, but don't be lured by false teachings. Keep faithful to the truth. The kingdom is eternal, indestructible, and the fire of love is intense. Take your place as valued citizens. Use your talents well, and you will influence many nations."

To Sardis: "Wake up from your slumber. Your clothes are soiled, but they can be made clean. Listen, if you can still hear, so your name won't be blotted from the Book of Life. Remember your shock when the Persians took you by surprise: The Son of Man comes as a thief."

To Philadelphia: "You may be small and weak, but you are strong. Stay faithful, and your works cannot fail. In the kingdom, those who oppose you now will study at your feet. You will be vindicated, honored pillars of God's temple which will stand firm despite sudden shifts in empire policy."

To Laodicea: "Use your wealth to care for the widow, orphan, the poor, and the disabled. Your present works are like your putrid, sulfur-laden, lukewarm water supply. Seek true riches, not that which passes

---

[132] Laban altered Jacob's wages ten time (Gen 31:41) indicating repeated occurrences, not exactly ten times. The word day is used in different ways in the scripture. In this case, I interpret day as a relatively short period of time.

away. Let's reason together so your scarlet sins can be turned white. I am knocking at the door of your heart."

Scene 2 (Throne Room)

Suddenly, an open door to heaven appears, and the thundering, trumpet-like voice bellows,

Come up here. I will show you what soon will take place.

There is no time to think. Instantly we are there, in God's place, seeing a throne surrounded by eternal glory. It is an overwhelming brilliance.

There is a figure present, mysterious beyond description, who sits on the throne having a body appearance like that of translucent green Jasper.[133] This reminds me of the promise of the new restored creation. There is also a hint of blood-red Carnelian,[134] bringing to mind the sacrifice of the Son. An emerald rainbow,[135] signifying the new covenant, overflows with brilliant green hues, surrounding the throne like a halo.

In front of the throne appears an awe-inspiring, transparent sea, like crystal.[136] It is a solid barrier between heaven and the mayhem on the earth below. Emanating from the throne are lightning flashes accompanied by a rumbling voice of thunder; I can't decipher the words. Seven lampstands are present, representing the seven congregations, each burning with the fire of the Holy Spirit. This fire is similar to what we saw in our previous vision, but it is incredibly intense and bright. There are seven lampstand spirits that seem to be able to communicate with the seven congregations, as much as they are willing to hear. I am struck by the sevens. This number, symbolizing perfection, completeness, and prominence repeats everywhere in this place.

---

[133] Pliny the Elder, in *Natural Histories,* chapter 35, describes iaspis (jasper) to be green and often transparent. This is likely the very valuable and rare gem stone to which Revelation refers.

[134] Carnelian (Sardius) was considered blood-colored by ancient writers according to Donald Grey Barnhouse, <u>Revelation</u> (Grand Rapids, MI: Zondervan Publishing House, 1971), 90.

[135] Gen. 9:13-16.

[136] Ezek. 1:22.

There are twenty-four elders seated on smaller thrones in a circle around the one in the center. Each one wears a white robe indicating victory and freedom from sin. They wear golden crowns representing the authority which God entrusts to them. The number twenty-four reminds me of the twelve patriarchs and the twelve disciples. I take it that these represent all of the believing Jews and Gentiles who are now alive with the Messiah in paradise.

There are four unusual living beings, who seem to be able to interpret the thundering voice coming from the throne. They respond accordingly to its commands. They have eyes all over, front and back, enabling them to see everything that is happening on heaven and earth. The first is ferocious like a lion, the second is strong as an ox, the third can soar like an eagle, and the fourth has the wisdom that true humanity exhibits. They each have six wings which also have eyes all over them. The first pair of their six wings connect to each other, signifying their interconnected harmony and cooperation. A second wing pair enables them to fly wherever action is needed. The last pair turns inward, representing their internal unity. I have the impression that these beings represent the hosts of heaven that maintain all of creation.

God's glory radiates outward from the throne. We feel the intense blessing of it as it overflows everything. There is no evil in this place. God has no rival in heaven, he is in all and over all. The blessings of his glory are immense; it leads to worship penetrating our spirits. Nothing else is possible. The four beings eternally sing:

> Holy, Holy, Holy
> Lord God Almighty
> Who Was and Who Is and Who is to Come.
> The twenty-four elders throw down their crowns and sing:
> O Lord our God
> All Glory, Honor, and Power is Yours.
> By You are All Things Created.
> By Your Will, they Exist and are Created.

The royal chorus continues for a long time. Then, suddenly, I see the right hand of the one sitting on the throne. He is holding a scroll with writing on both sides, but it is sealed with seven seals. A huge, powerful angel appears and bellows:

Does anyone deserve to undo the seals and open the scroll?

The sound goes out far and wide. On earth, only thunder is heard. In heaven the response is complete silence. We can barely look at the scroll, let alone open it. No one comes forward.

John bursts into tears. It seems that God's will to bring heaven together with earth fails. Perhaps this is because of the failings of the followers of the Way. Is there no hope? No one is worthy.

But then, one of the elders speaks. He says, **"Stop crying, Look!"** Then, in a loud voice, he announces a royal arrival:

> **The Lion from the Tribe of Judah**
> **The Root of David**
> **Has Won the Victory!**
> **He is Worthy to Open the Seals!**

We look to the throne among the elders and four living beings. Surprisingly, we see an innocent little lamb. It has fatal wounds from when it was slaughtered, and yet, it is standing. It has seven eyes that perceive what is happening everywhere on the earth and seven horns that direct the Holy Spirit's work among all of the congregations. This innocent, seemingly helpless lamb walks up and takes the scroll from the one sitting on the throne.

I look over and notice that the four living beings are holding bowls of incense; these are the prayers emanating from Jesus followers on earth saying:

> Our Father
> Who art in Heaven
> Hallowed be thy Name.
> Your Will be Done
> On Earth
> As it is in Heaven.

Then the four living beings, playing harps, begin to sing:

> You are Worthy to Take the Scroll.
> You are Worthy to Open its Seals.
> For You were Slaughtered and with your own Blood.

> You Purchased a People for God
> From every Tribe and Tongue
> From every People and Nation
> And made Them a Kingdom of Priests to our God
> And They Will Reign on the earth.

The elders and innumerable numbers of angels join in with the singing, all with full voice and perfect pitch.

> The Slaughtered Lamb has now Deserved
> To take the Riches and the Power
> To take the Wisdom, Strength, and Honor
> To take the Glory and the Blessing.

From everywhere in creation, I hear the words:

> To the One on the Throne and the Lamb
> Be Blessing and Honor and Glory
> And Power Forever and Ever.

A resounding, **"Amen!"** shouted from the four living beings.

> The elders fall down and worship!

Scene 3 (Seven Seals)

The innocent Lamb opens one of the seven seals. Then simultaneously, one of the four living beings thunders:

Come forward and do your thing!

A white horse appears. The rider is raising a Persian archer's bow and wears a victory wreath on his head. He is bent on conquest. This reminds me of attacks at the eastern Roman border by the Parthians and their recent military victories.

The Lamb snaps open a second seal from the scroll, and another of the four living beings thunders:

Come forward and do your thing!

This time, a red horse appears. I see an image of internal dissent in the Roman empire. Uprisings appear everywhere, leading to much bloodshed.

The Lamb breaks another seal, and I hear thundering, just like before. A black horse appears. The economy is in shambles. A daily minimum wage purchases only a loaf of bread or a pot of barley soup. None of this affects the rich. They still enjoy their fine wine and their expensive spas.

The next seal snaps open with another thundering, and the horse that appears is pale. People are dying everywhere. Disease, famine, and looting trouble roughly a quarter of the empire. The violent don't hesitate to murder and kill to get what they want.

The fifth seal opens. There is no horse image this time, and no thundering announcement of some empire-wide calamity. This time, I see Way-followers. A large number are killed; some are crucified, others beheaded. As they enter into paradise, they are given white robes of righteousness. They are now free from all of the evils of the world. But then I hear them ask:

> Holy and True Master
> How much longer will you tolerate this evil?
> When will things be set right?
> When will final judgment come?

Then I hear the answer:
> Relax. Not yet.
> There are many more to be sealed into the kingdom.
> They will stand firm, just as you did.

The next seal snaps and the images are frightening. A solar eclipse is accompanied by a red blood moon. I feel a tremendous earthquake with a seismic rating of at least 9.0. Now stars are falling out of the sky and heaven itself disappears. This is a nightmare. I sense that this imagery symbolizes something big coming upon the earth, but what? People are afraid. The wealthy power-brokers are hiding their wealth. Many are storing emergency food supplies. Some are even committing suicide to avoid the anticipated calamities. Some are asking: "Is this the end? What is happening? Will anyone survive?"

Four angels appear; these are the ones who restrain evil. They seem ready to let go of their restraint. If they do, evil will immediately run its full course. But then, another angel emerges with the signet ring of God's authority. He shouts:

> **Not yet. It is not time.**
> **Leave the earth, the sea, and everything living alone.**
> **There are many more to be granted kingdom citizenship.**

I'm relieved! Calamity is avoided, at least for now. I wonder, "How long will this take?", and "How many will be sealed into the kingdom?"

Another vision appears, as if to answer my second question. It displays a military census. I see each of the twelve Israel tribes lined up for a count. It symbolizes the ordained number (144,000) of faithful descendants of Abraham, the true Israelites. These are the first fruits of God's kingdom. They will begin the battle to spread God's kingdom to the ends of the earth.

Suddenly, the census vision disappears and another one takes its place. All kingdom citizens, from every tribe and nation are before me, an uncountable number. Each person wears the white robe of righteousness and holds palm branches of peace. They bellow triumphantly:

> Salvation belongs to our God
> To the one who sits on the throne
> And to the Lamb.

Then all of the myriad of angels around the throne and the four living beings fall down and worship. They echo:

> **Yes, Amen!**
> Blessing and glory and wisdom
> Thanks, and honor and power and strength
> Be to our God forever and ever
> **Amen!**

One of the elders asks John, "So, who are all of those in white robes?" John replies, "How should I know? Don't you know?" The elder answers:

> These are the ones who have endured persecution and suffering.
>
> Their robes are white because they are transformed through the sacrifice of the Lamb.
>
> The LORD is their shepherd; they lack nothing.
> He makes them lie down in green pastures.
> He leads them beside living water.
> He restores their soul.
> He leads them in paths of righteousness for his name's sake.
> His shepherd's staff comforts them forever.
> His presence wipes away all tears
> He destroys all fear and conquers all evil.
> He prepares a feast of blessings and their cup overflows.
> Surely goodness and mercy shall follow them
>   as they dwell in the temple of the LORD eternally.

As I ponder these two images, I realize that the initial 144,000 warrior vision leads to the second, which portrays the more complete picture. It includes everyone that will be adopted into the family of Abraham, that is, the entire family of God.

The Lamb opens the seventh seal. I feel a sense of excitement. We are finally going to see what is in the scroll! What is it? But there is only silence. There is more silence. A short time passes. The silence seems so endless.

Act 2: **Trumpets, Woes, and Witnesses**

Scene 1 (The Seven Trumpets)

As the silence continues, seven angels appear, each holding a trumpet. There's another holding a golden censer containing the prayers of Way-followers, which are rising from the earth, mingled with much anger, pain, and fear. I see the angel mixing those prayers on a golden alter with burning incense and then releasing them. The perfected requests rise before God's throne and I sense the Father carefully, individually considering each one. The period of silence continues. I'm reminded of when the children of Israel groaned in Egyptian slavery and when they cried to God for help. Is another deliverance about to take place? Another Exodus?

Suddenly, the silence ends. God hears. The angel takes the fire of the Holy Spirit from the altar and casts it down to earth. I hear thunder and loud rumblings, see lightning, and feel another earthquake. I'm filled with both anticipation and fear.

The seven angels lift their trumpets; I hear the first resounding blast. God is removing his hand of protection, not because he loses patience, but because the fire of his love is calling for repentance. His desire is to redeem all of humanity. A hail of calamities rain down including war, invasion, and civil disturbances. There is much bloodshed that seriously shakes the entire empire.

Grass and trees are burning up. The prophet Isaiah sometimes describes people as grass and the rich and powerful as trees.[137] Now I get it. The strife affects all of the grass, the lower classes, but only some of the trees, the rich and powerful. The *little people* always seem to suffer the most.

The second trumpet blows. This time I see a huge flaming mountain, Rome, the superpower, along with its institutions,[138] breaking apart. It is disappearing as it sinks into the symbolic sea of turmoil caused by the raging of peoples, multitudes, nations, and languages.[139] A third of this sea turns to blood; a superpower doesn't give up easily; its fall is never without consequences. A third of the creatures that live in the sea and a third of the ships are destroyed. The foundations of commerce, careers, and enterprise shake apart.

I hear the echo of the next trumpet and see the emperor, that admired and worshipped luminary, burning up in flames and brought down suddenly like a torch. His influence, spreading out as rivers and streams through the Roman world, is made bitter, killing the hopes and dreams of those that depend on them.

---

[137] Isa. 40:6, 1 Pet 1:24-25, Isa. 2:11-13
[138] Jer. 51:24-25, Isa. 2:13-17, Matt. 21:21.
[139] Rev. 17:15.

Another trumpet sounds and I see a third of the Sun, Moon, stars, and light darkened, affecting both day and night. This is a time of gloom and sorrow. Human wisdom is failing as chaos is advancing in the empire. Everything is falling apart. What will become of the world? What will become of Rome?

Scene 2 (The First Two Woes)

John and I are back on earth and a flying eagle is hovering in mid-heaven. Does this portend even greater calamities?

The eagle shouts:

Woe one, Woe two, and Woe three are coming.
These will be announced when the last three trumpets sound.
The time is at hand.

The first four trumpets revealed the Roman empire shaking to the core; that was hard enough. What are these woes? No time to think; the sound of the fifth trumpet reverberates, which is also the first woe.

The Satan, like a star, falls from the sky and uses a key to open a shaft leading to the abyss. Evil is about to run its course. What emerges first appears like fumes from a smokestack. But then I see it more clearly; It is a swarm of locusts that darken everything. They have human faces, lion's teeth, gold crowns, women's hair, and scorpion tails, which represent people controlled by the Destroyer with the full power of evil. These locusts claim authority through force, threats, and seduction, hoping to end the havoc and restore order to the empire. They proceed like a rumbling army of chariots, devouring everything in their path. The populace is in anguish from these locusts' scorpion-like stings, which bring much unnecessary pain and hardship. Many give up and want to die.

Way-followers are not affected by this woe, whether they be those of lower rank or those of means. Their eternal future is secure, so they have no fear. After a short time, five months, which is the actual lifespan of locusts in the Middle East, things settle down.

There are two more trumpets and two more woes to come. I'm nervous. As with the Exodus, things likely will get worse before they get better.

The sixth trumpet sounds signifying the second woe, and a voice reverberates from before the throne, which addresses the sixth angel.

Release the four angels who are tied up by the River Euphrates.

The Euphrates is the natural border between the Romans and the Parthians to the East. The empire is most vulnerable here. Rome is in shambles, and invasions are imminent. The enemies have been waiting for a long time for this exact moment. It is time. These enemies, totaling 200 million (the approximate total population of the Roman empire), present a serious threat. I see the fire, sulphur and brimstone of hatred coming from the invaders' mouths. Their chest plates reflect their intentions; they have the color of fire, dark purple, and brimstone. They show no mercy. Millions fall in the battles.

After all of this, most continue to resist the almighty God. They still worship the false pagan gods and indulge in thefts, murders, and immoralities. Apparently, even this is not enough to get them to repent. What will it take? Is it even possible?

Scene 3 (Establishing the Kingdom of God)

I expect to hear the seventh trumpet and experience the third woe. But instead, a strong, powerful, angel covered by a cloud is descending from heaven. This angel is much more imposing than the one we saw earlier. He is holding the scroll, now open with the seals removed. Oh yes, I remember now. We still have no idea of what the scroll contains. I guess we are about to find out.

This huge angel has one foot on the land and another on the sea. He shouts with a loud voice, and seven thunders answer. I can't make out what they say. Apparently, John can. I see him begin to write. But then, another voice from heaven shouts:

Seal up what the Seven Thunders say.
Don't write it down.

I'm relieved. Those thunders likely portend even more severe warnings than those which we have experienced already. It occurs to me that judgments alone cannot lead to repentance.

The huge angel swears an oath by the power of the Creator of all things.

All of God's mysteries will be made clear
when the seventh trumpet sounds.

Another voice speaks to John:

Go, take the scroll that is now open from the angel standing on the land and sea.

John obeys and says to the angel, "Give me the little scroll." The angel replies, "Take it and eat it." John takes the scroll and consumes its contents. He tells me that it contains the sweet good news that God will victoriously merge heaven with a restored earth. But there is also the bitter realization that there are battles on the horizon which are necessary to bring this about.

The angel speaks again as he hands John a measuring stick.

Get up and measure God's temple, the altar,
and those who are worshipping in it.
Leave out the outer court.
It is for the Gentiles who will trample the holy city
for forty-two months.
Prophecy again to many peoples, kingdoms, and nations.

I get it! Abraham's descendants will not fully control Jerusalem until the time of the gentiles is complete. In the meantime, Way-followers figuratively are the holy temple that John sees and measures.[140] It rests upon the foundation established by the apostles with Messiah Jesus as

---

[140] Ephesians 2:20-22

the cornerstone. Its construction will be complete after the Good News message spreads worldwide.

This is a difficult task because worldly temptations pollute the outer court. As the temple is constructed, many proclaim allegiance to Jesus and sit under his teachings, but fail to live by his message. This holy temple sits within Spiritual Sodom and Egypt where the wheat and chaff grow together. It is where the message of Jesus is weakened or even denied. I call this place the city of wheat and tares.

Then, John and I see two witnesses appear on the horizon. They resemble Moses and Elijah in their appearance and behavior. Their speech has the fire of the Holy Spirit as it burns the hearts of God's enemies. Those that resist are shut off from the gentle rain of God's blessings. Instead they are devoured with unnecessary hardships coming from the plagues of life.

The witnesses wear sackcloth as they groan in prayer for those who are enslaved to sin. Their desire is for God to reconcile the whole world to himself, including all peoples, multitudes, nations, and tongues.

Suddenly, a voice speaks to provide further clarification. These witnesses are lampstands, just like John's seven congregations. They are also olive trees, like Joshua the priest and Zerubbabel the royal descendent of David in Zechariah's prophecy.[141] These witnesses represent all of the congregations of Way-followers, Jew and Gentile, who are priests to our God and adopted as royal sons of the King.

The voice speaks again and gives us additional information. "The ministry of my two witnesses will continue for 42 months." If we add this to the 42 months that Jesus spent with his disciples, we get seven years. This is the perfect symbolic length for the time needed for God's kingdom to achieve complete victory.

But what happens after this? The witnesses die. We see their dead bodies in the streets of the city of wheat and tares, yet they are not buried. They still present a silent witness. Those in the city who remain enslaved by sin refuse to turn towards God. They celebrate wildly as they stubbornly follow their worldly pursuits. Their glee is short-lived, however. Suddenly and unexpectedly, the witnesses stand to their feet and we hear: "Come up here!" The two witnesses rise up on a cloud of vindication towards heaven to greet the Messiah who is about to return

---

[141] Zech. 4

in victory to judge the living and the dead. Fear overwhelms those that remain as they look on expecting judgment.

As we watch, John and I feel a huge earthquake causing a tenth of the city of wheat and tares to fall; seven thousand spiritually die from this event. In Elijah's day, only seven thousand remain faithful. Now all but seven thousand are faithful. In Isaiah's day, only one tenth of the holy seed remained, now it is nine tenths. The message: only a few are left behind.

Scene 4 (The End is Near)

John and I hear:

Two woes are past, the third is at hand.

The seventh trumpet sounds, but instead of witnessing the third woe, we find ourselves back in the throne room and hear voices:

> Now the kingdom of the world has passed
> to our Lord and his Messiah
> And he will reign forever and ever.

The twenty-four elders fall on their faces and we join them as they sing in unified worship:

> Almighty Lord God, we give you thanks.
> Who Is and Who Was.
> Because by your power, you have begun to reign.
> The nations are raging; your anger came down
> And with it the time for judging the dead
> To give the reward to your servants the prophets.
> The holy ones, too, and the small and the great
> Those who fear your name
> It is time to destroy the destroyers of earth.

God's temple in heaven opens and the ark of his new covenant appears within it. We witness flashes of lightning and feel rumblings, thunderclaps, an earthquake, and heavy hail. I sense that Day of the Lord is soon. The future is now.

Act 3: Journey Through Time

Scene 1 (The Woman, Dragon, and Two-Horned Lamb)

Just when I think that things are wrapping up, an amazing sign appears in heaven. We are back in time. This must be an interlude. Maybe it will help us understand what is coming later, that last *woe*.

We see a woman representing the faithful remnant of Israel, clothed with glistening sunbeams of the Messiah's light. Her crown is a diadem of twelve sparkling, gemstone stars, one for each of the twelve tribes. The Moon which imperfectly reflects sunlight portrays the Imperial, false religion to be under the woman's feet in submission. This vision is very different from the woman on Roman coinage. Those display the Sun, the Moon, and the goddess Faustina. They give glory to the emperor.

A second sign appears in heaven. It is a fiery red dragon, which symbolizes the devil who is the deceiver of mankind. A quick, deceptive, seductive sweep of its tail casts a third of the angels down from their heavenly ranks. They join his rebellion against God. The dragon has seven heads, each with a crown or diadem, and ten horns. These reveal the spiritual authority that he exercised to rule the sevenfold, former empires that exhibited tenfold, worldwide, oppressive power.

The woman is groaning in the pain of childbirth. I remember when Israel was anticipating the coming of the Messiah and was experiencing the pain of Roman oppression. The woman gives birth; the man-child is Jesus. He is the one who will rule God's kingdom with a *rod of iron*, which is that shepherd's staff which he uses to protect his flock. The hook end of the rod gently pulls back the sheep when they go astray. The thick band of iron at the other end strikes hard at the enemy when they threaten to attack. Way-followers will suffer persecution, but they will be protected.

The government shall be upon the child's shoulder. His name shall be called Wonderful Counselor, Mighty God, Everlasting Father, Prince of Peace. The dragon is angry. He attempts to stop the child and his mission in its tracks. I recall Herod killing all the young boys under two years of age. I also recall the wilderness temptations. The dragon's two main weapons, violence and deception, both fail. The Son fulfills his destiny and is snatched away to heaven.

A war breaks out, but the battle is short. The dragon, the accuser, and all of his angels have no chance. It is not even close. Michael and his angels win the war. The dragon and his followers are expelled from heaven and thrown to earth. The accuser is defeated; Jesus is Lord. John and I hear a victory celebration from the throne room:

> Now at last has come salvation and power
> The kingdom of our God and the authority of the Messiah!
> The accuser of our family has been thrown down.
> The one who accuses them before God, day and night.
> They conquered him by the blood of the Lamb
> And by the word of their testimony
> Because they did not love their lives unto death.
> So, heavens rejoice and all those that live there!
> But woe to the earth and to the sea
> Because the devil has come down to you in great anger
> Knowing that he only has a short time.

The dragon hits the ground, stunned, but there is no way that he is about to give up. He begins to bring harsh persecution onto the woman, that faithful remnant, but God protects her in the wilderness. This brings to mind the Exodus. This woman, like the ancient children of Israel, is not yet in the promised land; there is a time in the wilderness that she must endure. God is faithful; he provides manna from heaven and living water for nourishment. All will be fulfilled in time.

The dragon, now on earth, incites a flood of opposition. The populace is agitated and reacts with hostility because this woman refuses to conform either to Jewish legalism or to the requirements of the Roman Imperial Cult. The mob is replete with rage, but these trials diffuse after a time. The hostility rose like a river, but then it sinks beneath the surface, soon to be forgotten.

The dragon switches his focus to the woman's followers. These include the many Jews and Gentiles who hear and respond to the Good News. Things are getting out of hand for the dragon; Way-followers are quickly increasing their numbers. He needs a new strategy. The dragon stands by the sand of the sea as he considers his options.

He recruits the full force of empire to his cause. We see two monsters rising. The first, arises from the restless sea of humanity. It is an imposing sight. It has characteristics of a leopard, lion, and bear. It is quick as a leopard to pounce on all enemy threats. Its proclamations are as fierce and threatening as a lion. Its feet are as strong and stable as a bear. Its seven heads represent an amalgam of seven-fold worldwide kingdoms that rule through time. It has ten horns with diadems that portray the local authorities positioned throughout the world to enforce its will. This monster appears invincible. It operates with the full force of the dragon's power and authority.

One of the monster's seven heads suddenly is seriously wounded. After Nero's suicide, the three subsequent emperors, Galba, Ortho, and Vitellus, couldn't rule for even one year. Each fell by murder or suicide. Rome's wound, at that time, was as if to death. Many predicted its imminent demise, but the empire stabilized and now is as strong as ever. People are amazed at its recovery, saying, "Who is like it? Who can fight against it?" Every province again gives full allegiance to the empire and the divine emperor. By this, they also worship the dragon, in whose authority the empire operates. Power and blasphemous claims that should only belong to God will last until Jesus returns to fully establish his kingdom.

This monster continues to oppress the Way-followers by blaspheming their God and denying his ultimate victory. It uses its authority over all peoples of the empire to attack and overcome, either by exile or execution. All who are not sealed into the foundation of God's new kingdom cooperate and assimilate into this evil beastly system. Anyone who can hear this warning should take notice. Resist! If we have to die, then so be it. If we are shunned, then so be it. This is not easy. It takes great patience and faith.

The second monster comes from the land and appears as a lamb with two horns, but its words sound like those of the dragon. It consists of all the governors who enforce the first monster's rule. As a lamb, it promotes education, modern philosophies, diversity, sexual liberation, and wealth. Yet it behaves just like the dragon. With one horn it deceives. If that fails, the other horn persecutes. It operates on the land, which comprises the stable areas of cultural influence. All of its actions advance the interests of the revived empire and those of the dragon.

The power of this lamblike monster to subdue its enemies emanates outward, like fire from heaven. Amazing miraculous demonstrations are performed before everyone in plain sight. The eloquence and glitter of these subtle deceptions are possible because of major incredible scientific and technological advancements. This second monster breathes life into the first by speaking for it. It demands that all of the empire's subjects give full allegiance to its idolatrous religious system. Many, now convinced, willingly give their full devotion. The threat of death greets anyone who dares to resist.

The empire officially stamps everyone who submits. Without this stamp, one cannot participate in the guilds to market their goods; they cannot buy or sell. The mark of the monster has the number 666 in the west and 616 in the east. This is derived by summing the numeric values for Neron on western coins and Nero on eastern coins. It is the mark of the emperor, Nero in particular, but generally it applies to every world ruler. It is the imperfect number of man.

Scene 2 (The Fall of Babylon)

We see the Lamb standing at his stronghold in the heavenly city. He is accompanied by his army of 144,000 followers, the first fruits of the kingdom, aligned and prepared for battle. We are again at the time when the Way-followers are beginning their mission to establish God's kingdom.

A voice thunders. It sounds like the rumbling of ocean waves. As I listen closely, I'm surprised to realize that it is the music of harps. The players are singing a new song in front of the elders and four living beings. Only the 144,000 seem to be able to hear and understand this song. It contains their marching orders: conquer by love and peace. These warriors are pure, satisfying an important Mosaic military requirement. The impure cannot engage in this kind of battle. The 144,000 will fight with their words, in which there are no lies; they only proclaim truth. They demonstrate lives without blemish and are ready to completely follow the Lord's commands. They are charged with the task of implementing the new kingdom whose foundation was set in place by Jesus and his apostles.

John's Revelation Visions: Act 3: Journey through Time

An angel flies directly overhead, proclaiming with a loud voice:

> **Eternal good tidings to all who live on the earth**
> **to every tribe, nation, and language.**
> **Fear God! Give him glory!**
> **The time has come for his judgment!**
> **Worship the one who made heaven, the earth, the sea, and the springs of water.**

Another angel appears shouting:

> **Babylon the Great, Rome, has been defeated.**
> **She has fallen.**
> **She is the one who made the nations drink the wine of the anger that comes upon her fornication.**

The demise of empire is imminent because Jesus has defeated the power of death. He is the way, the truth, and the life. The question remains: "What will humanity do when the Roman evils of violence and deception are destroyed for all to see?"

A third angel comes forth and speaks as if to answer this question:

> If anyone worships the monster or its image
> or belongs to its evil system
> that person will experience the wine of God's anger.
> It will be poured straight into the cup of his wrath
> that burns as fire and sulphur against all evil
> before the holy angels and also before the Lamb.
>
> Those who worship the monster and give homage to its image,
> the smoke of their torment goes up,
> and they will have no respite, day or night till the end of the age.

This demands patience from God's holy people who live according to the spirit of the Lamb; deliverance will take time. The entire world will have time and opportunity to accept the Good News. Those who refuse to repent undoubtedly will persist in aligning with the defeated monster. This kind of behavior only leads to torment; the smoke of that memory will never end. Isaiah teaches that the wicked are like the troubled sea, which cannot rest, and its waters cast up mire and dirt. How terrible. After the evil systems are destroyed, one hopes that all will turn to the loving God whose will is to redeem all of creation.

Another loud voice bellows:

Blessed are the dead who from this time forward, die in the Lord.

God's spirit replies: "Yes, so they may rest from their works for the deeds that they have done follow after them." The multitudes who repent are those who were spiritually dead, but then die in faith. They will have rest.

Scene 3 (The Harvest)

In the fullness of time, one like the son of man appears wearing a gold crown. He holds a sharp sickle and sits on a white cloud of vindication. An angel comes out of heaven's temple with a bold request:

It's harvest time. Put in your sickle and reap. The harvest of the earth is ripe.

I think I see some hesitation as the Son of Man considers whether the harvest truly is ready. Have the 144,000 true Israelites and their multitudes of disciples from all nations completed their conquest? Has the Good News message permeated the entire world? The Lamb then concurs and thrusts his sickle to gather the Way-followers together; they are ready for deliverance.

Then, another angel comes into view from heaven's temple holding another sharp sickle. Just behind this second angel is a third. He emerges from the temple's altar, and with the fire of the Holy Spirit, he calls out:

Go to work and gather the clusters of fruit from the vine of the earth. The grapes are in ripe bunches!

This second angel with the sickle gathers the fruit, which he throws into a winepress of God's judgment where the unrepentant will be made accountable for their evil deeds. It is trodden outside the holy city of wheat and tares, where the righteous reside.

Out of the winepress, I see blood coming out as high as a horse's bridle for a distance of two-hundred miles. This is the approximate length of the Jordan River originating from its headwaters at the base of Mt. Herman and ending at the Dead Sea where nothing lives. This blood river image is sharply different than Ezekiel's temple vision. There, fresh water is trickling from the entrance of this temple. As it flows downhill, it becomes deeper and deeper. Eventually, it turns into a river flowing directly into the dead sea. This lake that was dead became fresh, teeming with life. All kinds of fruit bearing trees, good for both nourishment and healing, flourish beside the river. Ezekiel presents a vision of living water which brings life.

The winepress image and the figurative river of blood depicts the alternative. Ezekiel's river brings life; the winepress river brings violence, deception, bloodshed, and despair. Moses pleaded with the Israelites to choose life, not death. Those outside the holy city in this vision apparently choose the latter. They prefer death rather than facing the fiery love of God.

Now we see the other harvest, the millions upon millions that the Son of Man gathered together with his sickle. They, having defeated the monster and his image, are lifted up and are standing upon a glassy sea above the chaos. This harvest is mixed with the fire of God's love that seeks to restore all things and bring in the new creation. The multitudes sing the song of Moses:

> Great and amazing are your works
> O Lord God, the Almighty One.
> Just and true are your ways
> O king of the nations.
> Who will not fear you Lord and glorify your name?
> For you alone are holy.
> For all nations shall come
> And worship before you
> Because your judgments have been revealed.

As I listen to this song, I realize that it is nothing like the original song of Moses. Yes, they are both songs of victory that celebrate an Exodus-like deliverance from oppression. That is where the comparison ends.

This song glorifies God without a tinge of violence. The original song of Moses glorifies a warrior God who conquers and destroys his enemies by force. Victory by words of truth replace victory by bloodshed and humiliation. Glory goes to a God who reveals his true nature, a god of love, not a god of force. The victors celebrate the defeat of the monster, which was achieved by this unique strategy.

Act 4: The Final Battles and the New Creation

Scene 1 (The Seven Vials)

Another sign comes into view in heaven. It is an overwhelming sight. We see the temple and tabernacle of witnesses, which is the physical reminder of God's covenantal promises. It opens in heaven, and seven angels holding seven plagues come out. They are clothed in clean, shining linen of purity and are wearing golden belts of righteousness across their chests. One of the four living beings comes over and hands them seven golden vials of God's passion to set things right. Smoke from God's glory, presence, and power fill the temple.

I thought that the previous vision completed the victory, but oh, that was an interlude. We've seen a glimpse of the coming victory, but now it is time to complete the previous visions. Sin and evil have reached a climax, the time for intercession and prayer is over.

A mighty voice thunders from the temple addressing the seven angels,

> **Go your way and pour the seven vials of God's indignation to the earth.**

The first angel releases their vial and it splashes down, breaking the restraints that limit evil. I see foul, painful sores break out on those who aligned themselves with the monster and his image. I notice that Way-followers are protected. Can these sores represent, consumerism, wealth, fame, and greed? It is grievously painful to experience the disappointment when these things fail to satisfy one's expectations.

Another angel drops a second vial on the sea. More restraints break. The sea of humanity's chaos turns to blood like a corpse. Everything that was living there dies. I recall the second trumpet where only a third of the creatures died. That was a warning, but now I sense complete destruction. This causes great distress to those relying on Roman agencies.

The next angel drops their vial. It hits the streams and rivers, which also turn to blood. Similar to the previous vial, this judgment echoes the third trumpet judgment on the rivers and streams of authority branching out from the center. Like the previous vial, the impact is drastically more intense. This vial-angel shouts to God:

> You are the One Who Is and Was.
> You are the Holy One, and you are just.
> You have passed the righteous sentence.
> They spilled the blood of saints and prophets
> And you have given them blood to drink
> They deserve it.

Surprisingly, these words are missing something. It is missing *the One to Come*. Perhaps the *to Come* part is already upon us.

A voice coming from the altar responds in affirmation:

> Yes, Lord God Almighty, your judgments are true and just.

The fourth vial hits the Sun. People are burning from its great heat. Truth burns. As the heat turns up, people become angry. They curse God because of the pain, but they persist in their wickedness anyway. There is no turning back towards the loving Father.

The fifth vial strikes the very seat of the empire and breaks it apart. This causes great agony. The people shiver in distress. The darkness of despair covers everything. The people curse God. Even now, they refuse to relent in their evils.

The sixth vial dries up the river Euphrates, the barrier that holds back conquest from outside the Empire. When the natural border is gone, invasions from the barbarous hordes are imminent.

Spirits of evil spew from the dragon, from the emperor, and from the false prophet, who speaks for the empire and promises victory. These forces desperately are trying to hold things together. False promises appear as frogs; they are foul, impure lies. Through deceiving signs, the demonic spirits demonstrate a show of force and travel through their areas of remaining influence to gather a huge army for the great upcoming final battle.

Meanwhile, the Lamb speaks to his followers:

> Look, I come as a thief.
> God's blessing is on those who are awake.
> Those that remain are clothed with the robes of purity.
> Don't be found naked in shame.

A huge army gathers at that iconic battlefield, Mt. Megiddo. This place, the site where so many previous armies met, symbolizes all battlefields, past and future. In my time, it represents Gettysburg, Normandy, Pearl Harbor, even the Twin Towers.

The seventh vial disperses into the air and I hear a loud voice from the throne, **"It is done!"** I see lightnings. Shortly after, there are rumblings and thunder claps. I feel a huge earthquake, one unlike any that previously occurred on earth. No, not like anything I could ever imagine.

Rome splits in three; it is utterly destroyed. The cities of her provinces collapse. God remembers all of the evil done by this empire. It is time for her to experience her just rewards.

The mountains and islands of Roman institutions which seemed so permanent disappear under the raining of calamities, each one like a one hundred-pound hailstone. The peoples curse God in their distress. All of this imagery depicts the momentous event when Rome, the greatest empire of all time, falls. The dark ages are upon us.

Scene 2 (The Cycle of Empires' Rise and Fall)

One of the vial-angels comes over and speaks:

> Come with me.
> I will show you the judgment of the great whore who
> sits on many waters.
> She is the one with whom the kings of the earth
> committed fornication.
> She is the one whose fornication has the wine
> that has made all earth-dwellers drunk.

As the vial-angel leads us away to the desert, I wonder, "Who is this great whore that controls the peoples of many nations?" Then, I see her, sitting on a scarlet monster. She is called by many diverse names because the Satan has many ways to entice and lure humanity away from God. The monster on which she sits has seven heads and ten horns. These heads and horns are just like the previous monster aligned with the dragon. The woman is wearing purple and scarlet, decked out with gold, precious stones, and pearls. She is holding a golden goblet full of abominations and the impurities of her fornications. There is writing on her forehead. It reads:

Mystery!
Babylon the Great, Mother of Whores and the earth's Abominations
The city that exploited the world to satisfy its evil desires.
She is drunk from the blood of Jesus followers, God's people.

John and I are astonished at this image. It is very confusing and mysterious.

The vial-angel asks: Why are you astonished? I'll explain all of this. It takes discernment to understand this revelation.

Then, the vial-angel explains:

> That monster is from the abyss, the pit of evil. It is destined for eternal destruction. This will shock those who were devoted to it.
>
> The seven heads exemplify the hills of Rome. Five of its kings are gone. The sixth, Nero, now rules. The seventh has not yet appeared, but will at some time in the future. His reign will be short. He is part of this evil system and is destined for destruction along with the empire.
>
> The ten horns symbolize many kings who haven't yet been born. Their reigns will also be short. They are in full agreement with the cause of the monster and use their power accordingly. They will fight the Lamb, but

fear not, the Lamb will prevail because he is the Lord of Lords and King of Kings. His followers are called, chosen, and faithful.

Eventually, the coming kings will destroy the whore, consuming all her wealth, leaving her naked and poor. She symbolizes the evil of that great city, Rome, the center of empire from which its royal dominion emanates. She is the one who selfishly and oppressively drained the resources from around the world.

It is God's purpose to allow these future kings to reign in allegiance with the monster till all is fulfilled.

As I ponder all of this imagery, I begin to understand the rhythm of these revelatory visions. They embody the repeating war of Good versus Evil. Over and over, the story is retold. Empires rise along with their monsters of power and propaganda. They expand through force and then oppress. The static of false ideologies, sometimes political but often religious, overwhelms the voices of truth. Those voices are mocked, persecuted, and ultimately defeated. Then when evil reaches its zenith, judgment comes. The whole seductive system comes crashing down on itself. We observe this pattern in history, we experience it now, and we can expect it to appear again. Time after time it repeats. Why not simply turn to the loving Father? Instead: "The nations rage, the kingdoms totter; he utters his voice, the earth melts (Ps. 46:6)." All is vanity.

> What has been is what will be,
> and what has been done is what will be done;
> there is nothing new under the Sun.
> Is there a thing of which it is said,
> "See, this is new?"
> It has already been,
> in the ages before us.
> The people of long ago are not remembered,
> nor will there be any remembrance

of people yet to come
by those who come after them.[142]

I see another pattern. Each cycle brings a greater intensity of evil. The trumpet judgments were harsher than the warnings of the seals. The vial judgments were even more intense. At some point, the living God will step in and put things right. He'll come as a thief, at a time most unexpected. Way-followers, take notice! Be found faithful.

Scene 3 (The Ultimate Collapse)

Another mighty angel appears surrounded by the glory of God; his light fills all of the earth and he shouts loudly:

> **Babylon the Great has fallen**
> **She has fallen!**
> **All that remains are ghosts of her past**
> **Dark memories of her evils.**
> **All the nations drank from the wine of her sexual immorality.**
> **The kings of the earth committed idolatry with her.**
> **The traders of the earth became rich from her luxurious living.**

The glory surrounding this angel is overwhelming. When light shines on the shadow of empire, its glitter reflects only gloom.

> Those who walk in darkness, and whose eyes the god of this world hath blinded through their lusts, look only on the material side, upon prosperous times, large revenues, rapidly developing resources. The great city of the world looks fair and glorious in their eyes, and even the godly are dazzled by her beauty; but when the light of heaven shines, her fall is seen to be inevitable, for she is seen to be hateful; her palaces are seen to be prisons, her highest wisdom little more than low cunning, her most exalted intelligence base-born, her sweetest songs discordant cries; the evil spirit,

---

[142] Eccles. 1:9-11 NRSV.

welcomed back, has come in sevenfold power; for the dry places afford no rest to those who still love sin and the pleasures of sin.[143]

Another voice from heaven speaks:

> Come out of her my people, so that you don't become embroiled in her sins, and so you don't receive any of her plagues.
>
> Her sins are piled to the sky, and God has remembered her wickedness.

This declaration implores the Way-followers to resist. Do not assimilate into and participate with darkness. Live according to the light, regardless of the consequences. Remain faithful.

The voice continues to speak, describing in detail the superpower's sudden, complete, and unexpected demise. Mass marketing bubbles burst. There is no longer a demand for all the upscale trendy clothing, devices, delicacies, expensive furniture, luxury items, and investment opportunities. Merchants, traders, and financial advisors who promote these enterprises mourn:

> The global network was so strong and efficient. We earned so much money from its systems. Now, in a single day, the market has collapsed.

Meanwhile, there is celebration in heaven. There is vindication for the oppressed who suffered under the dominance of the rich and powerful.

Another angel appears and picks up a huge rock, throwing it into the sea, saying:

> Babylon the Great will be thrown down like that with a splash
> Never again will she rise.
> Never again will her entertainment industry flourish.
> Never again will skilled workmen be employed in her factories.
> Never again will you see her businesses open till late at night.

---

[143] Ellicott's Commentary for English Readers on Revelation 18.

Never again will you see the joy of weddings in her streets.

The allure of her mighty global enterprises misled all of the nations. By them, masses of peoples all over the earth were deceived, oppressed, and killed. Prophets who tried to shine the mirror of truth on her evils were silenced. Many of God's people were slaughtered in oppression. In the end, the entire system implodes upon itself.

Loud voices sound out from a huge crowd in heaven.

Alleluia

Salvation and glory and power belong to our God.
His judgments are true and just.
He has judged the great whore who corrupted the earth
and he has judged her for spilling the blood of his servants.

Alleluia

Smoke, representing the memory of her destruction, rises up forever.

Scene 4 (Return of the King)

Suddenly, John and I are back in the throne room. The twenty-four elders and the four creatures fall down and worship God who sits on the throne. They say, "Amen" and "Alleluia."

A voice comes from the throne, "Give praise to our God, all you his servants, and you who fear him, both small and great."

We hear a powerful second voice rumbling like the sound of many ocean waves and booming like strong thunder:

Alleluia.

The Lord our God, the Almighty has become king.
Let us celebrate and rejoice and give him the glory
because the marriage of the Lamb has come,
and his bride has prepared herself.

She has been given shining pure linen, to wear,

the righteous deeds of God's holy people.

The angel tells John to write: *God's blessing is on those who are invited to the Lamb's marriage supper.*

John feels an impulse to worship, but the angel said: "Hey! What are you doing? I'm a fellow servant along with you and all who testify about Jesus, which is the spirit of prophecy. Worship only God."

As I ponder all of this, it occurs to me that we are witnessing the ultimate victory: The cycles of empire are over.

Scene 5 (The Day of the Lord)

We are back on earth. Heaven opens, revealing a white horse with Jesus, the Faithful and True, sitting upon it. I see a name written there, but only he knows it. His eyes are flaming and he, the King of Kings, wears many crowns, encompassing universal reach. His white robe is dipped in his own blood, which was shed at his crucifixion. The armies of heaven follow, wearing white robes of righteousness. His title is: Word of Truth. He is ready to make war by the sharp two-edged sword protruding from his mouth. He strikes down the nations, not by bloodshed, but by the pure word of God. He, the Good Shepherd, rules with a shepherd's rod of iron to protect his flock. He, himself, will tread the winepress of the wine of his passion for Almighty God's justice. The fruit that springs forth from the wicked are the consequences due them from their own actions. The emblem on his thigh reads: Lord of Lords and King of Kings.

An angel appears in the middle of the Sun shouting a call to the birds of prey flying in the sky. It is a quote from Ezekiel 39:17:

> **Come here! Gather around! Witness God's great feast! Eat the flesh of kings, military leaders, the strong, the cavalry, people of all ranks.**

We then witness the ultimate devastation of identifying with evil. The birds of prey symbolically consume the remaining dregs of wickedness. The magnitude of this humiliation is in clear sight, yet the monster is not giving up; he prepares for his last stand.

His assembled worldwide army gathers as he prepares to go to war against the King of Kings. But to my surprise, *there is no war*. The monster is simply captured. So is the false prophet whose lies and empire-sponsored propaganda had deceived so many. Both are cast into the lake of fire surrounded with burning sulphur, the Dead Sea, where there is no spiritual life. The rest of the military are judged according to the righteousness of the two-edged sword, God's Word. By this, the evil ones go to Hades where they wait to be raised at the end of the age to face the final judgment.

An angel now descends from heaven, holding a large chain. He grabs the dragon, known as the ancient serpent, the devil, and the Satan. He ties him up and throws him into the Abyss, locked and sealed. There can be no more deceiving of the nations till after a full measure of time goes by. Hopefully, those who were deceived in life will now have their chance to hear the Good News. This period is known by many as the millennium reign.

Back in God's place, I see many thrones. Seated on them are the faithful Way-followers who were persecuted and killed in life. They have the authority to judge and reign with the Messiah. He is the Great Shepherd who looks after his flock with an iron rod, his shepherd's staff. Blessed are those who share in this first resurrection. They have no fear of death and will be Priests to God and the Messiah for this full measure of time. Those who gave devotion to the monster and dragon, do not rise at this time.

At the appointed time, I see the Satan released from his prison in the abyss. He emerges determined to once more deceive the nations. An army, designated by the title Gog and Magog, rise up and surround God's people who are centered in the spiritual Holy City, Jerusalem. But God's word comes as fire from heaven judging the whole bunch. The Satan and these hordes wind up in the Lake of Fire, the Dead Sea, outer darkness.

A large white throne appears with one sitting on it. Heaven and earth disappear from sight and all of the dead, rich and poor, are standing there. Books open, and then one more opens. It is the Book of Life. I see Death and Hades empty. Each person faces judgment based on what they did in life. Now, Death and Hades are destroyed, symbolized by being thrown into the Lake of Fire. Those not recorded in the Book of Life are thrown there also. This is the second death.

Scene 6 (The New Creation)

The new heaven and earth appear. I notice that there is no crystal sea separation because heaven and earth are now together. The chaos of the world is gone; all is set right. The new Jerusalem, consisting of all Way-followers, is coming down, adorned like a bride. A voice exclaims from the throne:

> Look! God has come to dwell with humans!
> He will dwell with them.
> They will be his people, and he will be their God.
> God himself will be with them and will be their God.
> He will wipe away every tear from their eyes.
>
> There will be no more death, or weeping, or pain.
> The first things are no more.
> The one, sitting on the throne, speaks:
> Look, I am making all things new.
> Write these words which are faithful and true.
> It is done!
> I am the Alpha and Omega
> The beginning and the end.
>
> I will freely give water from the springs of life to the thirsty.
> The one who conquers will inherit these things.
> I will be their god and they shall be my children.
> But as for cowards, faithless people, murderers,
> fornicators, sorcerers, idolaters, and all liars,
> their destiny is the lake of fire and sulfur, the Dead Sea, the second death.

One of the vial-angels comes over. "Come with me," he says. "I will show you the bride of the Lamb." Up, in the spirit, we ascend to a high mountain. There's the holy city, a new Jerusalem, descending down to earth. It is glorious, having the appearance of rare, transparent, crystal-clear, green jasper. Its walls are super-high. There are twelve angels at twelve gates, individually inscribed with the names of Israel's tribes. The city is square, with three gates on each side. There are inscriptions on the twelve foundations stones. These respectively are names of the twelve apostles.

The vial-angel measures the city with his measuring rod. It is a cube, with length, breadth, and height being fifteen-hundred miles. The base is the size of the Roman empire. This city encompasses the entire civilized world. I recall that the Holy of Holies in the previous temples were also cubes. No evil is allowed in this city. The city itself is like golden transparent, glass. Nothing is hidden. The foundations have the radiance of twelve precious stones, similar to those of the breast plates worn by Israel's priests. Each gate to the city is constructed from a single pearl of an incredibly great price. The streets are magnificent pure clear, transparent gold, where righteousness reigns.

There is no temple in this holy city because God and the Lamb serve that purpose. Their light fills the whole place; there is no need for sun and moon to light up the darkness, because evil is no more. Her gates are never shut and the nations and rulers can enter at any time. But the blazing light excludes anything that is impure. This keeps outside anyone who lies or commits abominations. Only those written in the Lamb's Book of Life are welcome.

The vial-angel shows us a river, sparkling like crystal, flowing from God and the Lamb's throne. It runs through the center of the city with the Tree of Life on both banks. Every month this tree produces twelve kinds of fruits and its leaves provide healing to the nations. Nothing is cursed. The servants of the Lamb, his devoted followers, directly see the face of God and worship him on his throne, right there in the city. There is no darkness because God's light shines bright. Lamb-followers reign forever.

The vial-angel says: "These words are trustworthy and true."

John again wants to worship, but the vial-angel stops him and says: "Hey! Stop that! I'm simply a fellow servant along with all who heed the words of this prophecy. Worship God only!"

He then says:

> Don't keep these words to yourself.
> You see, the time is near.
> The unjust will persist in their evils.
> The righteous will continue doing good.
> Let those who are holy continue being holy.

> Then the Lamb says:
> Look! I am coming soon.
> I will come to judge everyone according to their deeds.
> I am the Alpha and Omega, the first and the last, the beginning and the end.
> Blessed are those who are found worthy to enter the city and eat of the tree of life,
> but outsiders, sorcerers, fornicators, murderers, idolaters, and slanderers must be excluded.
> I, Jesus, have sent my angel to testify to the seven congregations.
> I am David's root and of his lineage, the Bright Morning Star.
> Come! Anyone who hears, Come!
> Anyone who is thirsty, come and freely drink from the water of life.

The visions end. Wow, what a trip that was. We are back at Patmos. It will take time to process all of this. John writes, "To anyone who hears this testimony and then adds or removes anything from it, God will add to them the plagues herein. They will not share in the blessings of the holy city or be able to eat from the tree of life. Remember, Jesus is coming soon! Amen! Come Lord Jesus. The grace of the Lord Jesus be with you all."

John, forgive me for my paraphrase and added commentary. The exact, original words of your Revelation scroll remain a blessing to us all.

Chapter 15

Concluding Remarks

John had to be very careful when he constructed his letter. If he was direct and clear, the Romans would have reacted violently. John would be tortured, probably killed, and the seven congregations possibly destroyed. He and the Way gatherings obviously were steeped in their knowledge of Old Testament prophetic scripture. If the Romans read the book about dragons, monsters, winepresses of blood, and all of the other imagery, they likely would have concluded, "This fool has a wild imagination."

The seven congregations heard the message differently. The Revelation scroll presents calls for subversive political resistance. It insists that disciples remain faithful to the Way teachings and not assimilate with evils of the Imperial Cult or any false religion for that matter. It calls for patience and trust, even at the point of death. On the positive side, John's visions pledge the ultimate victory, a timely and needed encouragement for congregations that were despised and illegal. This book was a very important and applicable message to first-century Way-followers.

Is it relevant to us today? Yes, most definitely. Rome is long gone, but its fragmented pieces are all about. Christians, in many nations worldwide, experience persecution just as severe as did the seven congregations. The Imperial Cult is gone, but the secular religions of enlightenment and postmodernism are alive and well. The lure of New Age mysticism is powerful. It is leading many away from the faith. It's tenets often even mix with mainstream Church practices as supposed prophets put forth their private revelations and, at the same time, mock orthodox Christianity. In Western civilization, Way-followers don't encounter violent persecution, but we do face lots of empire propaganda. The two-horned lamb may have lost its weapon of violence, but its remaining strategy of deception is quite potent. Crafty indoctrinations can be as much of a danger as violence, especially when mixed with biblical teachings. It can lull us to sleep and miss the slow walk towards evil. We might not notice the cultural shifts where society calls evil good and good evil. In our time, the reach of the empire system subtly affects every area of life.

Our job is to:

1. Make sure that we as individuals do not assimilate and give allegiance to evil.
2. Have realistic expectations and shine the light of truth on iniquity wherever it appears.
3. Share the Good News of God's love in word and deed.

History demonstrates that God works in recognizable paradigms throughout the ages, and those who oppose God also follow predictable patterns. Events may not repeat, but often they rhyme. Persons, events, places, and institutions of an earlier time foreshadow those that come later. This is building to the ultimate climax. At some point, evil will run its course and the Lamb will return. This is the hope of every Way-follower. In the meantime, our job is to reflect love back to God and to his creation. What we do in this life matters. Seeking to escape before things get hard is the wrong focus.

Final Thoughts

There are a few reasons why you might be reading this page. You could be deciding whether the book is worth considering at all. You might have scanned parts of the book and want to see how it ends. Or you plowed all the way through. Congratulations!

After experiencing the loss of a child and learning about abuse that my wife experienced at a Christian boarding school, my family experienced a crisis of faith. I realize that we are not alone in this. Many are questioning, especially now in this new century. The faith of countless millions is hanging by a thread. In some cases, it is already gone. Doubting, questioning, and probing are healthy and normal. But after confronting the chaos of doubt, I believe that it is possible to embrace a deeper, living faith that can withstand life's tragedies.

Over the years, I've worked through those parts of the Christian faith that I considered to be problematic. Each chapter of this book delves into one of those areas. Hopefully, this effort will bring some fresh perspectives to the fore. I don't claim credit for any new insights; I've learned a great deal from studying the work of many excellent biblical scholars.

The Christian faith rests on one central question. Did Jesus physically rise from the dead? If the answer to this is no, then Christianity has nothing to offer. If the answer is yes, then Jesus' teachings need to be seriously considered, and the Bible needs to be interpreted through the lens of those teachings. In my journey, I've come to the conclusion that the resurrection is indeed a real historical event. Once coming to this position, I've found that when I use Jesus as a guide, the many obstacles to faith disappear. You, the reader, can agree or disagree. It is your choice. Note though that this book says nothing about how one should live out the Christian faith, once convinced that the message is true. Maybe it would be more appropriate for me to ask: "How do I, as imperfect as I am, live it out?" This is a topic for another day.

So, there you have it; I hope that my work proves useful. Thanks for listening.

CPSIA information can be obtained
at www.ICGtesting.com
Printed in the USA
FSHW022341061019
62721FS